Valeriu

A Roman Story

J. G. Lockhart

Alpha Editions

This edition published in 2024

ISBN : 9789362099549

Design and Setting By
Alpha Editions
www.alphaedis.com
Email - info@alphaedis.com

Contents

BOOK I.

CHAPTER I.

Since you are desirous, my friends, that I should relate to you, at length and in order, the things which happened to me during my journey to Rome, notwithstanding the pain which it must cost me to throw myself back into some of the feelings of that time, I cannot refuse to comply with your request. After threescore years spent in this remote province of an empire, happy, for the most part, in the protection of enlightened, just, and benevolent princes, I remember, far more accurately than things which occurred only a few months ago, the minutest particulars of what I saw and heard while I sojourned, young and a stranger, among the luxuries and cruelties of the capital of the world, as yet imperfectly recovered from the effects of the flagitious tyranny of the last of the Flavii.

My father, as you have heard, came with his legion into this island, and married a lady of native blood, some years before the first arrival of Agricola. In the wars of that illustrious commander, during the reigns of Vespasian and Titus, he had the fortune to find opportunities of distinguishing himself; but when his general was recalled, by the jealousy of Domitian, he retired from public life, and determined to spend the remainder of his days in peace, on the lands which belonged to him in right of his wife here in Britain. He laid the foundations of the house in which I have now the pleasure of receiving you; and here, in the cultivation of his fields, and in the superintendence of my education, he found sufficient employment for an active, though no longer an ambitious mind. Early in the reign of Trajan he died. Never did either Roman or British dwelling lament a more generous master.

I cannot pretend to regret the accident which immediately afterwards separated me from a gentle mother—never to see her more upon the earth. Yet deeply was the happiness of my returning hour stained by that privation. It is the common rule of nature, that our parents should precede us to the grave; and it is also her rule, that our grief for them should not be of such power as to prevent us from entering, after they are gone, into a zealous participation both of the business and the pleasures of life. Yet, in after years, the memory of that buried tenderness rises up ever and anon, and wins rather than warns us to a deliberate contemplation of our own dissolution.

Towards the end of the winter following the death of my father, there arrived letters which engaged anxious consideration. They were from members of his family, none of whom either my mother or myself had seen. It was explained, especially by Caius Licinius, the lawyer, (who was near of kin to our house,) that by the death of a certain Patrician, Cneius Valerius by name,

I had become legally entitled to a very considerable fortune, to claim and take possession of which, demanded my immediate presence in the metropolis. My rights, said this jurist, were indeed called in question by another branch of the family, but were I on the spot, his professional exertions, with whatever interest he or any of his friends could command, should be at my service, for the sake of my father and of my name.

The love of travel had never before been excited in my bosom; but now that I knew I was so soon to embark for Italy, the delights which I might there hope to experience came crowding upon my imagination. The dark and pine-clad banks of my native Anton, said I, shall now be exchanged for that golden-waved Tiber, of which so many illustrious poets have sung. Instead of moving here among the ill-cemented and motley fabric of an insulated colony, and seeing only the sullen submission of barbarians on the one hand, or the paltry vanity of provincial deputies on the other, I shall tread the same ground with the rulers of the earth, and wear, among native Romans, the gown of my ancestors. I shall behold the Forum, which has heard the eloquence of Cicero and Hortensius; I shall ascend to the Capitol, where Cæsar triumphed; I shall wander in the luxurious gardens of Sallust, or breathe the fresh air in the fields of Cato: I shall gaze upon the antique majesty of temples and palaces, and open my eyes on all that art and nature have been able to heap together through eight centuries, for the ornament of the chosen seat of wisdom and valour.

A single trusty slave was selected to accompany me. It was not certainly on account of his accomplishments that Boto had been chosen for this duty; for although he had lived all his days in the vicinity of the colonists at Venta, there was scarcely a person within the bounds of the British Belgæ that spoke worse Latin. He was, however, a man of natural sagacity, possessing shrewd discernment concerning whatever things had fallen under his customary observation; and he shewed no symptom either of diffidence respecting his qualifications for this new office, or of regret at being separated from those in whose company many years of gentle servitude had glided over his sun-burnt countenance. It was reported to me, that he invited several of our rustics to drink with him in one of the out-houses, where his exultation knew no limits. He was going to Rome, for his young master very well knew he could never get on in such a journey without the helping eye and hand of Boto; and he had a brother in Italy already, (he had gone over with a distinguished legionary some ten years before,) and from him (for he would of course meet with him as soon as our arrival should be known) he would receive all requisite information concerning the doings of the great city. The usefulness which, he doubted not, I should be constrained to acknowledge in his manifold qualifications, would, without all question, entitle him to some signal reward—perhaps nothing less than manumission on his return.

Two days passed more quickly than any I ever remember to have spent amidst a strange mixture of mirth, and sorrow, and noisy preparation.

Where that single tall naked pine now stands buffeted by the wind, then grew a thick grove, of which that relic alone survives. It was there that I turned round to gaze once more on the quiet verdure of these paternal fields, and our small pastoral stream glistening here and there beneath the shady covert of its margin.

I had at first intended to cross over to Gaul, and traversing that province, enter Italy, either by the route of the Alps, in case we could procure convenient guides and companions, or by some vessel sailing from Marseilles or Forum Julii to Ostium. But the advice of one of my neighbours, who had himself been a great traveller, made me alter this plan, and resolve to commit myself to the care of an experienced mariner who was just about to sail for Italy, by the way of the pillars of Hercules, in a vessel laden chiefly with tin; and on reaching the Clausentum, I found this man, with several passengers, ready for the voyage.

For the first three or four days, I was so afflicted by the motion of the vessel, that I could bestow little attention on any external object; my eyes were so confused and dazzled, that I saw nothing beyond the corner of the deck on which I had caused my carpets to be laid; and a few ejaculations to Castor and Pollux were all the articulate sounds that I uttered. By degrees, however, the weight of my depression began to be alleviated; and at intervals, more particularly during the night watches, if I was not altogether in possession of myself, I was at least well enough to enjoy a sort of giddy delight in watching the billows as they rose and retreated from the prow. There were moments, also, in which the behaviour of Boto, under this new species of calamity, could furnish me, as it had already done the more hardy of my fellow-voyagers, with store of mirth. Near us frequently, upon the deck, sat a Captain of the Prætorian Bands, who, more than any other of these, displayed a florid complexion and cheerful eye, unalterable by the fluctuation of the waters. This Sabinus had served in all the wars of Agricola, and accompanied him even in his perilous circumnavigation of the islands which lie scattered to the north of Britain. He had also gone back to Rome with his commander, not, like him, to extenuate imperial jealousy by the affectation of indolence, but to seek for new occupation on some other disturbed frontier of the Empire. In Syria and Cappadocia he had spent some years; after which, he had attended the Emperor himself through Mæsia and Illyricum, and all those countries he traversed and retraversed, during that shameful contest in which so many Roman eagles were made the prey of barbarous enemies, and which terminated at last in that cowardly treaty, by which Domitian granted a diadem to Decebalus, and condescended to place the Roman Senate among the tributaries of a Dacian. Our friend had also strutted his part in that gorgeous triumph, or rather succession of triumphs, by which the defeated and disgraced Prince, on his return from the Ister, mocked the eyes and ears of the incredulous and indignant Romans. In a word, he had partaken in all kinds of fortune, good and evil, and preserved his rubicundity and equanimity unaltered in them all. Having attained to a situation of some dignity, he had now been visiting Britain on a special message from the new Emperor, and was returning in the hope that no future accident of fortune, or princely caprice, would ever again make it necessary for him to quit the shows and festivities of the capital.

This good-natured man sat down beside my suffering peasant, endeavouring to withdraw his attention from the pangs of his sickness, by pointing out the different boats which came in view as we held on from the Gobæan rocks, keeping close to the shore as we went, in order to shun, as well as we could, the customary fury of the Aquitanic Ocean. "Behold these fishing-vessels," he would cry, "which have undoubtedly been upon the coast of Rutupia for oysters, or it may be about the mouth of yonder Ligoris for turbot, and are now stretching all their canvass to get home with their booty to Italy. Smooth be your winds and fair your passage, oh rare fish!" To which the downcast Boto would reply, "Lavish not, oh master, your good wishes upon the mute fish, which have been tossed about all their lives, but reserve them rather for me (unhappy) who am thus tormented in an unnatural and intolerable manner;" or perhaps, "Speak not, I beseech you, of oysters, or of turbot, or of any other eatable, for I believe I shall never again feel hungry, so grievously are all my internal parts discomposed. Oh, that I had never left my native fields, and bartered the repose of my whole body for the vain hope of gratification to my eyes!"

By degrees, however, custom reconciled all of us to the motion of the bark, and the weather being calm during the greater part of the voyage, I enjoyed, at my leisure, the beauties, both of the sea, and of the shores alongst which we glided. From time to time, we put in for water and other necessaries, to various sea-ports of the Spanish Peninsula; but our stay was never so long at any place as to admit of us losing sight of our vessel. Our chief delight, indeed, consisted in the softness and amenity of the moonlight nights we spent in sailing along the coasts of Mauritania,—now the dark mountains of the family of Atlas throwing their shadows far into the sea—and anon, its margin glittering with the white towers of Siga, or Gilba, or Cartenna, or some other of the rich cities of that old Carthaginian region. On such nights it was the custom of all the passengers to be congregated together upon the deck, where the silent pleasures of contemplation were, from time to time, interrupted by some merry song chanted in chorus by the mariners, or perhaps some wild barbarian ditty, consecrated by the zeal of Boto to the honour of some ancient indigenous hero of the North. Nor did our jovial Prætorian disdain to contribute now and then to the amusement of the assembly, by some boisterous war-song, composed, perhaps, by some light-hearted young spearman, which our centurion might have learned by heart, without any regular exertion, from hearing it sung around many a British and Dacian watch-fire.

Thus we contrived to pass the time in a cheerful manner, till we reached the Lilybæan promontory. We tarried there two days to refit some part of our rigging, and then stretched boldly across the lower sea, towards the mouth of the Tiber. We were becalmed, however, for a whole day and night, after we had come within sight of the Pharos of Ostium, where, but for the small boats that came out to us with fresh fish and fruit, we should have had some difficulty in preserving our patience; for, by this time, our stock of wine was run to the last cup, and nothing remained to be eat but some mouldy biscuit which had survived two voyages between Italy and Britain. During this unwelcome delay, the Prætorian endeavoured to give me as much information as he could about the steps necessary to be pursued on my arrival in the city. But, to say truth, his experience had lain chiefly among martial expeditions and jovial recreations, so that I could easily perceive he was no great master of the rules of civil life. From him, however, I was glad to find, that the reputation of Licinius was really as great at Rome as it had been represented in our province; and, indeed, he treated me with a yet greater measure of attention after he was informed of my relationship to that celebrated jurist.

Early in the morning, a light breeze sprung up from the west, and with joyful acclamations the sails were once again uplifted. The number of mariners on board was insufficient for impelling the heavily laden vessel altogether by the force of oars, but now they did not refuse to assist the favouring breeze with strenuous and lively exertion. The Prætorian cheered and incited them by his merry voice, and even the passengers were not loath to assist them in this labour. My slave, among the rest, joined in the toil; but his awkwardness soon relieved him from his seat on the bench; a disgrace which he would have shared with his master, had I been equally officious.

Ere long, we could trace with exactness those enormous structures by which the munificence of Augustus had guarded and adorned that great avenue of nations to the imperial city. Those mountains of marble, projected on either side into the deep, surpassed every notion I had formed of the extent to which art may carry its rivalry of nature. Their immovable masses were garnished here and there with towers and battlements, on which the Prætorian pointed out to me the frame-work of those terrible catapults, and other engines of warfare, of which no specimens have ever been seen in Britain.

No sooner had we stept upon the shore, than we were surrounded by a great throng of hard-favoured persons, who pulled us by the cloak, with innumerable interrogations and offers of service. Among these, the varieties of form, complexion, and accent, were such, that we could not regard them without especial wonder; for it appeared as if every tribe and language under heaven had sent some representative to this great seaport of Rome. The fair hair and blue eye of the Gaul or German, might here be seen close by the tawny skin of the Numidian or Getulian slave, or the shining blackness of the Ethiopian visage. The Greek merchant was ready, with his Thracian bondsman carrying his glittering wares upon his back; the usurer was there, with his arms folded closely in his mantle; nor was the Chaldean or Assyrian soothsayer awanting, with his air of abstraction and his flowing beard.

Boto, as if alarmed with the prevailing bustle, and fearful lest some untoward accident should separate us, kept close behind me, grasping my gown. But our good friend Sabinus did not long leave us in this perplexity; for, having hastily engaged the master of a small barge to carry him to Rome, he insisted that I should partake of this easy method of conveyance. We found the vessel small but convenient, furnished with a red awning, under which cushions and carpets were already stretched out for our repose. The oars were soon in motion, and we began to emerge from among the forest of masts with a rapidity which astonished me; for the multitude of vessels of all sizes, continually crossing and re-crossing, was so great, that at first I expected every moment some dangerous accident might occur.

By degrees, however, such objects failed to keep alive my attention; the sleeplessness of the preceding night, and the abundance of an Ostian repast, conspiring to lull me into a gentle doze, which continued for I know not what space. I awoke, greatly refreshed, and found we had made considerable progress; for the continual succession of stately edifices already indicated the vicinity of the metropolis. The dark green of the venerable groves, amidst which the buildings were, for the most part, embosomed, and the livelier beauties of the parterres which here and there intervened between these and the river, afforded a soft delight to my eyes, which had so long been fatigued with the uniform flash and dazzle of the Mediterranean waves, and the roughness of the sea-beaten precipices. The minute and elaborate cultivation every where visible, the smoothness of the shorn turf on the margin, the graceful foliage of the ancient planes and sycamores,—but, above all, the sublimity of the porticos and arcades, and the air of established and inviolable elegance which pervaded the whole region, kept my mind in pleasurable wonder. Here and there, a gentle winding conducted us through some deep and massy shade of oaks and elms; whose branches, stretching far out from either side, diffused a sombre and melancholy blackness almost entirely over the face of Tiber. Loitering carelessly, or couched supinely, beneath some of these hoary branches, we could see, from time to time, the figure of some stately Roman, or white-robed lady, with her favourite scroll of parchment in her hand. The cool and glassy rippling of the water produced a humming music of stillness in the air, which nothing disturbed, save only the regular dash of the oars, and, now and then, the deep and strenuous voice of our cautious helmsman. Anon would ensue some glimpse of the open champaign, descending with all its wealth of golden sheaves to the very brink of the river—or, perhaps, the lively courts of a farmyard stretching along the margin of some tributary streamlet—or some long expanse of level meadow, with herds of snow-white heifers. I could not gaze upon the rich and splendid scene without reverting, with a strange mixture of emotions, to the image of this my native land; its wild forests, shaggy with brushwood and unprofitable coppice, through which of old the enormous wild deer stalked undisturbed, except by the adder of the grass, or the obscene fly of the thicket; its little patches of corn and meadow, laboriously rescued from the domain of the wild beast, and rudely fortified against his continual incursions;—the scattered hamlets of this Brigian valley, and my own humble villa—then humbler than it is now. Trees, and temples, and gardens, and meadows, and towns, and villages, were, ere long, lost in one uniform sobriety of twilight; and it was already quite dark, when the centurion, pointing to the left bank, said, "Behold the Gardens of Cæsar: beyond, is the Portian Gate, and the street of the Rural Lares. In a few moments we shall see the lights of the Sublician Bridge, and be in the city." At these words I started up, and gazing forward, could penetrate through the mists of evening into the busy glare of a thousand streets and lanes, opening upon the river. The old wall was already visible; where, after having swept round the region towards the Vatican and Janicular Hills, it brings the last of its turrets close down to the Tiber, over against the great dock-yards by the Field of Brutus.

Through a forest of triremes, galleys, and all sorts of craft, we then shot on to the bridge—beneath the centre arch of which our steersman conducted us. Beyond, such was the hum of people on the quays, and such the star-like profusion of lights reflected in the water, that we doubted not we had already reached the chief seat of the bustle of Rome. On, however, we still held our course, till the theatre of Marcellus rose like a mountain on our right. It was there that we ran our bark into the shore, not far from the little bridge—the third as you ascend the river—which conducts to the Island and the Temple of Æsculapius. While our friend was settling matters with the master, and the attendants were bringing out our baggage, I stood by myself on the elevated quay. Here a long tier of reflected radiance bespoke, it may be, the vicinity of some splendid portico—of palace, or temple, or bath, or theatre; there a broad and steady blaze of burning red, indicated the abode of artizans, resolved, as it seemed, on carrying their toil into the bosom of the night. Between—some speck of lustre betrayed, perhaps, the lamp of the solitary student, or the sober social hour of some peaceful family, assembled around the hearth of their modest lares. Behold me then, said I, in the capital of the globe; but were I to be swallowed up this moment in the waves of Tiber, not one of all these lights would be dimmed.

CHAPTER II.

Being told that my relation had his residence at no great distance, the friendly Sabinus insisted upon escorting me thither in safety. We walked, therefore, along two or three proud streets, which brought us near to the Pantheon of Agrippa, and there the house was easily pointed out to us; its porch decorated with recent palm-branches, which the Centurion said must have been placed there by the joyful hands of some fortunate client. Here having thanked this kind person, and left honest Boto among the crowd of slaves in the vestibule, I was speedily conducted into the presence of the Patrician.

I found him in a small upper chamber, lighted by a single silver lamp suspended from the roof, enjoying, as it appeared, repose and relaxation after the exertions of the day. He was reclining when I entered; and although supper was long over, some fruits and other trifling things still remained on the board. At table with him there was no one present, excepting a Greek of solemn aspect, whom he introduced to me as the superintendent of his son's education, and Sextus himself, a modest and ingenuous youth, who sat at the lower extremity of his father's couch. He was indeed a very mild and amiable young man, and I had more pleasure, after a space, in surveying his features, than the more marked lineaments of the other two. At first, however, nothing riveted my attention so much as the energetic physiognomy of the Senator. The forepart of his head was already quite bald, although the darkness of the short curls behind testified that age was not the cause of this deformity. His eyes were black and rapid, and his eyebrows vibrated in a remarkable manner, not only when he spoke, but even when he was silent; indicating, as it appeared, by their transitions, every new train of thought and imagination within his mind. His style of conversation was quick and fervid, and his gestures vehement as he spake; it being apparent, that, from restlessness and vanity of disposition, he was continually exercising a needless measure of mental activity and anxiety. Not satisfied with his own sufficient richness of ideas, no thought could be expressed which he did not immediately seize upon, and explain, even to him by whom it had been first suggested, with much fluency and earnestness of illustration. On the other hand, the guest, who wore a long beard reaching to his girdle, preserved in all things an uncommon demureness of manner, restraining every salient movement of his mind, and watching, with the gravity of a Numa, the glancing eyes and sharp features of his patron. A roll of yellow parchment graced his left hand, but the other was employed in selecting from the table such articles as were most agreeable to his palate. Licinius, although meagre in person, and at that time parched with declamation, seemed to live in such a state of intellectual excitement, that he thought little either of eating or drinking; therefore, the Athenian, resigning, for the most part, his share of the conversation, amused himself, in exchange, with the more trivial gratifications abandoned to him by his host. Nor, if one might draw any conclusion from his complexion and figure, was this the first occasion on which Xerophrastes had exercised that species of humility.

When Licinius had inquired of me concerning my native place, and also given a few words to the affairs which had brought me to the city, his conversation was naturally directed to subjects more new to me, if not more interesting to him. "You would observe," said he, "the palm branches at my door. They were won to-day by a five hours' harangue before the Centumviri. It is only in contests such as these that men of my order have now any opportunity to exercise themselves, and preserve some remembrance of those ancient worthies and great public characters that once adorned the state. To these things, therefore, young kinsman, I entirely devote myself; nor aim, like other citizens of rank, at passing the day in diversion, and ending it with luxuries. At supper my table is furnished with moderate fare, while in other houses I know not how many roasted boars and pompous sturgeons have been regaling with the rich perfume of their sauces and stuffing, guests who love the meat more than the man who gives it. This learned person knows how laborious is my course of life, and what an impatient crowd awaits my appearance every morning. His pupil will, I hope, tread in the same steps, and afford to a future generation the image of the former Licinius." With these, and the like discourses, he occupied our ears till it was time to retire; and then intimated that he had allotted to me an apartment which he expected I would continually occupy during my residence in the city. But being informed that I had a British slave with me, he insisted on having this man sent for, that he might see him, as he expressed it, before the genuine unsophisticated barbarian had been corrupted by keeping company with the cunning menials of the metropolis. Whereupon, it was commanded that Boto should come up, and he was forthwith ushered in by a certain leering varlet, with rings in his ears, whose face resembled some comic mask in the habitual archness of its malicious and inquisitive look.

Not few were the bows and scrapes with which my Briton entered these penetralia; nor was the astonishment inconsiderable with which the orator regarded Boto. "So, friend," said Licinius,—"and you have ventured to come to Rome, without so much as shaving your beard?" But the merry and good-natured tone in which these words were uttered, having somewhat reassured the bashful rustic, he gave a sly side-look towards the philosopher, (who, I think, had never once glanced at him,) and replied to Licinius, "Pardon me, O master, for coming thus into your presence; but I knew not, till Dromo told me, that beards were worn in Rome only by goats and the wisest of mankind." The words of the barbarian amused the orator—but, turning round to his own slave, "Ah! Dromo," said he, "do I already recognize the effects of your teaching?—beware the whip, corrupt not this good Briton, at your peril." He then asked of Boto various questions concerning his recent voyage; to all of which he made answers after his own fashion, sufficiently sagacious. Great contempt, however, was depicted on the face of the silent stoic during this conversation; which he, no doubt, looked upon as a very unworthy condescension on the part of Licinius; till at last, having, in a leisurely manner, poured out the last of the flagon, Xerophrastes arose from his couch and departed. As he withdrew, he unfortunately struck his knee on the corner of the table, which elicited from his stubborn features a sudden contortion. This, however, he immediately smoothed of, twisting his involuntary stoop into an obeisance to the Senator.

Young Sextus conducted me to my chamber; and we conversed together with easy juvenile confidence for some time before he left me.

CHAPTER III.

My sleep was sound and sweet; nevertheless, when the morning began to dawn, I was awakened by its first glimmerings, and found that my thoughts became at once too busy to admit of a return to slumber. I therefore arose, and went to walk in an open gallery, with which my chamber was connected. This gallery commanded a prospect of a great part of the city, which at that hour appeared no less tranquil than stately, nothing being in motion except a few small boats gliding here and there upon the river. Neither as yet had any smoke begun to darken the atmosphere; so that all things were seen in a serene and steady light, the shadows falling broadly westward over streets and squares—but pillars, and obelisks, and arches, rising up every where with unsullied magnificence into the bright air of the morning. The numerous poplars and other lofty trees of the gardens, also, seemed to be rejoicing in the hour of dew and silence; so fresh and cheerful was the intermixture of their branches among the piles of white and yellow marble. Near at hand, over the groves of the Philoclean Mansion, I could see the dome of the Pantheon, all burnished with living gold, and the proud colonnades of the Flaminian Circus, loaded with armies of brazen statues. Between these and the river, the theatres of Pompey and Marcellus, and I know not how many temples, were visible. Across a more crowded region, to the westward, my eye ascended to the cliffs and towers of the Capitol; while, still farther removed from me, (although less elevated in natural situation,) the gorgeous mansion of the Emperor was seen, lifted up, like some new and separate city, upon its enormous fabric of arcades. Behind me, the Flavian Amphitheatre, the newest and the most majestic of all Roman edifices, detained the eye for a space from all that lay beyond it—the splendid mass of the Esquiline—and those innumerable aqueducts which lie stretched out, arch after arch, and pillar after pillar, across the surrounding plain.

As I stood upon a projecting balcony, I heard some person stepping softly along the floor, and, being screened by some pillars, looked back into the gallery without subjecting myself to observation in return. The noise, I found, was occasioned by one of the slaves of Licinius, (the same I had remarked over night,) who had an air of anxious vigilance on this occasion, looking about from side to side as if afraid of being detected in some impropriety. I heard him tap at one of the apartments adjoining my own, and young Sextus, opening the door, eagerly asked, "Well, Dromo, good Dromo, what news?—Have you seen or heard any thing of her?—Speak low, I beseech you, and remember that my preceptor is near." "Which preceptor?" replied Dromo; "count me your best, and I will teach you how to manage all besides."—"Hush!" whispered the young man; "he may be astir with these eternal parchments."—"Be easy," returned the slave; "I have found out facts which will serve to bridle that tongue at any time."—"Dromo," said Sextus, "have a care; remember the thong of sleek leather which hangs at the foot of the stair-case; and many is the time I have saved you from it; for which you may, perhaps, have to thank the beauty of her who has rendered you necessary to me, as much as my own good nature. But no more idle words at present—what have you to tell me?"

"I have just been down," answered he, "to the herb-market. I had made my bargain, and was coming away, when I met one of old Capito's men, driving an ass laden with articles from the country. So I asked if he was carrying a present to his master's brother. He said he had brought nothing for Lucius but a letter; and that he believed its purport was to invite the two young ladies, to come out to-day and enjoy the beauty of the season. I no sooner got this information, than I ran hither as swiftly as my legs would carry me. You can easily go out, as if by chance, to pay your respects to the Patrician."

"Ah, Sempronia!" sighed Sextus, "shall I approach you at last?—What will she think when she sees me there?—Oh, how will she speak to me?"

While he was uttering these words, Dromo suddenly started, and came peeping on tiptoe towards the place where I stood. I stepped from behind my pillar, and said to the astonished youth, "Fear not, Sextus, that I shall intermeddle with your secrets, or make any use of what I have accidentally overheard. But I wish you would satisfy my curiosity, and inform me who is this lady, and what may be the meaning of all this concealment?"

Here Dromo, perceiving that his young master was a good deal confused, came forward and said, "From observing your looks last night, when I was making a handle of yon barbarian to torture our friend of the porch, I think you are a good-natured person, who would not willingly bring any of us into trouble. The truth is, that Licinius wishes my young master here to marry a certain lady, who has already had wet eyes over the ashes of a first husband; but who is of noble birth, and very rich. Now Sextus, being only eighteen, does not like this great lady so well as she likes him; and has, in fact, lost his heart elsewhere."—"Dromo," answered I, taking young Sextus by the hand as I spoke, "this is a pretty common sort of story; but I shall take no side till I have seen both of the ladies; and the sooner your ingenuity can bring that about, the more shall I be beholden to you."—"We shall try," replied the slave, observing that I had overcome the reluctance of the lover; "but in the meantime I observe that the clients are beginning to assemble in the porch, to await the forthcoming of Licinius. Go, therefore, and get some breakfast, for, by and by, you will both be expected to accompany the Senator to the Forum, to hear him plead; which, between ourselves, will be a six hours' job for you, unless you manage matters dexterously."

This hint produced a visible effect on Sextus; but we went down together immediately to an apartment, where some bread and grapes were prepared for us; and there, with much ingenuousness, he opened his heart to me. But what surprised me most of all, was to hear, that although he had been enamoured of Sempronia for several months, and was well acquainted with several of her relations, he had never yet seen her, except at certain places of public resort, nor enjoyed any opportunity of making known his passion.

While I was expressing my astonishment at this circumstance, we were interrupted by Xerophrastes, who came to inform us that Licinius, having already descended into the hall, was about to issue forth, and desirous of my company, if no other occupation detained me. We accordingly followed the philosopher, and found his patron where he had indicated, pacing to and fro, in the highest state of excitation, like a generous steed about to scour the field of battle. The waxen effigies of his ancestors stood at one end of the hall, some of them defaced with age; and upon these he frequently fixed his ardent eyes. Seeing me enter, he immediately cried out, "Come hither, young friend, and I shall presently conduct you to a scene worthy, above all others, of the curiosity of a stranger."

With this, arranging his gown, and putting himself into a dignified attitude, he ordered the porter, who stood chained by the door, to throw wide its massy valves; which being done, the litigants and consulters, who were without, received the orator with acclamations, and surrounded him on all sides. Some of the poorer ones, I observed kissing the hem of his garment, and dodging wistfully at his elbows, without ever attracting a word or look from him; while those of a higher class came forward more familiarly, seeking to impress particular circumstances upon his memory, and paying him compliments on the appearance he had made the day before in the Centumviral Court. Encircled by this motley group, he walked towards the great Forum, followed at a little distance by Sextus, the preceptor, myself, and some freedmen of his household. In moving on, we passed, by accident, the door of another great pleader, by name Bruttianus, who stood there attended in a similar manner. When he perceived Licinius, this man took from his door-post a green palm-branch, and waved it towards us in a vaunting manner; but our friend, saluting him courteously, cried out, with his sharp and cutting voice, "We shall try it again." Whereon Xerophrastes, immediately stepping up to his patron, began thus, "How this vain-glorious person exposes himself!—he is certainly a weak man; and his tones, by Hermes, are more detestable than those of an African fowl."—At which words, Sextus tipped me the wink; but I did not observe that Licinius was at all displeased with them. Yet, soon after, Bruttianus having overtaken us, the processions were joined, and the two pleaders walked the rest of the way together in a loving manner, exchanging complimentary speeches; to which Xerophrastes listened with edifying gravity of visage.

At length we entered that venerable space, every yard of whose surface is consecrated to the peculiar memory of some great incident in the history of Rome. Young Sextus allowed me to contemplate for some time, with silent wonder, the memorable objects which conspired to the decoration of this remarkable place; but after the first gaze of astonishment was satisfied, proceeded to point out, in order, the names and uses of the principal structures which rose on every side over its porticos—above all, of its sublime temples—into whose cool and shady recesses the eye could here and there penetrate through the open valves. Nor did the ancient rostrum from which Tully had declaimed, escape our observation—nor within its guarding rail of silver, the rising shoots of the old mysterious fig-tree of Romulus— nor the rich tesselated pavement which covered the spot that had once yawned an abyss before the steady eye of Curtius—nor the resplendent Milliary pillar which marked the centre of the place. In a word, had the gathering crowds permitted, I could have willingly spent many hours in listening to the explanation of such magnificent objects; but these, and the elevated voice of Licinius, who was just beginning his harangue, soon compelled me to attend to things of another description.

Within one of the proud ranges of arcade, on the side nearest to the Capitoline stairs, a majestic Patrician had already taken his seat on an elevated tribunal—his assessors being arranged on a lower bench by his side, and the orators and clients congregated beneath. When I heard the clear and harmonious periods of my kinsman; when I observed with what apparent simplicity he laid his foundations in a few plain facts and propositions; with what admirable art he upreared from these a superstructure of conclusions, equally easy as unexpected; when he had conducted us to the end of his argument, and closed with a burst of passionate eloquence, in which he seemed to leave even himself behind him, I could not but feel as if I had now for the first time contemplated the practised strength of intellect. Yet I have lived to discover that the talent which so greatly excited my wonder is often possessed from nature, or acquired through practice, in a measure which at that time would have afforded me scarcely inferior delight, by men of no extraordinary rank.

The keen and lively gestures of the fervid Licinius, whose soul seemed to speak out of every finger he moved, and who appeared to be altogether immersed in the cause he pleaded, were succeeded by the solemn and somewhat pompous stateliness of Bruttianus, who made a brief pause between every two sentences, as if he were apprehensive that the mind of the judge could not keep pace with the stream of his illustrations, and looked round ever and anon upon the spectators with a placid and assured smile, rather, as it seemed to me, to signify his approbation of their taste in applauding him, than his own pleasure in their applauses. Nevertheless, he also was a splendid speaker, and his affectation displeased the more, because it was evidently unworthy of his understanding. While he was speaking, I observed that the Stoic preceptor was frequently shifting his place among the crowd, and muttering every where expressions of high contempt. But this did not disgust me so much as the fixed attitude of ecstasy in which he listened to the discourse of his own patron, and the pretended involuntary exclamations of his delight. "Oh, admirable cadence!" he would say, "I feel as if I were draining a honey-comb. Oh, harmonious man, where have I, or any other person here, sucked in such sweetness!" These absurd phrases, however, were caught up forthwith, and repeated by the numerous young men who hung upon the skirts of the orator, and seemed, indeed, to be drinking in nectar from the speech, if one might judge from their countenances. From their taking notes in their tablets from time to time, and from the knowing looks they assumed at the commencement of every new chain of argument, I guessed that these might be embryo jurisconsults, preparing themselves by their attendance for future exertions of the same species; and, indeed, when I listened to their conversation at the close of every speech, I thought I could perceive in their tones and accents, studied mimicry of the natural peculiarities of Licinius, Bruttianus, and the other orators. Altogether, the scene was as full of amusement as of novelty, and I could willingly have remained to the end of the discussion. But my eyes chanced to fall upon young Sextus, and I could not but see that his mind was occupied in matters remote from the business of the Forum. He stood with his arms folded in his gown, and his eyes fixed upon the ground, only lifting them up from time to time with an impatient air towards a side entrance, or to observe by the shadows on the porticos what progress the sun was making.

Perceiving, at length, that Xerophrastes had his back turned to us, and that his father was engaged with his tablets, he plucked me by the sleeve. I understood his meaning, and followed him quickly through the crowd; nor did we look back till we had left the noise of the Forensic assembly entirely behind us. "I am depriving you," he said, "of no great gratification, for that old creature is, indeed, possessed of much natural shrewdness, but he is bitter from observing that his reputation is rather eclipsed by younger people, and looks like some worn-out and discarded cat, grinning from the top of the wall at the dalliance of some sleeker rival. You could find no delight in the angry sneerings of such an envious person; and his age would prevent you, at the same time, from willingly giving way to contemptuous emotions. I will be your guide to the villa. But if any questions be asked on our return, you can say I was anxious to shew you something of the other regions of the city."

He hurried me through noble streets, and past innumerable edifices, before each of which I would gladly have paused. Nevertheless, seeing him wrapped up in anxious thoughts, I did not oppose myself to his inclinations; and ere long, having passed the Hill of Gardens, I found that we had gained the eastern limit of the city.

CHAPTER IV.

A sharp walk of about an hour and a half on the Salarean Way, brought us within sight of the Suburban of Capito.

A lofty wall protected the fields of this retirement from the intrusive eyes of passengers. We entered by a small side-door, and found ourselves, as if by some magical delusion, transported from the glare of a Roman highway, into the depth and silence of some primeval forest. No nicely trimmed path conducted our feet. Every thing had at least the appearance of being left as nature had formed it. The fern rustled beneath us as we moved; the ivy was seen spreading its careless tresses from tree to tree; the fawn bounded from the thicket. By degrees, however, the gloom lessened, till at length, over an open space of lawn, we perceived the porch of entrance, and a long line of colonnade. We passed under the porch, and across a paved court where a fountain was playing, into the great hall, which commanded all the other side of the place—a noble prospect of elaborate gardens gradually rising into shady hills, and lost in a distance of impenetrable wood.

Here a freedman attended us, who informed us that Capito had retired into a sequestered part of the grounds with some friends from the city; but that if we chose we could easily join him there. We assented, and, following his guidance, ere long traversed no narrow space of luxuriant cultivation. From one perfumed terrace we descended to another; till, having reached a certain green and mossy walk, darkened by a natural arching of vines and mulberries, the freedman pointed to a statue at the farther end, and told us it stood over against the entrance of his master's summer-house. When we reached the statue, however, we could perceive no building. The shaded avenue terminated in face of a precipitous rock, from which there fell a small stream that was received in a massive basin, where the waters foamed into spray without transgressing the margin. A thousand delicious plants and far-sought flowers clustered around the base of the rock and the brink of the fountain, and the humming of innumerable bees mingled with the whispers of the stream. We stood for a moment uncertain whether we should move on or retire, when we heard one calling to us from beyond; and passing to the other side of the basin, descried, between the rock and the falling water, a low entrance into what seemed to be a natural cave or grotto. We stooped, and found ourselves within one of the most luxurious retirements ever haunted by the foot of Dryad. A sparry roof hung like a canopy of gems and crystals over a group of sculptured Nymphs and Fawns, which were placed on a rustic pedestal within a circular bath shaped out of the living stone. Around the edge of the waveless waters that slumbered in this green recess, were spread carpets rich with the dyes of Tyrian art, whereon Capito was reposing with his friends. He received Sextus with kindness, and me with politeness, introducing us both to his companions, who were three in number—all of them, like himself, advanced in years, and two of them wearing long beards, though their demeanour was destitute of any thing like the affected stateliness of our friend Xerophrastes. These two, as our host informed us, were Greeks and Rhetoricians—the third, a Patrician of the house of the Pontii, devoted, like himself, to the pursuits of philosophy and the pleasures of a literary retirement.

They were engaged, when we joined them, in a conversation which had sprung from the perusal of some new metaphysical treatise. One of the Greeks, the more serene-looking of the pair, was defending its doctrines with earnestness of manner, although in a low and measured cadence of voice; the other espoused the opposite side, with quickness of utterance and severe animation of look; while the two lordly Romans seemed to be contenting themselves, for the most part, with listening, although it was not difficult to perceive from their countenances, that the one sided in opinion with the Stoic, and Capito himself with the Epicurean.

They all arose presently, and proceeded to walk together, without interrupting the conversation, along the same shaded avenue which Sextus and myself had already traversed. He and I moved along with them, but a little in their rear—my companion being still too much abstracted to bestow his attention on what they were saying; while I myself, being but little an adept in such mysteries, amused myself rather with the exterior and manners of the men, than with the merits of the opinions they were severally defending. The Greeks were attired in the graceful costume of their country, which was worn, however, far more gracefully by the Epicurean than his brother,—the materials of his robe being delicate, and its folds arranged with studied elegance, whereas the coarse garment of the Stoic had apparently engaged less attention. Nevertheless, there was a more marked difference between the attire of Capito and that of Pontius Mamurra; for the former was arrayed in a tunic of the whitest cloth, beneath which appeared fine linen rollers, swathing his thighs and legs, to protect them, as I supposed, from the heat and the insects, and a pair of slippers, of dark violet-coloured cloth, embroidered with silver flowers; while the other held his arms folded in the drapery of an old but genuine toga, which left his yet strong and sinewy nether limbs exposed to the weather, all except what was covered by his tall black sandals and their senatorian crescents.

As we passed on, our host from time to time directed the attention of his visiters, more particularly of the two Greeks, to the statues of bronze and marble, which were placed at convenient intervals along the terraces of his garden. The symmetry of these figures, and the graceful simplicity of their attitudes, inspired me with I know not what of calm and soothing pleasure such as I had never before tasted, so that I thought I could have lingered for ever amidst these haunts of philosophic luxury. The images were, for the most part, portraits of illustrious men—Greeks, Romans—sages and heroes; but beautiful female forms were not wanting, nor majestic representations of gods and demi-gods, and all the ethereal imaginations of the Grecian poets. Seeing the name of Jupiter inscribed upon one of the pedestals, I paused for a moment to contemplate the glorious personification of might and wisdom, depositing, at the same time, a handful of roses at the feet of the statue—upon which I could observe that my behaviour furnished some mirth to the Epicurean Demochares; while, on the contrary, Euphranor, the disciple of the Porch, approved of what I did, and rebuked his companion for saying any thing that might even by possibility disturb the natural piety of an innocent youth. But the Roman Stoic stood by with a smile of stately scorn; and utter indifference was painted on the countenance of Capito. At another time, Sextus having staid behind to examine the beauties of a certain statue of Diana, which represented the goddess stretched out in careless slumber on the turf, with a slender grayhound at her feet, the Epicurean began to rally me on having a taste inferior to that of my friend, whose devotion, he said, could not be blamed, being paid to an exquisite imitation of what the great Nature of things had decreed should ever be the most agreeable of all objects in the eyes of a person of his age.—"Whereas you," continued he, "appear to be more occupied with deep-hung eye-brows, ambrosial beards, and fantastic thunderbolts, and the other exuberances of Homeric imagination."

To this reproach I made no reply, but Capito immediately began to recite some verses of a Hymn of Calimachus, in which both the Greeks joined him; nor could any thing be more delightful than the harmonious numbers. A sudden exclamation of my friend, however, interrupted them, and Capito, looking up a long straight pathway, said, "Come, Valerius, we shall see whether you or Sextus is the more gallant to living beauties, for here come my nieces. I assure you, I know not of which of them I am the more proud; but Sempronia has more of the Diana about her, so it is probable she may find a ready slave in our Sextus."

We advanced, and the uncle, having tenderly saluted them, soon presented us to their notice. Sextus blushed deeply when he found himself introduced to Sempronia, while in her smile, although she looked at him as if to say she had never seen him before, I thought I could detect a certain half-suppressed something of half-disdainful archness—the colour in her cheeks, at the same time, being not entirely unmoved. She was, indeed, a very lovely girl, and in looking on her light dancing play of features, I could easily sympathize with the young raptures of my friend. Her dress was such as to set off her charms to the utmost advantage, for the bright green of her Byssine robe, although it would have been a severe trial to any ordinary complexion, served only to heighten the delicious brilliancy of hers. A veil, of the same substance and colour, richly embroidered with flowers of silver tissue, fell in flowing drapery well-nigh to her knees. Her hair was almost entirely concealed by this part of her dress, but a single braid of the brightest nut-brown was visible low down on her polished forehead. Her eyes were black as jet, and full of a nymph-like vivacity.

The other, Athanasia, was not a dazzling beauty. Taller than her cousin, and darker-haired, but with eyes rather light than otherwise, of a clear, somewhat melancholy gray—with a complexion paler than is usual in Italy, a demeanour hovering between cheerfulness and innocent gravity, and attired with a vestal simplicity in the old Roman tunic, and cloak of white cloth—it is possible that most men might have regarded her less than the other. A single star of diamonds, planted high up among her black hair, was the only ornament she wore.

At the request of the younger lady, we all returned to the grotto, in the neighbourhood of which, as I have already mentioned, our tasteful host had placed the rarest of his exotic plants, some of which Sempronia was now desirous of inspecting. As we paced again slowly over those smooth-shaven alleys of turf, and between those rows of yews and box, clipped into regular shapes, which abounded in this more artificial region, the conversation, which the appearance of the cousins had disturbed, was resumed; although, as out of regard to their presence, the voices of the disputants preserved a lower and milder tone than before. I must confess, however, that mild as was the manner of the discourse, I could not help being somewhat astonished, that a polite Roman could permit such topics to be discussed in the hearing of females; above all, that he did not interpose to prevent Demochares from throwing out so many sarcastic reflections concerning the deities whose statues decorated the garden. A beautiful Mercury, in particular, which we all paused to admire, elicited many observations, that I could easily see were far from being agreeable to the fair cousins. But greatest of all was my wonder at the behaviour of Capito himself, who, after we had again entered that delightful grotto, turned himself to me as if peculiarly, and began a deliberate and ingenious piece of declamation concerning the tenets of his favourite philosophy;—such as the fortuitous concourse of atoms, the transitory and fluctuating nature of all things, and the necessity of snatching present enjoyments, as nothing permanent can be discovered whereon to repose the mind. With great elegance, indeed, did he enlarge on these golden theories, nor did he fail to intersperse his discourse with many exquisite verses from Lucretius and other poetical followers of his sect. Such, however, was the earnestness of his declamation, that I could not help believing him to be quite sincere to what he said, and asked him, not without anxiety, whether he had all his life been an Epicurean, or whether it was only of late that he had espoused that discipline.

"Valerius," said he, "the question is not discreditable to your tender age and provincial education. To be born wise, Fate or Heaven has denied to the human race. It is their privilege to win wisdom for themselves; the fault is their own, if they do not die wise. When the stripling enters upon the theatre of the world, bright hopes are around him, and he moves onward in the buoyancy of conscious power. The pride of young existence is the essence and extract of all his innumerable sensations. Rejoicing in the feeling of the real might that is, it is his delight to think—to dream—of might existing and exerted as for ever. New to the material, but still more to the moral world, he believes in the stability of all things whose transitory nature has not been exhibited before him. New to the tricks of mankind, he believes that to be said truly, which, why it should be said falsely, he is unable to conjecture. For him, superstition has equal potency to darken the past, and illuminate the future. At that early period, when ignorance is of itself sufficient to produce a certain happiness, the ambition is too high to admit such doctrines as I have no shame in avowing. But time moves on, and every hour some tender plant is crushed beneath his tread. The spirit clings long to its delusions. The promise that is destroyed to-day springs into life to-morrow in some new shape; and Hope, like some warring deity of your poets, bleeds and sickens only to revive again. But disappointment at length gathers to itself the vigour of an enduring form. The horizon becomes colder around us—the soul waxes faint and more faint within. It is then that man begins to recognize the true state, not of his own nature alone, but of all things that surround him—that having tasted much of evil, he is taught to feel the value of good—and weaning himself from vain-glorious dreams, learns the great lesson of wisdom, to enjoy the moments as they pass—to snatch some solid pleasure, at least, amidst a world of vision and imagination; so, in a word, as the poet has expressed it, he may not have reason to complain in the hour of death that he has never lived.

"In me," he continued, "you behold one that has gone through the experience necessary to produce an entire acquiescence in these doctrines. I am one of those, Valerius, who have resolved to concentrate, after this fashion, the whole of my dreams upon the hour that is. There are not wanting, indeed, here and elsewhere, persons who profess the same theories, only in the view of finding excuse and shelter for the practice of vice. But till it be proved that the practice of vice is the best means of enjoyment, in vain shall it be asserted that our doctrine is essentially adverse to virtue. The mistakes or the misdeeds of individuals must be estimated for nothing; for where is the doctrine that may not be shewn to have been defended by impure livers? The founder of our sect is acknowledged, by its most virulent enemies, to have been the most blameless of men, and they, I must take leave to believe, can never be sincere friends of virtue, who doubt, that he who is a true worshipper of pleasure, may also be the worshipper of virtue."

There was a certain something, as I thought, more like suppressed melancholy than genuine hilarity, in the expression of the old man's face, as well as in the tone of his voice, while he gave utterance to these sentiments; nor did any of those present appear desirous of protracting the argument; although I did not imagine from their looks that any of them had altered their opinion. What, however, I could not help remarking in a particular manner, was the gentle regret painted in the countenance of the elder niece, while Capito was speaking. The maiden sate over against him all the while, her cheek supported on her left hand, with an expression of tender affection. From time to time, indeed, she cast her eye upward with a calm smile, but immediately resumed her attitude of pensive abstraction. Her uncle took her hand in his when he had done speaking, and kissed it gently, as if to apologize for having said any thing disagreeable to her. She smiled again upon the sceptic, and walked by herself, (for I could not help following her with my eye,) down into a dark walk of pines that branched off at the right hand from the entrance into the grotto. There I saw her stoop and pluck a pale flower. This she placed in her bosom, and then rejoined us with a more cheerful aspect; after which, we all walked towards the villa. Nor did it escape my notice, that, although Sempronia appeared willing to avoid Sextus as we went, it always happened, by some accident or other, that he was nearer to her than any other person of the company.

They were both at a little distance behind the rest of the party, when Euphranor addressed himself to me, saying, "Is not this youth, your companion, the same that is under the guidance of a certain Xerophrastes?"—"The same," said I, "and a wary, sage-looking Athenian is his tutor. I believe he also is of the Porch."—"No doubt," interrupted Demochares; "he has a beard that Zeno might have been proud of, and walks as if he conceived himself to be the chief pillar of the Porch, if not the Porch itself."—"Who shall prevent Demochares from having his jest?" replied Euphranor. "The man is by birth a Thessalian, and his gutturals still remind one strongly of his native hills."—I would gladly have heard more of it, but he was interrupted by the nearer approach of the rest.

CHAPTER V.

Before the hour of taking the bath, we exercised ourselves for some time in the tennis-court, where I could not but admire, especially after having heard Capito philosophise, the vigour and agility displayed by him as well as his companions. I was then conducted into the baths, where, after being washed and perfumed in the most luxurious manner, I was arrayed in an elegant supper-garment by one of the slaves of our host. At table we were joined again by the ladies, who both reclined on the same couch with their uncle. Three comely youths attended us, in short tunics, and girt with napkins of fine linen; but, during the repast, an ancient female slave stood in silence behind the couch of the young ladies. A small fountain of alabaster played between two tall candelabra of the same material, at the farther end of the apartment; and a young damsel stood beside them, swinging slowly from time to time a silver censer, from which clouds of delicate odour rolled up to the mirrored roof.

In all things the feast was splendid; but there was no appearance of useless or vain ostentation. Every thing was conducted in a style of great calmness and order, without the least formality. The repast interrupted not the conversation, which went on in a manner to me equally instructive as entertaining; although I must confess the presence of Athanasia sometimes rendered me inattentive to what was spoken. I could not divest myself of the idea, that some unknown circumstance was pressing on the mind of the fair creature, and that when she smiled upon those who addressed her, it was sometimes to conceal her ignorance of that which had been said.

Being asked by Capito, I endeavoured, among other things, to inform him and his friends, as far as I could, concerning the then condition of this island, which, more particularly after the exploits of Agricola, had come to be a subject of some interest. In return, the chief topics which then occupied the capital were discussed by them, as I perceived, in a great measure on my account; and I listened with delight to the praises, which they all agreed on bestowing on the new Emperor. Many anecdotes were narrated, which tended to strengthen the feelings of admiration, with which I had already been accustomed to contemplate his character. But others were told, as the conversation went on, which I could not so easily reconcile with the idea I had formed of him.

For example, I was somewhat disturbed with what they told me concerning his treatment of the Christians, who, as we understood in Britain, had been suffered to live in tranquillity ever since Nerva acceded to the empire. But now, from the circumstances related, it appeared that the mild and humane Trajan had taken up, in regard to this sect, the whole aversion of Domitian;

every day some cruel catastrophe was made known of some person who had adopted their tenets. Being ignorant of the nature of those tenets, and having heard only in general terms that they were of Jewish origin, dark, and mystical, I was at a loss to account for the extreme hatred of the Prince, or rather for his condescending to give himself so much trouble concerning a matter so obscure and seemingly trifling.

Capito, however, assured me, that although I might have good occasion to wonder at the steps taken by the Emperor, it would no longer be said by any one, that the progress of the Christian sect deserved to be considered as a matter either of obscurity, or of no consequence. "On the contrary," said he, "from what you have just heard of the numbers and quality of those that have lately suffered various punishments, you cannot hesitate to admit that the head of the empire has been justified in considering it as a subject worthy his attention."

"We have adopted the gods of many nations," said Pontius Mamurra, "nor do I see why, because the Jews have been unfortunate in a contest with Rome, we should take it for granted that theirs are unworthy of respect. If, however, as we have heard asserted, he who embraces this creed becomes an infidel in regard to the deities of Rome, I say Cæsar does well in refusing toleration to the intolerant superstition. Domitian was a tyrant, and a monster of humanity; the late prince was wise and good; and yet it may be, that, in regard to these Christians, the principle of Domitian's conduct was right in the main, and that of Nerva's wrong. But you, Capito, regard both sides of the question, I have no doubt, with the same indifference."

"I hope," replied Capito, "I shall never regard with indifference any question, in which the interest of the empire and the honour of Trajan are concerned. But if you mean only that I am indifferent about the nature of this Syrian superstition, you are in the right. I have no knowledge of its dogmas, nor desire to have. I presume they have their share of that old eastern barbarity, in the shady places of which the elder Greeks used to think they could discover the outlines of something really grand and majestic."

"It may be so," said Mamurra; "but if the superstition be found dangerous to the state, the Prince does well in repressing its progress. That is the only question of which I spake."—"There is, indeed, no other," said Capito; "I thought of none."—"And how do you answer it, dear uncle?" said Athanasia, (lifting herself up, for the first time, to take part in the conversation.)—"Nay, my love," said the old man, "to answer that is the business of Cæsar, and of the Senate. I only regret, that blood should be shed, and citizens exiled; above all, in the reign of a just and merciful Prince.—Sempronia," continued he, "what is that strange story your father was telling about one of the daughters of Serennius?"

"They only allege," replied Sempronia, with a smile, "that Tertulla had a flirtation with a handsome young Greek, and the Greek happened to be a Christian,—and she was converted by the Greek,—and she was found out in going with him to some secret assembly of these people, in a vault by the Vatican Hill,—and her father has been glad to send her to Corsica, partly to escape the lawyers, and partly, I suppose, in hopes that the quietness of the island, and the absence of handsome young Christians, may perhaps, in time, restore poor Tertulla to her right mind—This is all. Do you think that a strange story, uncle?" "Not, if it be exactly as you have told it, Sempronia. What says Athanasia?" Athanasia answered gravely, that she was sorry for Tertulla, and had never heard any thing of the young Greek before.

By this time, the increasing darkness of the chamber had warned me that we ought to be thinking of our return. I had more than once looked towards Sextus, but he refused to meet my eye. When I was on the point of speaking, Sempronia, starting from her couch, exclaimed, that she was sure there was thunder in the skies; and presently flash after flash gleamed along the horizon. All sat silent, as if awe-struck; but Sempronia was the only one that seemed to be in terror from the tempest. Nevertheless, my eyes rested more on Athanasia, who looked paler than she had done, although her countenance preserved its serenity. "How awful," said I, "is the voice of Jupiter!" Athanasia folded her arms upon her bosom, and lifting her eyes to heaven, said in a whisper,—"How awful is the voice of God!" She then dropt her hand on the end of her couch, and half unconsciously taking hold of it in mine, I asked her if she was afraid. "No," said she, "I am not afraid, but the heaviness of the air makes me faint, and I never can listen to thunder without feeling something extraordinary within me."

Capito said, he could not think of our going into the city that evening, and that we must all make up our minds to remain in the villa. The countenance of Sextus brightened up, and he looked to me as if to ask my assent. I was easily persuaded, and our host despatched a messenger to inform Licinius of the cause of our absence. The old man then led us into another apartment, which was richly furnished with books and paintings. Here he read for some time out of one of the poets, to a party, none of whom, I am afraid, were very attentive in listening to him, till, the hour of rest being come, we were conducted to our several apartments, Sextus and myself, indeed, being lodged in the same chamber.

We were no sooner left alone than I began to rally my friend on the beauty of his mistress, and the earnest court he had been paying her. The youth listened with blushes of delight to her praises, but seemed not to have the least idea that he had been so fortunate as to make any impression on her mind. On the contrary, he scarcely appeared to be aware of having done any thing to attract attention from her, and expressed astonishment when I assured him, that his behaviour had been such as could not possibly admit of more than one explanation in the eyes of a person so quick and vivacious as the lovely Sempronia.

After we had both retired to our beds, and the lights were extinguished, we still continued for some time to talk over the incidents of our visit, and the future prospects of Sextus and his love; until at length sleep overpowered us in easy bonds, and agreeable dreams followed, I doubt not, in the hearts of us both, the thoughts and sights of a delightful day. Mine surely were delightful, for they were all of Athanasia. Yet, even in the visions of the night, I could never gaze on her face without some strange impression of mystery. I saw her placid smile—I heard the sweet low cadence of her voice—but I felt, and I could not feel it without a certain indescribable anxiety, that her deep thoughts were far away.

CHAPTER VI.

I awoke early, and drew near to the bed of Sextus; but seeing that he was fast asleep, and that a quiet smile was on his lips, I could not think of awakening him. The sun shone bright into the apartment, and I resolved to walk forth and breathe the balmy air of the garden.

The moisture was still heavy on the green paths, and the birds were singing among glittering leaves; the god-like statues stood unscathed in their silent beauty. I walked to and fro, enjoying the enchantment of the scene;—a new feeling of the beauty of all things seemed to have been breathed into my soul; and the pensive grace of Athanasia hovered over my imagination, like some presiding genius of the groves.

I found myself near the favourite grotto, and had stood over against its entrance for some space, contemplating the augmented stream as it fell from the superincumbent rock, and regretting the ravage which the nightly tempest had made among the delicate flowers round its basin. Twice I thought I heard the murmurs of a voice, and twice I persuaded myself that it was only the rippling of the waters; but the third time I was satisfied that some person must be near. I passed between the water and the rock, and beheld the fair creature that had been occupying so many of my thoughts, kneeling far within the grotto, as it seemed, in supplication. To disturb her by advancing farther, would have been impious; to retire, without the risk of disturbing her, almost impossible; but I remained there fixed to the spot, without perhaps considering all these things as I should have done. The virgin modesty of her attitude was holy in my eyes, and the thought never occurred to me, that I might be doing wrong in permitting myself to witness the simple devotions of Athanasia. "Great God, listen to my prayers," was all I understood of what she said; but she whispered for some moments in a lowly and fervent tone, and I saw that she kissed something with her lips ere she arose from her knees. She then plunged her hands into the well, by whose brink she had knelt, and turned round to the light. "Athanasia, forgive me," was already on my lips; but on seeing me, she uttered a faint cry and fell prostrate upon the marble. I rushed forward, lifted up her head, and laved water from the fountain, till I saw her lips tremble. At last she opened her eyes, and after gazing on me wildly for a moment, she gathered her strength, and stood quite upright, supporting herself against the wall of the grotto. "Great heavens!" cried I, "in what have I offended, that I should be rendered the cause of affliction to Athanasia? Speak, lady, and say that you forgive me."

"I thought," said she, with a proud calmness, "that Valerius was of Roman—of Patrician blood. What brings him to be a spy upon the secret moments of a Patrician maiden?"—Then bursting into a tone of unutterable fervour, "Speak," said she, "young man, what have you heard? How long have you stood here? Am I betrayed?"

"Witness, heaven and earth!" cried I, kneeling, "and witness every god, that I have heard nothing, except to know that you were praying. I have only seen you kneeling, and been guilty of gazing on your beauty." "You heard not the words of my prayer?" said she. "No, not its words, Athanasia, nor any thing of its purpose." "Do you swear this to me, young man?" "Yes, I swear by Jupiter and by Rome—as I am a man and a Roman, I know not, neither do I desire to know, any thing of what you said. Forgive me for the fault of my indiscretion—you have no other to forgive."

Athanasia paused for a moment, and then resuming more of her usual tone of voice, (although its accents were still somewhat disturbed and faltering,) said to me, "Valerius, since the thing is so, I have nothing to forgive. It is you that must pardon me for my suspicion." "Distress me not, Athanasia," said I, "by speaking such words." "From this hour, then," said she, "what has passed here is forgotten. We blot it from our memories;"—and with that, as if in token of the paction, she extended to me her hand. I kissed it as I knelt, and swore that all things were safe with me; but added, as I arose, "that I was afraid I should be promising more than I should be able to perform,—did I say I should be able to forget any hour, or any place, where I had seen Athanasia." "Nay," said she, "no compliment, or I shall begin to suspect you of insincerity." I was then about to withdraw from the grotto; but seeing a scroll of parchment lying at the feet of Athanasia, I stooped, and presented it to her, saying, "I was afraid she might forget it." She took it eagerly, and saying, "Of that there was no danger," placed it in her bosom, within the folds of her tunic. She was then gathering up her black tresses, and fastening them hastily on the back part of her head, when we heard the sound of footsteps not far off, and beckoning to me to remain where I was, she darted from me, and in a moment vanished among the trees. I waited for a few minutes, and then stepping forth, beheld her walking at a distance, beside her sister, in the direction of the villa. They were soon lost among the paths, and I returned alone into the grotto.

I sat down beside the dark well, wherein she had dipt her hands, and mused in a most disturbed mood on all the particulars of this strange and unexpected interview. Every motion of her features—every modulation of her voice, was present with me; I had gathered them all into my heart, and I felt that I must cherish them there for ever. From the first moment I saw her, my eyes had been constrained to gaze upon her with an interest quite novel to me; but now I knew that she could not smile, without making my heart faint within me, and that the least whisper of her voice was able to bring tears into mine eyes. Now I thought of my own unworthiness, and could not help saying to myself, "Why should a poor ignorant provincial, such as I am, be torturing myself with the thoughts of such a creature as this?" Then, again, some benign glance of hers would return before me, and I could not help having some faint hopes, that her innocent heart might be won to me by faithful unwearied love. But what always threw me back into despair, was the recollection of the mystery that I knew hung over her mind, although what it was I could not know. That she had been saying something in her prayers which could not be overheard without betraying her, she had herself confessed. What could be this secret, so cherished in dread, and in darkness?—A crime?—No crime could sully the clear bosom of her innocence. No consciousness of guilt could be concealed beneath that heavenly visage. But perhaps she had been made the confidante of some erring,—some unhappy friend. Perhaps, in her prayer, she had made mention of another's name, and implored the pardon of another's guilt. Last of all, why might it not be so, that the maiden loved, and was beloved again; that she might have some reason to regard any casual betrayal of her affection as a calamity; and that, having uttered the name of her lover in her secret supplications, her terrors might all have been occasioned by her apprehensions of my having overheard it? And yet there was something in the demeanour of Athanasia, that I could not bring myself to reconcile entirely with any one of these suppositions. Had she feared that I had overheard any confession of guilt,—even of the guilt of another,—surely some semblance of shame would have been mingled with her looks of terror. Had she apprehended only the discovery of an innocent love, surely her blushes would have been deeper, and her boldness less. Yet the last solution of the difficulty was that which haunted me the most powerfully.

When I came forth into the open air, I perceived that the sun was already high in heaven, and proceeded in haste towards the villa, not doubting that Sextus and Capito would be astonished by the length of my absence. I found them and the ladies walking under the northern colonnade, having returned, as they told me, from a fruitless search after me through almost the whole of the garden. I looked to Athanasia, as if to signify that she well knew where I might have been found; but, although I saw that she understood my meaning, she said nothing in explanation. Sextus drew me aside shortly after, and told me, that his father had sent to inform him, that our presence was necessary in the city before supper-time, to attend a great entertainment which was to be given that evening by the lady whose cause he had successfully pleaded in the Forum on the preceding day; which lady, I now for the first time learned, was no other than the same Marcia Rubellia, to whom his father was very anxious the youth should be married. The success of this pleading had increased very much the wealth of the lady, and, of course, as Sextus well knew, the anxiety of Licinius for the proposed union; and to remain at the villa any longer, was, he said, entirely impossible, since he already suspected his father had not been quite pleased with him for leaving the Forum the day before, without staying to hear out a cause in which his duty, if not his inclination, ought to have made him feel so greatly interested.

We bade adieu, therefore, to our kind host and the young ladies, not without more reluctance than either of us durst express, and ready promises to return soon again to the villa. We found Dromo and Boto waiting for us at the gate, the former of whom looked unutterable things, while the latter appeared to be as joyful in seeing me again, as if we had been parted for a twelvemonth. The two slaves were mounted on asses, but they led horses for our conveyance; so we mounted with all speed, and were soon beyond the beautiful enclosures of Capito. As soon as we were fairly out of sight of the house, Dromo began to ply Sextus with innumerable questions about the result of the visit, all of them in bad Greek; that, as he said, there might be no chance of what passed being understood by the Druid; for by that venerable designation, he informed us, the primitive Boto had already come to be best known in the vestibule of Licinius. "Ah!" quoth he, "there is no need for many words; I am sure my young master has not been behindhand with himself. If he has, it is no fault of mine, however. I put Opportunity into his hands, and she, you know, as the poets say, has only one lock of hair, and that is in front."

Sextus being very shy of entering into particulars, I found myself obliged to take upon me the satisfying of the curiosity of this inquisitive varlet, which I did in a manner that much astonished Sextus, who by no means suspected, that in the midst of my own attention to the other cousin, I had been able to take so much notice of what passed between him and Sempronia. However, the gentle youth took a little raillery all in good part, and we laughed loudly in unison at the triumphant capers which the whip of Dromo made his poor ass exhibit, in testimony of his satisfaction with the progress which all things appeared to be making. We reached the city about three hours after noon, and were told by the slaves in attendance, that Xerophrastes had gone out some time before, and that Licinius was already busy in arraying himself for the feast of Rubellia.

CHAPTER VII.

Her mansion was situated about the middle of the Suburra, in a neighbourhood nowise splendid, and itself distinguished, on the side fronting to the street, by no uncommon marks of elegance or opulence. A plain brick wall covered almost the whole of the building from the eye of the passenger; and what was seen deserved the praise of neatness, rather than of magnificence. Nevertheless, the moment one had passed the gate, and entered the court, one could not help perceiving, that taste and wealth had been alike expended abundantly on the residence; for the broad terrace and gallery behind were lavishly adorned, the one with sculpture and the other with paintings; and the gardens, which these overlooked, appeared to be both extensive and elaborate.

We were conducted through several pillared halls, and then up a wide staircase, of somewhat sombre magnificence, into the chamber where the company were already in part assembled, and busy in offering their congratulations to the mistress of the feast. She was so much engaged with their flatteries that she did not at first perceive our entrance; but as soon as she knew who had come, the chief part of her attention was divided between her victorious advocate and his blushing son.

Rapidly as we have been advancing in our imitation of the manners of the capital, our island, most unquestionably, has never yet displayed any thing that could sustain the smallest comparison with what then met my eyes in the stately saloon of this widow. The group around her was gay and various, and she was worthy of forming its centre; young and handsome, dressed in a style of the utmost splendour, her deportment equally elegant and vivacious. Her complexion was of that clear rich brown which lends to the eye a greater brilliancy than the most exquisite contrast of red and white; and over which the blood, when it does come into the face, diffuses at once the warmest and the deepest of blushes. Her hair appeared to be perfectly black, unless where the light, streaming from behind, gave an edging of glossy brown to the thick masses of her curls. Her robe of crimson silk was fastened by a girdle, which seemed to consist of nothing but rubies and emeralds, strung upon threads of gold. She wore a tiara that rose high above her tresses, and was all over resplendent with flowers woven in jewellery; and around her delicate wrists and ankles were twined broad chains of virgin gold, interspersed with alternate wreaths of sapphire. Her form was the perfection of luxury; and although I have said that her deportment was in general lively and brilliant, yet there was a soft seriousness that every now and then settled in her eyes, which gave her, for a moment, a look of melancholy that seemed to me more likely to be in harmony with the secret nature of her disposition. I watched her in particular when she spoke to Sextus; her full rich-toned voice was then merry, and her large eyes sparkled; but when she was engaged with any other person, she could not help gazing on the beautiful youth in silence; and then it was that her countenance wore its deepest expression of calmness—I had almost said, of sadness.

I had been gazing on her, I know not how long, from another part of the room, when I heard a hearty chuckle from behind me, and thought I could not be unacquainted with the voice. Looking round, I saw, not without delight, the stately figure of my Prætorian Captain, Sabinus, whose cheerful eye soon distinguished me, and who forthwith came up to salute me in the most friendly manner. I introduced him to Licinius and Sextus, the former of whom expressed himself as being much gratified with the attention the centurion had shewn to me during our voyage; so that I felt myself, as it were, no longer a stranger in the place; and the lutes and trumpets at that moment announcing that supper was ready to be served up, I took care to keep close to Sabinus, and to place myself near him on the couch.

The room in which the feast was prepared, communicated by a pair of brazen folding doors, richly sculptured, with that in which the company had assembled; but from it, although the sun had not yet gone down, all light was excluded, excepting what streamed from golden candelabra, and broad lamps of bronze suspended overhead from the high and painted ceiling. The party might consist of about twenty, who reclined along one demi-circular couch, the covers of which were of the softest down, and the frame-work inlaid with ivory;—the part of the room enclosed by its outline being occupied with the table, and an open space to which the attendants had free access. We had no sooner taken our seats than a crowd of slaves entered, carrying large boards upon their heads, which being forthwith arranged on the table, were seen to be loaded with dishes of gold and silver, and all manner of drinking vessels, also with vases of rare flowers, and urns of perfume. But how did the countenance of Sabinus brighten, when the trumpet sounded a second time as if from below, and the floor of the chamber was suddenly, as it were, pierced in twain, and the pealing music ushered up a huge roasted boar, all wreathed with stately garnishings, and standing erect on his golden platform as on a chariot of triumph! "Ah! my dear boy," cries he, "here comes the true king of beasts, and only legitimate monarch of the woods. What should we not have given for a slice of him when we were pent up, half-starved and fainting, in that abominable ship of ours?—All hail, most potent conqueror! but whether Germanic or Asiatic be thy proper title, I shall soon know, when that expert Ionian has daintily carved and divided thee." But why should I attempt to describe to you the particulars of the feast? Let it suffice, that whatever idea I had formed of Roman profusion was surpassed, and that the splendour of the entertainment engaged the attention of all except Rubellia herself, who, reclining immediately above Sextus, kept her eyes fixed almost all the time it lasted, upon his luxuriant curls of dark hair, unless when she caused the young damsel, her cup-bearer, to pour out to her wine in a goblet of onyx, which she touched with her lips, and then handed to the indifferent boy. When the supper was half over, the folding-doors were again thrown open, and there entered a group of maidens and beautiful youths, who danced before us to the music of the lute, and scattered crowns of roses at the feet of Rubellia and her guests. She herself placed one of them on the head of Sextus, and another on that of his father, who lay on the other side of her, and then caused a large cup of wine to be carried all around, whereof each of us tasted, and drank to the health of the orator, in whose honour the entertainment was made. The ladies that were present imitated the example of the hostess, and crowned such as were by them; but Sabinus and I, not being near enough to any of them, received that courtesy from some of the dancing maidens. Libations were poured out abundantly on the marble floor, and all the gods were invoked to shower down their blessings on Rubellia, and those that had been so fortunate as to serve her. Sweet strains of music resounded through the tall pillars of the banqueting-room, and the lamps burned heavily in an atmosphere overloaded with perfumes.

It appeared to me, from the beginning, that my friend Sabinus witnessed, not without some feelings of displeasure, the excessive attentions which Rubellia lavished on young Sextus; and I gathered, from the way in which he every now and then looked towards them during the supper, that, had the place permitted, he would not have allowed such things to go on without some comment. But when we had left the banqueting-room, and removed to another apartment, where, amidst various entertainments of dancing, music, and recitation, Rubellia still retained close to herself the heir of Licinius, the centurion made to himself abundant amends for the previous restraint to which his temper had been subjected. "Confess now," said he, "that she is a lovely creature, and that your British beauties are tame and insipid, when compared with such a specimen of Roman fascination; and confess, withal, that this curled boy is either the most ignorant, or the most insusceptible of his sex. Good heavens! in what a different style was she treated by the old magistrate, whose very bust there, in the corner, looks quite blank and disconsolate with its great white eyes, while she, that sate for so many months pale and weeping by his bed-side, is thinking of nothing but to bestow all the wealth he left her on a beardless stripling, who appears to regard the bust and the beauty with almost equal indifference.—Alas! poor old withered Leberinus, little did you imagine that so small a phial would suffice to hold all her tears. My only wonder is, that she still permits your marble image to occupy even a corner of her mansion; but, no doubt, you will soon be sent on your travels. I dare say, some cold pedestal in the garden will, ere long, be the best birth you need look for.—Well, well, you see what fools we may be made by the cunning of these pretty crocodiles. I trust my dotage, when it does come, will not shew itself in the same shape with that of my good old friend. I hope the ghost of the worthy Prætor will not frown unseen the night she takes this Adonis to her arms. If I were in his place, I should give her curtains a pretty shake. By Hermes! it would not be a pretty monument and a flowery epitaph that would make me lie still."

"How long is it," said I, "since this venerable magistrate died? Surely she has allowed him the decency of a tenmonth's grief, before she began to give suppers, and perceive the beauty of Sextus?" "Whether it be a tenmonth ago or not," replied the Centurion, "is more than I can take upon me to decide; all I know is, that it appears to me as if it were but yesterday that I supped here, (it was just before I set off for Britain,) and saw the young lady reclining, even at table, with those long black curls of her's, in the bosom of the emaciated Leberinus. By Jupiter! the old man would not taste a drop of wine unless she kissed the cup—she coaxed every morsel he swallowed down his throat, and clasped the garland round his bald pate with her own fingers; ay, twice before that sleek physician—that solemn-faced Greek, whom you see at this moment talking with your kinsman, advised her to have him carried to his bed. For all the gravity of his looks, I would lay a trifle, that worthy Bœotian has his own thoughts about what is passing, as well as I. But the worst-pleased face in the whole room is, I think, that of old Rubellius himself yonder, who has just come in, without, it is evident, being aware that any feast was going forward. Without question, the crafty usurer is of opinion he might have been invited. I promise you, I can interpret the glances of that gray-headed extortioner; and well I may, for it is not the first time I have had an opportunity of studying them. Ay, ay, quoth he to himself, she may do as she will with the bonds of Leberinus; but she might have remembered, that a codicil can be easily tacked to the end of a living man's testament."

"But, after all," said I, "one must admit, that if she married old Leberinus to please her father, the widow has some right to choose her second husband according to the pattern of her own fancy." "Oh! by all means," answered he; "let her please herself; let her make a fool of herself now, if she will. She may perhaps learn, some time or other, that it is as possible to have too young a husband, as to have too old a one." "Come now," said I, "Sabinus, confess that if she had selected some well-made, middle-aged man—some respectable man—some man of note and distinction, you would have judged less harshly of poor Rubellia." "Ah! you cunning dog," said he; "who would have thought that you had brought so much wickedness from that new world of yours? But do you really think she will wed Sextus? The boy appears strangely cold. I should not wonder, when all is done, if the match were more of the orator's seeking than his own." "I can only tell you," said I, "that I have never heard Licinius mention any thing about it; and, I dare say, Sextus would be very sorry to think of losing his liberty for the sake of the wealth of Leberinus—ay, or for that of old Rubellius to boot." "Young friend," quoth he, "you are not quite acquainted with the way in which these matters are managed at Rome. If we had you six weeks at the other side of the Viminal, we should teach you better."

I know not how long this sort of talk might have lasted; but Licinius put an end to it by joining us, and soon engaged the worthy Centurion, and several more of us, with some lively, but unintelligible discussion on the merits of some new edict, of which none of us had ever heard, or were likely ever to hear any thing again. We were glad to escape from the lawyer into another room, where some Greek slaves were performing a sort of comic pantomime, that appeared to give more delight to old Rubellius than any other of the spectators. As for Sextus, I saw plainly that he was quite weary of the entertainment, and anxious to get away; but we were obliged to remain till after Licinius was gone, for it was evident that he wished his son to see out the last. But no sooner had we heard his chariot drive off, than the young man and I took leave of the lady, and withdrew. Sabinus lingered a moment behind us, and then joined us in the vestibule, from which, his course lying so far in the same direction as ours, we all proceeded homewards on foot.

We had proceeded along the street of the Suburra for a considerable space, and were already beneath the shade of the great Temple of Isis and Serapis, (which stands on the northern side of the Esquiline Hill, nigh over against the Amphitheatre of Vespasian,) when, from the opposite side of the way, we were hailed by a small party of soldiers, who, as it turned out, had been sent from the Prætorian camp in search of Sabinus, and one of whom had now recognized his gait and stature, notwithstanding the obscurity of the hour. The Centurion went aside with the leader of these men for some moments, and then informed us that it was very fortunate they had so easily recognized him, as the business on which they had been sent was such as did not admit of being negligently dealt with. "To-morrow," said he, pointing to the Amphitheatre before us, "that glorious edifice is to be the scene of one of the grandest shows exhibited by Trajan since his accession to the empire. It is the anniversary of the day on which he was adopted by Nerva, and the splendour of the spectacle will be in proportion to the gratitude and veneration with which he at all times regards the memory of that excellent benefactor. But there are some parts of the exhibition that I am afraid old Nerva, could he be present to behold them, would not regard with the same feelings as his successor." "Surely," said I, "the beneficent Trajan will not stain the expression of his gratitude by any thing unworthy of himself, or that could give displeasure to Nerva?" "Nay," replied the Centurion, "it is not for me to talk about any thing that Trajan chooses to do being unworthy of Trajan; but you well know that Nerva would never suffer any of the Christians to be molested during his reign, and now here are some of these unhappy fanatics, that are to be compelled either to renounce their faith in the face of the assembly to-morrow, or to die in the arena. It is to inspect the condition of these unfortunates, who, I know not for what reason, are confined in a dungeon below the ramparts in the vicinity of our camp, and to announce to them the final determination of their fate, that I, as Centurion of the night, have now been summoned. If you are curious to see the men, you are at liberty to go with me, and I shall be obliged to you for your company."

My curiosity having been excited in regard to the new faith and its adherents, I was very desirous to accept of this offer. Nor did Sextus any sooner perceive that such was my inclination, than he advised me to gratify it, undertaking, at the same time, to satisfy his father, in case of any inquiry, that I was in a place of safety, and under the protection of Sabinus. With him, therefore, and with his Prætorians, I proceeded along various streets which led us by the skirts of the Esquiline and Viminal Hills, on to the region of the Mounds of Tarquin, over against which, as you have heard, the great camp of those bands is situated;—if indeed that ought of right to be called by the name of a camp, which is itself a city of no slender dimensions, and built with great splendour of architecture, spread out beyond the limits of Rome, for the accommodation of that proud soldiery. There my friend took me into his chamber, and furnished me with a cloak and helmet, that I might excite no suspicion by accompanying him on his errand. The watch-word of the night also was given me, *Silent faith*; and proceeding again, we shortly reached the place where the Christians were lying.

CHAPTER VIII.

Entering the guard-room, we found it crowded with spearmen of Sabinus's band, some playing at dice, others carousing jovially, many wrapt up in their mantles, and asleep upon the floor; while a few only were sitting beneath the porch, with their spears in their hands, and leaning upon their bucklers. From one of these, the Centurion, having drawn him aside, made inquiry concerning the names and condition of the prisoners, and whether as yet they had received any intelligence as to the morrow. The soldier, who was a grave man, well stricken in years, made answer, "that the men were free-born and of decent estate, and that he had not heard of any thing else being laid to their charge, excepting that which concerned their religion. Since they have been here," he continued, "I have been several times set on watch over them, and twice have I lain with one of them in his dungeon; yet have I heard no complaints from any of them, for in all things they are patient. One of them only is to suffer to-morrow—but for him I am especially concerned, for he was known to me of old, having served often with me when I was a horseman in the army of Titus, all through the war of Palestine, and at the siege of Jerusalem."

"And of what country is he?" said Sabinus. "Is he also a Roman?" "No, sir," answered the spearman, "he is no Roman; but he was of a troop of the allies that was joined often to our legion, and I have seen him bear himself on the day of battle as well as any Roman. He is by birth a Greek of the Syrian coast; but his mother was of the nation of the Jews." "And yet, although the son of a Jewess, he was with us, say you, at the siege of Jerusalem?" "Even so," replied the man; "and not he only, but many others; for the Jews were divided against themselves; and of all them that were Christians, not one abode in the city, or gave help to defend it. As this man himself said, the oracles of the Christians, and their prophets, had of old given warning that the city must fall into the hands of Cæsar, by reason of the wickedness of that people; therefore, when we set our camp against Jerusalem, these all passed out from the city, with their wives and children, and dwelt safely in the mountainous country until the fate was fulfilled. But some of their young men fought in our camp, and did good service, because the place was known to them, and they had acquaintance with all the secrets of the Rock. Of these, this man was one. He and all his household had departed from the ancient religion of the Jews, and were believers in the doctrines of the Christians, for which cause he is now to suffer; and of that, although I have not spoken to him this evening, I think he has already received some intelligence, for certain of his friends passed in to him, and they covered their faces as they went in, as if weeping." "Are these friends still with him?" said Sabinus. "Yes," answered he, "for I must have seen them had they come forth again. Without doubt, the two women are still with him in his dungeon." "Women?" quoth Sabinus; "and of what condition think you they may be?" "That I know not," replied the soldier; "for, as I have said, they were muffled in their mantles. But one of them, at least, is a Roman, for I heard her speak to him that is by the door of the dungeon." "How long is it," said the Centurion, "since they went in to the prisoner?" "More than an hour," replied the soldier, looking at the water-clock that stood beneath the porch; "and if they be Christians, they are not yet about to depart, for they never separate without singing together, which is said to be their favourite manner of worship."

He had scarcely uttered these words, when the soldiers that were carousing within the guard-room became silent, and we heard the voices of those that were in the dungeon singing together in a sweet and lowly manner. "Ah, sir!" said the old soldier, "I thought it would be even so—there is not a spearman in the band that would not willingly watch here a whole night, could he be sure of hearing that melody. Well do I know that soft voice—Hear now, how she sings by herself—and there again, that deep strong note—that is the voice of the prisoner."

"Hush!" quoth the Centurion, "heard you ever any thing half so divine? Are these words Greek or Syrian?" "What the words are I know not," said the soldier; "but I know the tune well.—I have heard it played many a night with hautboy, clarion, and dulcimer, on the high walls of Jerusalem, while the city was beleaguered." "It is some old Jewish tune then," said Sabinus; "I knew not those barbarians had had half so much art."

"Why, as for that, sir," replied the man, "I have been all over Greece and Egypt—to say nothing of Italy—and I never heard any music like that music of the Jews. When they came down to join the battle, their trumpets sounded so gloriously, that we wondered how it was possible for them ever to be driven back; and then, when their gates were closed, and they sent out to beg their dead, they would play such solemn awful notes of lamentation, that the plunderers stood still to listen, and their warriors were delivered to them with all their mail as they had fallen." "And the Christians also," said Sabinus, "had the same tunes?" "Oh yes, sir—why, for that matter, these very tunes may have been among them, for aught we know, since the beginning of their nation. I have stood sentinel with this very man, and seen the tears run down his cheeks by the star-light, when he heard the music from the city, as the Jewish captains were going their rounds upon the battlements." "But this, surely," said the Centurion, "is no warlike melody." "I know not," quoth the old soldier, "whether it be or not—but I am sure it sounds not like any music of sorrow,—and yet what plaintive tones are in the part of that female voice!"

"The bass sounds triumphantly, in good sooth." "Ay, sir, but that is the old man's own voice—I am sure he will keep a good heart to the end, even though they should be singing their farewell to him. Well, the Emperor loses a good soldier, the hour Tisias dies. I wish to Jupiter he had not been a Christian, or had kept his religion to himself. But as for changing now—you might as well think of persuading the Prince himself to be a Jew."

"That last high strain, however," quoth Sabinus, "has ended their singing. Let us speak to the women as they come out; and if it be so that the man is already aware of what is to be done to-morrow, I see not why we should trouble him with entering his cell. He has but a few hours to live, and I would not willingly disturb him." "I hear them coming," said the soldier. "Then do you meet them," said Sabinus, "and tell them that the Centurion wishes to speak to them ere they go away—we will retire out of hearing of the guard."

With that he and I withdrew to the other side of the way, over against the door of the prison; and we stood there waiting for the women under a fig-tree, close by the city wall. In a few minutes two persons, arrayed as the soldier had described, drew near to us; and one of them, without uncovering her countenance, said,—"Master, we trust we have done no evil in visiting the prisoners; had it been so, surely we should not have been permitted to enter without question."

These words were spoken in a voice tremulous, as if with grief rather than with terror; but I could not help starting when I heard them. However, I commanded myself, and heard in silence what Sabinus replied.—"Be not alarmed," said he; "there is no offence committed, for no orders have been issued to prevent these men from seeing their friends. I sent for you, not to find fault with what you have done, but only to ask whether this prisoner has already been told that the Emperor has announced his resolution concerning him, and that he must die to-morrow, in the Amphitheatre of Vespasian, unless he renounce his superstition."—"He knows all," answered the same voice; "and is prepared for all."

"By heavens! Valerius," whispered Sabinus; "it is no mean person that speaks so—this is the accent and the gesture of a Roman lady." Then raising his voice, "In that case there is no need for my going into the dungeon; and yet, could I hope to say any thing that might tend to make him change his purpose, I would most gladly do so. The Emperor is as humane as he is just, and unless when rebellious obstinacy shuts the gates of mercy, he is the last that would consent to the shedding of any blood.—For this Tisias, of whose history I have just been hearing something, I am in a particular manner interested, and to save him, I wish only I had power equal to my inclination. Is there no chance of convincing him?"—"He is already convinced."—

"Could his friends do nothing?"—"His friends have been with him," said the voice.—This last sentence was spoken so distinctly, that I knew I could no longer be mistaken; and I was on the brink of speaking out, without thinking of the consequences that might occur, when she that had spoken, uttered a faint cry, and dropping on her knees before Sabinus, said,—"Oh, sir! to us also be merciful, and let us go hence ere any one behold us!"—"Go in peace, lady," answered the Centurion, "and henceforth be prudent as well as kind;" and they went away from us, and were soon lost to our sight in the windings of the street.

We stood there for some moments in silence, looking towards the place where they disappeared. "Strange superstition," said Sabinus; "what heroism dwells with this madness!—you see how little these men regard their lives;—nay, even women, and Roman women too—you see how their nature is changed by it."—"It is, indeed, a most strange spectacle," said I; "but what is to be the end of it, if this spirit become diffused widely among the people?"—"In truth I know not," answered the Centurion; "as yet we have heard of few who had once embraced this faith, renouncing it out of fear for their lives."—"And in the days of Nero and Domitian," said I, "were not many hundreds of them punished even here in the capital?"—"You are within the mark," said he; "and not a few of those who were sent into exile, because of their Christianity, were, as you may have heard, of no ordinary condition. Among these there were Flavius Clemens, the Consular, and his wife, Domitilla; both of whom I have often seen in my youth—both relations to the family of Vespasian—whom, notwithstanding, all the splendour of the imperial blood could not save from the common fate of their sect. But Nerva suffered all of them to live in peace, and recalled such as were in exile, excepting only Domitilla, whose fate has been regretted by all men; but I suppose it was not at first judged safe to recal her, lest any tumult should have been excited in her name, by those that regretted (and I am sorry to say these were not a few) the wicked license of which they had been deprived by the death of her tyrannical kinsman, and the transition of the imperial dignity into another line. She also with whom we have been speaking, is, I am sure, a Roman lady of condition; and you may judge of her zeal, when you see it brings her hither at midnight, to mingle tears and prayers with those of an obscure Asiatic. Did you observe, that the other female both walked and stood behind her."

"I observed all this," answered I. But little did Sabinus suspect that I had observed so much more than himself had done. Before parting from him, I said I should still be gratified with being permitted to see the prisoner; and although he declined entering himself, he accordingly gave command that the door of his dungeon should be opened for me, requesting me, at the same time, to refrain from saying any thing more than was necessary for the explaining the apparent purpose of my visit,—the communication, namely, of Trajan's decree.

The Centurion withdrew to his camp; and the same old spearman with whom we had conversed at the Porch, carried a torch in his hand, and shewed me the way into the dungeon.

Between the first door and the second, which appeared to be almost entirely formed of iron, there intervened a few broad steps of mason-work; and upon the lowest of these, I stood waiting till he should open the inner door. Several keys were applied before he discovered the right one; but at last the heavy door swung away from before him so speedily, that the air, rushing out of the vault, extinguished the torch; insomuch, that we had no light excepting that which streamed from an aperture high up in the wall of the dungeon itself; a feeble ray of star-light alone—for the moon had, long ere this time, been gone down—which, nevertheless, sufficed to shew us to the prisoner, although we at first could see nothing of him.

"Soldiers," said the old man, in a voice of perfect calmness, "for what reason are you come?"—"We come," said my companion, "by command of the Centurion, to inform you of things which we would willingly not have to tell—To-morrow Trajan opens the Amphitheatre of Vespasian."—"My comrade," said the prisoner, "is it your voice I hear? I knew all this already; and you know of old that I fear not the face of death."—"I know well, Tisias, you fear not death; yet why, when there is no need, should you cast away life? Think well, I beseech you, and reserve yourself for a better day."—"The dawn of that better day, Romans, already begins to open upon my eyes. I see the east red with the promise of its brightness. Would you have me tarry in darkness, when I am invited to walk forth into the light?"—"Your words rejoice me," answered the spearman; "and I am sure all will rejoice in hearing that you have at length come to think thus—Trajan himself will rejoice. You have but to say the word, and you are free,"—"You mean kindly," said the old man, rising from his pallet, and walking towards us as far as his fetters permitted; "but you are much mistaken—I have but to keep silence, and I am free."—"Alas! what mean you? Do you know what you say? You must worship the gods in the morning, else you die."—"Evening, and morning, and for ever, I must worship the God that made heaven and earth. If I bow down to the idols of Trajan, I buy the life of a day at the price of death everlasting. Tempt me not in your kindness: I fell once. Great God, preserve me from falling! I have bade farewell to my friends already. Leave me to spend these few hours by myself.—Leave me to prepare the flesh for that from which the spirit shrinks not." So saying, he extended his hand to the spearman, and the two old men embraced each other before me.

"Prisoner," said I, "if there be any thing in which we can serve you, command our aid. We have already done our duty; if we can also do any thing that may give ease to your mind now, or comfort to your kindred, you have but to speak."—"Sir," replied he, "I see by the eagle wings on your helmet, that you are one in authority, and I hear by your voice that you are young. There is a certain thing, concerning which I had some purpose to speak to this old brother."—"Speak with confidence," said I; "although I am a Roman, and bear all loyalty to Cæsar, yet this Prætorian helmet is not mine, and I have but assumed it for the sake of having access to your prison. I am no soldier of Trajan: Whatever I can do for you without harm to others, speak, and I will do it. I will swear to you——" "Nay, sir," said he, "swear not—mock not the God of heaven, by invoking idol or demon—I believe your word— but, since you will hear, there is no need why any other should be witness to my request."—"I will retire," said the other, "and keep watch at the door. I am but a poor spearman, and this young patrician can do more than I."— "Be it so," said the prisoner, a second time embracing him; "I would not willingly expose you to any needless danger; and yet I see not what danger there is in all that I have to ask."

With this the spearman withdrew; and being left alone with Tisias, I took his hand, and sitting down beside him on his pallet, shortly explained to him the circumstances under which I had come thither.

"Young sir," said he, "I know not what is about the sound of your voice, and the frankness of your demeanour, that makes me feel confidence enough to intrust you with a certain thing, which concerns not myself, nor any hope of mine, for that were little—but the interests of one that is far dearer to me than I can express, and who, I hope, will live many happy days upon earth, after I shall have sealed my belief in the message of God, by blood that has of old been exposed a thousand times to all mortal perils, for the sake of worthless things. But a very short while ago, and I might have executed this thing for myself; but weakness overcame me at the moment of parting."

"If it be any thing which you would have me convey to any one, say where I may find the person," said I, "and be assured I shall deliver it in safety."

"Sir," he proceeded, "I have here with me certain writings, which I have carried for these twenty years continually in my bosom. Among these, is one of the sacred books of the faith for which I am to die, and I would fain have it placed in the hands of one to whom I know it will be dearest of all for the sake of that which it contains; but, I hope, dear also for the sake of him that bequeaths it. Will you seek out a certain Roman lady, and undertake to give into her own hands, in secret, the scroll which I shall give you?"—"I will do my endeavour," said I; "and if I cannot find means to execute your command, I shall destroy the book with my own hands before I quit Rome—

for my stay here is uncertain."—"If you cannot find means to do what I ask safely," he replied, "I do not bid you destroy the book—*that* is yours to do with as it shall seem good to you—but I conjure you to read it before you throw it away. Nay, even as it is, I conjure you to read it before you seek to give it to her whose name I shall mention."—"Old man," said I, "almost I believe that I already know her name, and more besides. If it be so that I have conjectured aright, be assured that all you ask shall be fulfilled to the letter; be assured also, that I would die with you to-morrow, rather than live to be the cause or instrument of any evil thing to her that but now visited you in your dungeon."—"Alas!" cried the old man, starting up, "lay not this also, O Lord! upon my head. Let the old bear witness—but let the young be spared, to serve thee in happier years upon the earth!"—"Be not afraid," said I, "if it was Athanasia, no one suspected it but myself; and I have already told you that I would die rather than bring evil upon her head."

"Yes," he answered, after a pause—"it was, indeed, Athanasia. Who is it but she that would have left the halls of nobles, and the couches of peace, to breathe at midnight the air of a dungeon, that she might solace the last moments of a poor man, and, save the bond of Christ, a stranger! But if you have known her before, and spoken with her before, then surely she must indeed be safe in your hands. You know where she dwells—that I myself know not. Here is the scroll, from which that noble maiden has heard my humble voice essay to expound the words of eternal life. I charge you to approach her with reverence, and give into her own hands my dying bequest; yet, as I have said, deliver it not to her till you have yourself read what it contains."—"Christian," said I, placing the writing in my bosom, "have no fear—I will read your book, and ere two nights have gone over my head, I shall find means to place it in the hands of Athanasia; and now, farewell."— "Nay, not yet for the last time. Will you not come in the morning, and behold the death of a Christian?"—"Alas!" said I, "what will it avail that I should witness the shedding of your blood? The Prince may have reason to regard you as an offender against the state; but I have spoken with you in your solitude, and know that your heart is noble. Would to Heaven, that by going thither I could avert your fate!"—"Methinks, sir," he replied, "it may be weakness—but yet methinks it would give me some farther comfort in my death, to know that there was at least one Roman there, who would not see me die without pity; and besides I must have you constrain yourself, that you may be able to carry the tidings of my departure. Her prayers will be with me, but not her eyes. You must tell Athanasia the manner of my death."— "For that cause," said I, "I will constrain myself, and be present in the Amphitheatre."—"Then, farewell," said he; "——and yet go not. In whatsoever faith you live,—in whatsoever faith you die, the blessing of an old man and a Christian can do you no harm." So saying, the old man stood up, and leaning his hand on my head as I sat, pronounced over me a blessing which I never shall forget. "The Lord bless thee—the Lord enlighten thy darkness—the Lord plant his seed in thy kind heart—the Lord give thee also to die the death of a Christian!"

When he had said so, he sat down again; and I departed greatly oppressed in spirit, yet feeling, I know not how or why, as I would rather have lost many merry days, than that dark and sorrowful hour. The soldiers in the guard-room were so much engaged in their different occupations, that they heeded me not as, dropping my borrowed habiliments, I stept silently to the gate; and I was soon out of sight of their flaming watch-fires, and far from the sounds of their noisy mirth.

CHAPTER IX.

The Roman streets were totally silent and deserted. It was the first time that I had been in the presence of a human being, foreseeing distinctly, and quietly waiting, the termination of his mortal existence, and I could not help asking of myself, how, under similar circumstances of terror, I should have been able to sustain my spirits?—to what resources I should, in such a moment, look for the support which seemed to have been vouchsafed so abundantly to this old man; by what charm, in fine,—by what tenet of philosophy, or by what hope of religion,—I should, in the midst of life, be able to reconcile myself to a voluntary embrace of death! To avoid disgrace, indeed, and dishonour, said I, I think I could be Roman enough to dare the worst; but this poor man is willing to die, rather than acknowledge, by one offering on the altar, the deities in whose worship all his Greek ancestors have been trained; yet who, except perhaps a few obscure individuals that have adopted the same new superstition, would think this man dishonoured by returning to the religion of his fathers? Deep, indeed, must be his conviction of the truth of that which he professes to believe—serious indeed must be his faith, and high his trust. What if, after all, his faith should be true, and his trust wise? And the gentle Athanasia!—She too a Christian! Might not this mystery be hereafter explained to me by her lips?

Musing and meditating thus, it was no wonder that I, who knew so little of Rome, should have soon wandered from the straight way to the home of my kinsman. But that I at last caught, at the turning of a street, a glimpse of the Flavian Amphitheatre, which I had before passed on my way from the feast of Rubellia, I might, perhaps, have wandered long. I had some notion how that grand edifice was situated with respect to the house of Licinius, and therefore moved towards it immediately, intending to pass straight down from thence into the Sacred Way. But when I came close to the Amphitheatre, I found that, surrounded on all sides by a city of sleep and silence, that region was already filled with all manner of noise and tumult, in consequence of the preparations which had begun to be made for the spectacles. The east hardly yet indicated dawn; but the torches and lanterns of workmen and artificers were in motion every where. On one side, the whole way was blocked up with a throng of waggons; the conductors, almost all Ethiopians and Numidians, lashing each other's horses, and exchanging, in their barbarous tongues, outcries of wrath and execration. The bellowings that resounded from any of the waggons, which happened to be set in motion amidst the throng, intimated that savage beasts were confined within them; and when I had discovered this, and then regarded the prodigious multitude of the vehicles, I cannot say what horror came over me at thinking what cruel sights, and how lavish in cruelty, were become the favourite pastimes of the most refined of nations. I recognized the well-known short deep snort of the wild boar, and the long hollow bark of the wolf; but a thousand fierce sounds, mingled with these, were new to my ears. One voice, however, was so grand in its notes of sullen rage, that I could not help asking a soldier, who sate on horseback near me, from what monster it proceeded. The man answered, that it was a lion; but then what laughter arose among some of the rabble, that had overheard my interrogation; and what contemptuous looks were thrown upon me by the naked negroes, who sate grinning in the torch-light, on the tops of their carriages! Then one or two of the soldiers would be compelled to ride into the midst of the confusion, to separate some of these wretches, fighting with their whips about precedence in the approach; and it seemed to me that the horses could not away with the strong sickly smell of the wild beasts; for they would prance, and caper, and rear on end, and snort as if panic-struck, and dart themselves towards the other side; while some of the riders were thrown off in the midst of the tumult, and others, with fierce and strong bits, compelled the frightened or infuriated animals to endure the thing they abhorred—in their wrath and pride forcing them even nearer than was necessary. In another quarter, this close-mingled pile of carts and horses was surmounted by the enormous heads of elephants, thrust up into the air, some of them with their huge lithe trunks lashing and beating (for they, too, as you have heard, would rather die than snuff in the breath of these monsters of the woods,) while the tiara'd heads of their riders would be seen tossed to and fro by their contortions. What a cry of cursing, what cracking of whips and cords, what blowing of horns, and whistling and screaming; and all this mixed with what roaring and howling from the savage creatures caged in darkness!

I went, however, for a moment, into the Amphitheatre, by a little side-way, where admission was cheaply obtained. Here, as yet, all things were in order, for the hour had not yet come for giving the wild beasts entrance to the huge dens prepared for them. A few carpenters only were seen in one corner, erecting a sort of low stage, and singing merrily, of whom, when I made inquiry concerning the purpose of that erection, one of these fellows also began to jeer; "Whence come you, good sir, that you do not know a common scaffold when you see it? It is surely not the first time that a Christian has had his head chopped off in the Flavian?"—"By Pluto, I am not so sure about that matter," quoth another. "I don't know whether any of the dogs were ever beheaded here or not; if they have been, I can only say it was better than they deserved."—"There spoke a true man," cries a third. "No, no; keep beheading for Romans—let citizens have their own. Things are come to a pretty pass, when they shew us nothing but tigers against tigers. By Jove, I would rather see one of those misbelieving Atheists set right before the mouth of a true Getulian lion's cage, and hear his bones cracked ere all be over,—I say, I would rather see that, than fifty of your mere beast fights."—

"After all," rejoined the first, "it must be allowed that our Cæsar had a fine eye for the Amphitheatre."—"Who doubts it?" says the other. "Rome has never seen any thing that deserved to be called a show, since he was killed by sneaking traitors. They say, Nero was still better at that sort of work; but 'let the skinless Jew believe,' as the saying is. I desire to see no better sport than Domitian gave us the very week before his death. We shall never live to see his like again!"—"Come, boys," rejoins one of the rest; "no despairing! I had begun to think that these good princes, as they call them, would never shew us a bit of real sport again. Here, now, is at least something. Who can tell what may follow? and, besides, if the worst come to the worst, we shall still have lions against lions, tigers against tigers, Dacians against Dacians, and now and then a Jew or a Christian, or whatever you please to call him, exhibited *solus* on such a stage as this. Come, come, don't make matters worse than they are."

The ruffians shewed that they knew well enough I was displeased, and I half regretted, as I strode away from them, the want of that Prætorian helmet, which would have preserved me from the insolence of their mirth. However, I was well pleased to gain a distance at which I could no longer be troubled with them, and walked with rapid steps along the wide streets, over which morning was now beginning to shine; while the air, agitated with a quick breeze, refreshed my cheeks and temples—of which I had need, being heated with the glare and noise, and, perhaps, faint, too, after the manner of the young, from want of sleep.

I was admitted into the house by Dromo, who seemed to have been looking out for me; for he opened the door almost before I had time to knock at it. He regarded me as I entered with a very cunning face; insomuch, that I comprehended without difficulty, he believed me to have spent the night in some scene of debauch; but he, nevertheless, attended me, without saying a word, into my chamber. He then assumed a countenance of great reflection, and advised me, with much appearance of friendly concern, to go to bed, even although I could not stay long there; "because," said he, "you will feel much fresher when you get up; and let me tell you, you must be up early, for I have already been with Licinius, who intends to send Sextus with a present to Rubellia immediately after breakfast; and you may be sure he will insist on your company, for he can do nothing without you. Ah! had it not been for a certain pretty creature, the young gentleman would not, I am confident, have permitted you to be going the rounds in this way by yourself. But I take it something amiss, and shall tell him so, that he did not depute me (who am not particularly enamoured just at present) to go with you, and take care of your safety. I only wonder how you have got home so well as it is."—"Indeed," said I, "good Dromo, I cannot help wondering a little at that myself—for I have been all through the city, and lost my way half-a-dozen times over, and yet here you see I am."—"The more reason," quoth the slave, "that you should send some little offering to Mercury's Temple over the way, in the morning—a few sesterces will be sufficient—and if you have no objections, I shall willingly take care of them for you. Mercury is the guardian of all that travel about in the dark; and besides, he is the special patron of love expeditions. But to say the truth, you are not the only person that owes a gift to that shrine; for the worthy sage—Xerophrastes—he, too, has been a night-wanderer—and he has not yet come in. I have my doubts whether, when he does so, he will be as sober as you are; but I must take care to be at my post, and admit him in silence, for the time is not yet come to uncloak his doings. Trust me, this is not the only vagary I have set down to his account—all in good time. But what says my master Valerius, touching the offering to the great God Hermes?"

I saw, by the knave's face, that it was necessary the sesterces should be forthcoming. "Here they are," said I, "good Dromo; and remember, that although Mercury, among other things, is the god of thieves also, he will not be well pleased if you curtail his offering." "Never mind," answered the varlet, as he was shuffling out of the room, "Mercury and I understand each other of old. Go to bed, and try to get a little of your own old British red into your cheeks again; for Licinius has a hawk's eye, and will be sure to have his suspicions, if he sees you come down with such a haggard look. Remember you have not a beard to cover half your face, and all your iniquities."

So saying, he left me to my couch, indeed, but not to slumber; for busy thoughts kept me broad awake, till, after the lapse of perhaps an hour, young Sextus entered my apartment, already arrayed with more than usual elegance, to execute, however unwillingly, the message of his father. He had in his hand a small casket of open ivory-work, which he flung down on my bed, saying, "Get up, dear Valerius, and save me at least from the pain of going alone with these gewgaws. Would to Heaven my father would marry her himself, and then I should have no objection to carry as many caskets as he pleases. But do you get up and assist me; and as we go along, you shall tell me what you have seen and heard in company with your jovial Prætorian."

I was soon ready, and ascended, along with my young friend, the chariot which Licinius had commanded to be ready. I told him, as we glided through the streets, as much as I judged expedient; and, in particular, when I perceived that our charioteer was making a circuit, in order to avoid the neighbourhood of the Amphitheatre, I could not help expressing to him the effect which had been produced in my mind, by my casual inspection of the preparations. "I am afraid, then," said he, "that you will scarcely be willing to witness the exhibition itself; and yet I would fain have you to overcome your aversion, both because, whatever you may think of such things, it is not fitting that you should go from Rome without once, at least, seeing how they are conducted; and more particularly, because I much suspect Rubellia intends to be present at the festival—in which case I should be sorry to be compelled to attend upon her without you; and as to leaving her at the gate of the Amphitheatre, that, you know, would be quite impossible, unless I wished openly to contradict the wishes of my father."

I assured him he should not want any comfort my presence could afford him; although not without, at the same time, expressing my astonishment that he should consider it at all probable that his dainty Rubellia would choose to sit among the spectators of an exhibition so abounding in circumstances of cruelty, and, as I had understood, forbidden to her sex. "Nay," answered he, "laws and edicts are made to be broken in such cases; and as for the cruelty of the scene, there is scarcely a lady in Rome that would be more scrupulous on that head than my widow. To tell you the truth, one of the things that makes me most unwilling to go, is the fear that Sempronia also may be there; and, perhaps, when she sees me with Rubellia, give credence to some of the reports which have been circulated (not without my father's assent, I think, if all were known,) about this odious marriage, which I swear to you shall never take place, although Licinius were to drive me from his door, and adopt a stranger."—"Sextus," I made answer, "if Sempronia thinks there is any thing serious between the widow and you, she must think you a pretty rascal, for the violent love you made to herself at the Villa. But I am sure she will easily perceive, by your countenance, that you do not regard Rubellia, handsome as she is, with any extraordinary admiration; whereas—if you were not conscious of it, I am sure she must have been so—there was never a face of more passionate love than yours, all the time you were in *her* company. And, even now, the very mention of her name calls a glow into your cheeks,—yes, and even into your eyes,—that I think would flatter Rubellia, could she excite such another, more than all the jewels of all the caskets your father will ever send."—"Distract me not, O Valerius!" said the youth,— "distract me not with speaking of that too lovely, and, I fear, too scornful girl. Do you not perceive that we have at last struck into the Suburra, and are quite near to Rubellia's house?"—"It is so," said I, looking out of the carriage, "and I suspect you are right in thinking she means to be present at the Amphitheatre, for there is a crowd of urchins about her gate, and I perceive a brilliant group of equipages has attracted them. She purposes to go in all her splendour."—"Good Heavens!" replied he, "I believe all the world is to be there. I never passed so many chariots; and as for the rabble, see what a stream of heads continues pouring down out of every alley. My only hope is, that Rubellia may arrive too late for the best situations, and perhaps disdain to witness the spectacle from any inferior part of the Amphitheatre; and yet she must have interest, no doubt, to have secured good accommodation beforehand."

We were just in time to meet Rubellia stepping from her portico with a gay cluster of attendants. On seeing us, however, she beckoned with her finger, and said, "Oh, are you come at last? Well, I must take Valerius with myself, for I insist upon it that I shall be best able to point out what is worthy of his notice; and you, Sextus Licinius, come you also into my chariot; we will not separate you from your Orestes." She said so with an air of sprightly ease and indifference, and sprung into the carriage. An elderly lady, with a broad merry face, went into it also, but there was still room for Sextus and myself; and the rest of the party followed in other vehicles that were waiting.

The crowd by this time had so accumulated, that our horses could not advance but at leisurely pace; but the noise of the multitude as they rushed along, and the tumult of expectation visible on every countenance, prevented us from thinking of any thing but the festival. The variety, however, and great splendour of the equipages, could not but attract my attention. Now it was an open chariot, drawn by milk-white Thessalian horses, in which reclined some gorgeous female, blazing with jewellery, with a cluster of beautiful boys or girls administering odours to her nostril; and perhaps some haughty Knight or Senator now and then offering the refreshment of his flattery. Then, perhaps, would come rumbling along, a close clumsy waggon, of the old-fashioned matronly sort, stuck full with some substantial plebeian family—the fat, comfortable-looking citizen, and his demure spouse, sitting well back on their cushions, and having their knees loaded with an exulting progeny of lads and lasses, whose faces would, every now and then, be thrust half out of the window, in spite of the mother's tugging at their skirts. And then, again, a cry of "Place, place," and a group of lictors, shoving every body aside with their rods, before the litter of some dignified magistrate, who, from pride or gout, preferred that species of motion to the jolting of a chariot. Such a portly person as this would soon be hurried past us, but not before we had time to observe the richness of the silken cushions on which he lay extended, or the air of majesty with which he submitted himself to the fan of the favoured freedman, whose business it was to keep those authoritative cheeks free from the contamination of common dust and flies. Anon, a jolly band of young gallants, pushing their steeds along, to not a few of whom the fair Rubellia would vouchsafe her salutation. But wherever the carriage was stopped for an instant, it was wonderful to see the number of old emaciated men, and withered hags, that would make their way close up to the windows, imploring wherewithal to obtain a morsel. The widow herself leaned back on these occasions, as if to avoid the sight; but she pointed to a bag of small coin that hung in a corner of the chariot, and from it Sextus distributed to the one side, and I to the other; and yet it was impossible to give to every one; we were surrounded all the way with a mingled clamour of benedictions from those that had received, and execrations from those that had got nothing, and noisy ever-renewed solicitations from that ever-swelling army of mendicants. At last, however, we arrived in safety at the western gate—the same around which I had, the night before, witnessed such tumultuous preparation. One of the officers in waiting there, no sooner descried the equipage, than he caused a space to be laid open for its approach, and himself advanced to hand Rubellia into the interior, but she whispered to Sextus and me, by no means to separate from her in the crowd.

CHAPTER X.

Behold me, therefore, in the midst of the Flavian Amphitheatre, and seated, under the wing of the luxurious Rubellia, in a very convenient situation. There was a general silence in the place, because proclamation had just been made that the gladiators, with whose combats the exhibition was to commence, were about to enter upon the arena, and shew themselves in order to the people. As yet, however, they had not come forth from that place of concealment to which so many of their number would never return; so that I had leisure to collect my thoughts, and survey for a moment, without disturbance, the mighty and most motley multitude, piled above, below, and on every side around me, from the lordly senators, on their silken couches, along the parapet of the arena, up to the impenetrable mass of plebeian heads which skirted the horizon, above the topmost wall of the Amphitheatre itself. Such was the enormous crowd of human beings, high and low, that when any motion went through their assembly, the noise of their rising up or sitting down might be likened to the sullen roaring of the sea, or the rushing of a great night-wind in a forest. Not less than eighty thousand human beings, they told me, were here met together. Such a multitude could no where be regarded, without inspiring a certain indefinable sense of majesty; least of all, when congregated within the wide sweep of such a glorious edifice, and surrounded on all sides with every circumstance of ornament and splendour, befitting an everlasting monument of Roman victory and imperial munificence. Judge, then, with what eyes all this was surveyed by me, who had but of yesterday emerged from a British valley—who had been accustomed all my life to consider as among the most impressive of spectacles, the casual passage of a few scores of legionaries through some dark alley of a wood, or awe-struck village of barbarians.

Trajan himself was already present—his ivory chair distinguished only by its canopy from that of the other Consul who sate over against him; tall and majestic in his demeanour; grave, sedate, and benign in countenance, as you have seen in his medals and statues. He was arrayed in a plain gown, and appeared to converse quite familiarly, without affectation of condescension, with such Patricians as had their places near him; among whom Sextus and Rubellia pointed out many remarkable personages to my notice; as Adrian, afterwards emperor; Pliny, the orator, a man of courtly presence, and lively, agreeable aspect; and, above all, the historian Tacitus, the worthy son-in-law of our Agricola, in whose pallid countenance I could easily recognize the depth, but sought in vain to discover any traces of the sternness of his genius. Of all the then proud names that were whispered into my ear, could I recollect or repeat them now, how few would awaken any interest in your minds! Those, indeed, which I have mentioned, have an interest that will never die. Would that the greatest and the best of them all were to be remembered only for deeds of greatness and goodness!

The proclamation being repeated a second time, a door on the right hand of the arena was laid open, and a single trumpet sounded, as it seemed to me, mournfully, while the gladiators marched in with slow steps, each man—naked, except being girt with a cloth about his loins—bearing on his left arm a small buckler, and having a short straight sword suspended by a cord around his neck. They marched, as I have said, slowly and steadily; so that the whole assembly had full leisure to contemplate the forms of the men; while those skilled in such business were fixing, in their own minds, on such as they thought most likely to be victorious, and laying wagers concerning their chances of success, with as much unconcern as if they had been contemplating irrational animals, or rather, indeed, I should say, so many pieces of ingenious mechanism. The diversity of complexion and feature exhibited among these devoted athletes, afforded at once a majestic idea of the extent of the empire, and a terrible one of the purposes to which that wide sway had often been made subservient. The beautiful Greek, with a countenance of noble serenity, and limbs after which the sculptors of his country might have modelled their symbols of graceful power, walked side by side with the yellow-bearded savage, whose gigantic muscles had been nerved in the freezing waves of the Elbe or Ister, or whose thick strong hair was congealed and shagged on his brow with the breath of Scythian or Scandinavian winters. Many fierce Moors and Arabs, and curled Ethiopians, were there, with the beams of the southern sun burnt in every various shade of swarthiness upon their skins. Nor did our own remote island want her representatives in the deadly procession, for I saw among the armed multitude—not surely without some feelings of more peculiar interest—two or three gaunt barbarians, whose breasts and shoulders bore uncouth marks of blue and purple, so vivid in the tints, that I thought many months could not have elapsed since they must have been wandering in wild freedom along the native ridges of some Silurian or Caledonian forest. As they moved around the arena, some of these men were saluted by the whole multitude with noisy acclamations, in token, I suppose, of the approbation wherewith the feats of some former festival had deserved to be remembered. On the appearance of others, groans and hisses were heard from some parts of the Amphitheatre, mixed with contending cheers and huzzas from others of the spectators. But by far the greater part were suffered to pass on in silence;—this being in all likelihood the first—who could tell whether it might not also be the last day of their sharing in that fearful exhibition!

Their masters paired them shortly, and in succession they began to make proof of their fatal skill. At first, Scythian was matched against Scythian—Greek against Greek—Ethiopian against Ethiopian—Spaniard against

Spaniard; and I saw the sand dyed beneath their feet with blood streaming from the wounds of kindred hands. But these combats, although abundantly bloody and terrible, were regarded only as preludes to the serious business of the day, which consisted of duels between Europeans on the one side, and Africans on the other; wherein it was the well-nigh intransgressible law of the Amphitheatre, that at least one out of every pair of combatants should die. Instead of shrinking from these more desperate brutalities, the almost certainty of their termination seemed only to make the assembly gaze on them with a more intense curiosity and delight. Methinks I feel as if it were but of yesterday, when,—sickened with the protracted terrors of a conflict, that seemed as if it were never to have an end, although both the combatants were already covered all over with hideous gashes,—I at last bowed down my head, and clasped my hands upon my eyes. I had scarcely done so, when Rubellia laid her hand upon my elbow, whispering, "Look, look, now look," in a voice of low, steady impatience. I did look, but not to the arena: No; it was upon the beautiful features of that woman's face that I looked, and truly it seemed to me as if they presented a spectacle almost as fearful. I saw those rich lips parted, those dark eyes extended, those smooth cheeks suffused with a steadfast blush, that lovely bosom swelled and glowing; and I hated Rubellia, for I knew not before how utterly beauty can be brutalized by the throbbings of a cruel heart. But I looked round to escape from the sight of her;—and the hundreds of females that I saw fixed with equal earnestness on the same horrors, taught me, even at the moment, to think with more charity of that pitiless gaze of one.

At that instant all were silent in contemplation of the breathless strife; insomuch, that a groan, the first that had escaped from either of the combatants, although low and suppressed, sounded distinctly amidst the deep hush, and being constrained to turn once more downwards, I beheld that, at length, one of the two had received the sword of his adversary quite through his body, and had sunk upon the sand. A beautiful young man was he that had received this harm, with fair hair, clustered in glossy ringlets upon his neck and brows; but the sickness of his wound was already visible on his drooping eye-lids, and his lips were pale, as if the blood had rushed from them to the untimely outlet. Nevertheless, the Moorish gladiator who had fought with him had drawn forth again his weapon, and stood there awaiting in silence the decision, whether at once to slay the defenceless youth, or to assist in removing him from the arena, if perchance the blood might be stopped from flowing, and some hope of recovery even yet extended. There arose, on the instant, a loud voice of contention; and it seemed to me as if the wounded man regarded the multitude with a proud, contemptuous glance, being aware, without question, that he had executed all things so as to deserve their compassion, but aware, moreover, that even had that been freely vouchsafed to him, it was too late. But the cruelty of their faces, it may be, and the loudness of their cries, were a sorrow to him, and filled his dying breast with loathing. Whether or not the haughtiness of his countenance had been observed by them with displeasure, I cannot say; but those who had cried out to give him a chance of recovery, were speedily silent, and Cæsar looking round, and seeing all the thumbs turned downwards, was constrained to give the sign, and forthwith the young man, receiving again without a struggle the sword of the Moor into his gashed bosom, breathed forth his life, and lay stretched out in his blood upon the place of guilt. With that a joyous clamour was uplifted by many of those that looked upon it, and the victorious Moor, being crowned with an ivy garland, was carried in procession around the arena by certain young men, who leaped down for that purpose from the midst of the assembly. In the meantime, those that had the care of such things, dragged away, with a filthy hook, the corpse of him that had been slain; and then, raking up the sand over the blood that had fallen from him, prepared the place, with indifferent countenances, for some other tragedy,—while all around me, the spectators were seen rising from their places, and saluting each other; and there was a buzz of talking as universal as the silence had been during the combat; some speaking of this thrust and that ward, and paying and receiving money lost and won; some already discoursing of other matters, as if nothing uncommon had been witnessed; while others, again, appeared to be entirely occupied with the martial music which ever struck up majestically at such pauses, beating time upon the benches before them, or joining their voices with the proud notes of the trumpets and clarions. Rubellia talked gaily with Sextus, inviting him to ridicule me with her, for the strangeness of behaviour I had displayed.

The sun, by this, had already mounted high in the heavens, and the glare became so intolerable, that men could no longer fight on equal terms; which being perceived, Cæsar gave command to look after the wild beasts, and, in the meantime, (for I heard his voice distinctly,) to give warning to the Flamens that they should have their altar set forth.

CHAPTER XI.

Upon this, Trajan, with those immediately about his person, withdrew; but Rubellia told me he had only gone to the Palatine by the subterraneous path, for the purpose of taking some refreshment, and that there was no doubt he would return in time to witness the rest of the spectacle. This example, however, was followed in some sort by a great part of the spectators, for some departed altogether from the Amphitheatre, while many more were seen moving from place to place, crossing from one vomitory to another, and paying their respects to different parties of friends, who had occupied places at a distance from them during the combats. In the meantime, servants of Trajan's household were observed giving directions in the arena to a great number of persons, who afterwards began to distribute baskets of dried fish, bread, and other eatables, among such as chose to accept of them; while viands of a more costly description were introduced among the wealthy, by slaves and freedmen of their own. Neither were the bearers of water-jars idle, nor the street hawkers of fruit; least of all, those whose traffic is in snow,— of whom, I believe, hundreds were scrambling in all quarters over the benches, whistling shrilly, as is their method, to announce the article in which they dealt.

The Lady Rubellia was not one of those who would ever leave her friends destitute of the means of refreshment on such an occasion as this; and accordingly two or three of her household were soon with us, bearing jars of sweet-meats, baskets of fruit, flasks of wine, with other appurtenances of a luxurious collation. We had scarcely begun to taste of these things, when our attention was attracted by some one striding, with great activity, from one row of benches to another behind us, and looking round, I discovered the rosy countenance of Sabinus, whose anxiety to join us was, as I immediately suspected, the cause of this exertion. An ordinary person would have sought some circuitous method of approach, rather than attempt the sheer descent from one of the stone parapets which rose immediately in our rear; but the brawny limbs of the Centurion shrunk not from that adventurous leap, and, in a word, I soon found him seated beside us, bowing and smiling to Rubellia with his usual mixture of boldness and suavity. He delayed not from participation in her delicacies; but lifting a goblet of Falernian, drank down, without stopping, till he could see the foundation of its interior gold. His fingers also soon became acquainted with the receptacles of fruit and confectionary; and I was half-inclined to some suspicion, that he might perhaps have remained in his original situation, had he not chanced to observe the slaves of Rubellia, as they came up the vomitory, with their comely-looking, napkin-covered baskets upon their heads. As it was, his arrival was acceptable, except perhaps to Rubellia, who I thought looked as if she were not overmuch pleased with the interruption his mirthful talk occasioned to the conversation on which she had been endeavouring to fix the attention of young Licinius.

For that, however, another interruption had been already prepared in another part of the assembly, from which our Xerophrastes also had taken cognizance of our position. There was such a crowd, however, immediately below us, that I know not whether the philosopher would ever have been able to make his way to the region where we sat, had it not been that we heard his voice in disputation, and entreated those that opposed his passage, if possible, to make room for him. The first glimpse we had of his countenance, shewed us that the squeeze had been giving him serious inconvenience, for the drops of perspiration stood visible on his bald front. The persons whom he was addressing, however, seemed to listen with such unconcern, that it was impossible not to feel somewhat displeased with them, for treating so disrespectfully one whom his venerable aspect might have entitled to more courtesy. In vain did he represent to them, (for we heard his strong voice distinctly every now and then,) that it was not for the sake of any personal ease or convenience he was desirous of penetrating into an upper part. In vain did he reiterate "My pupil"—"my disciple"—"my young scholar, Sextus Licinius"—"the son of Caius Licinius"—"the son of the great orator Caius Licinius is there." In vain did he enlarge upon the constancy of attention which philosophers owe to those who are placed by the hands of parents under their superintendence. No sooner, however, did Sextus and I begin to shew the interest we took in his situation, than Sabinus raised himself up on the bench, and called aloud on those that surrounded the Stoic, with a voice of much sternness and authority, to let him pass immediately at their peril.

Many eyes were forthwith turned towards us; and whether it were the dignity and haughtiness of the Centurion's voice and attitude, or that his garb alone gave him much weight in the assembly, the resistance was relaxed, and Xerophrastes enjoyed an opportunity of almost entirely recovering his usual serenity of aspect before he reached us. The first thing he did was to accept of a cup which I held out to him, and then with much courtesy did he thank us all, but most the Centurion, for the part he had taken in working out his deliverance from the hands, as he expressed it, of those inhuman and illiterate persons; "while you," he continued, "brave warrior, have shewn that in your breast, as in that of Epaminondas—of Alexander—and of your own Julius— the reverence of the muses, and of divine philosophy, does not disdain to inhabit with the ardour of active patriotism, and the spirit-stirring delights of Mars."

"As for that," said Rubellia, with a smile, "all the world knows that Sabinus is quite a philosopher—he was just beginning a very learned harangue when we were attracted by your voice in the crowd; and you have the more reason to thank him, because he was cut very unseasonably short, in consequence of the distress in which we perceived you."

"Most noble lady!" replied the Stoic, "you know not how much you have delighted me; from the first moment, indeed, that my eyes rested upon the countenance of your heroic friend, I suspected that he had subjected himself to some other discipline besides that of camps. I saw the traces of thought, lady—and serious contemplation. The mind can never exercise its faculties, without conveying some symptoms of those internal operations to the external surface of the visage. The soul can never energize habitually, without betraying its activity in the delicacy and acumen, which the more elegant and susceptible parts of the corporeal frame acquire during those elaborate and mysterious processes of thought. I saw, therefore, and suspected. But what thanks are not due to you, for having so agreeably confirmed me in this happy suspicion! Of a surety, the noise and tumult of the camp is not so well adapted for the theoretic or contemplative life, as perfect leisure and retirement; yet, who shall doubt that the soul of great energy can overcome all such disadvantages? Who shall think that the spirit of Socrates did not eagerly philosophize during the campaign he served?—Who shall say that the Stagyrite must have suspended his acute, although imperfect investigations, even although he had accompanied his royal pupil across the Hellespont, and attended all the motions of his victorious army, instead of staying at home to teach the youth of Greece?—Who, finally," said he, casting his courteous eyes full on the Prætorian, "shall suspect but that this generous warrior has been effectually advancing the growth of philosophic science, within his own mind at least,—if not composing works, in his intervals of leisure, destined hereafter to benefit and instruct the world, even although he may have been attending the flight of the Eagle from utmost Britain to the desert frontiers of the Parthian?"—"Nobody, indeed," replied the sportive lady—"nobody, indeed, who has enjoyed any opportunity of being acquainted with the Centurion, can have any doubt on that head.— Sabinus," she continued, turning towards him, "what treatise are you at present engaged with? Come, now, speak out, and truly;—are you still busy with your περι της Φυσεως του οιστρου βακχικου,[1] that you were quoting from the other night?—or are you deep in '*the delight of contemplation*?'—or—
—"—"Not at all," quoth the Centurion, interrupting her; "I am only deep in *love*——" Saying so, he laid his hand in a very tender fashion upon his breast, and even, as I thought, began to throw a little sentiment into his eyes; but he had no opportunity of going on with his speech, for Xerophrastes had no sooner heard him utter the word *love*, than he immediately began to pour out a new rhapsody.

"Love!" quoth he; "Ha! love:—in good sooth, a noble subject, and one concerning which not a few laudable treatises have been composed. Yet, without question, much remains to be done in this matter; and I should be most proud if the illustrious Sabinus would vouchsafe to me a perusal of his speculations. Without question," he continued, "you have commenced with a proper definition and division of the subject. You have distinguished betwixt what is properly called *love*, and the other more or less kindred affections, with which hallucinating writers have too often committed the error of confounding it. You have described, in the first place, the difference between it and the *Storgé* or natural affection which parents have for their offspring—an affection in which not a few of the irrational tribes appear (if physiologists may be trusted) to be even superior to the human race."—"Hens, for example," quoth the Centurion, with a face of infinite gravity.—"Even so—*hens*," continued the sage; "an apt illustration.—I perceive, indeed, lady," whispered he to Rubellia, "that you have not deceived me concerning the attainments of this your noble friend.—Hens—a most acute illustration!—See you now, O Sextus!" he went on, "it is not the characteristic of true philosophy to despise those illustrations which are drawn from the affairs of ordinary life, and the common surfaces of things. No: it is rather her part to shew forth her own intrinsic excellence and splendour, by raising that which is in itself low and customary, to unexpected dignity, by her methods of felicitous application. See you, now, with what unexampled skill this hero—this philosopher, I should rather say—may I presume to add, this brother philosopher?—has illustrated the nature of love in this treatise of his, by introducing the domestic habits of your common household fowl. Such things should not pass unheeded by the young aspirants to learning, because these, more than any other circumstances, may furnish them with encouragement to proceed in their course, by shewing how many of the materials of philosophy lie every where under the eyes of the most common traveller of the path of life; and how assuredly it is the fault of the individual himself, if he neglect the means of spiritual advancement, which are sure to be afforded in whatever situation may chance to have been assigned to him."

"I beg your pardon for interrupting you," said Rubellia; "but Sabinus has almost finished the grapes while you have been speaking; and I would only just beg to suggest, that it is the fault of the individual, Xerophrastes, if he neglects the means of corporeal refreshment, which may yet be afforded to him by what remains in the basket."

"Most kind lady," resumed he, "your benevolence is worthy of your nobility.—But you know not how much the philosophy I have embraced, tends to lessen the natural desire of man for such things as you allude to— nevertheless," he continued, "I will not refuse to partake yet farther of your bounty; for I have been sorely dealt with in the multitude, as yourselves witnessed."

So saying, he took hold of the basket, and began to feel in the bottom of it, but found very little to his purpose; for, to say the truth, the rest of the party had been almost as eager in their attentions to it as the Centurion. A few slender bunches, notwithstanding, were still there, one of which the philosopher thrust into his mouth, and the rest he concealed beneath one of the folds of his huge mantle, until he should have made an end of his criticism. Meantime, the natural language of the broad, jovial, unreflective countenance of our worthy Centurion, seemed considerably at variance from the notion of his attainments and pursuits, which this merry lady had been instilling into the pedagogue. Rubellia herself, however, appeared to enjoy the thing far more keenly than either Sextus or I; insomuch, that I was afraid Xerophrastes would penetrate through the joke she was playing off upon him, before he had given himself his full swing in commendation of the Prætorian. But Sabinus, on his side, was, as it seemed, of opinion, that he had already heard enough of such disquisitions; for he had scarcely seen out the last cup of Falernian, ere he began to give hints that he wished very much to descend into the arena, for the purpose of observing the animals about to be exhibited, while they were yet in their cages. Xerophrastes, however, even when he had heard him signify this desire, appeared still to be resolved on considering him as one of the philosophic order of mankind; for he at once offered to accompany him, saying, that the visit was of course intended for the gratification of some scientific curiosity, and that therefore he should think himself culpable did he neglect the opportunity.

"Come, then," quoth the good-natured Sabinus, "by all means prepare yourself for the descent; but at least allow me to precede you, that there may be no risk of untimely obstructions."—"Most assuredly, noble Centurion," replied Xerophrastes, "in this, as in all things, I shall be proud to be enumerated among your followers. My pupil, also," he added, "and his friend, will no doubt accompany us, that they may benefit by our discourse on whatever may be subjected to observation."—"Venerated friend," said Rubellia, "would you leave the ladies by themselves in the midst of the Amphitheatre? I hope Sextus Licinius, at least, will consider our weakness, and remain for our protection."

She laid her hand on my companion's arm, with a look which was decisive. Her ancient crony whispered something about the impropriety of leaving only one of the party to attend upon two females; but I took advantage of her low tone to pretend ignorance of that hint, and rose with the Centurion.

"Go quickly," said Sextus, "for the interval must be well-nigh at an end; and if those that have gone out begin to rush in again, you may have difficulty in regaining your places."—"Give fear to the winds," quoth Sabinus; "am not I with them, that know every lion-feeder in Rome? No chance of the exhibition recommencing without my having sufficient warning. It is not for nothing that I have lost and won so many thousand sesterces in the Amphitheatre. Would to Hercules as much respect were paid to experience every where else, as in the Arena to your true old Better. Already, I perceive that half a dozen of those knowing characters down below, about the entrances to the dens, have detected me. They must fancy my purse is in a poor state indeed, when I don't seem to think it worth while to take even a single peep at the cages. Come, worthy brother in philosophy, and you, my fellow-voyager, let us be alert, lest we arrive after Platæa."

We obeyed with due alacrity, and, leaving the reluctant Sextus to his fate, touched presently the margin of the arena. We had no sooner arrived there, than an old skin-dried limping Numidian, with a bit of lion's hide fastened round his loins—one who, from his leanness and blackness, had very much the appearance of having been baked to a cinder, drew to the Centurion, with many nods and significant grins of recognition. Sabinus, on his part, seemed noways backward to acknowledge this acquaintance; but, on the contrary, began to talk volubly with him in a strange sort of broken dialect, chiefly composed, as I afterwards learned, of Punic vocables. After this had lasted some minutes, he took Xerophrastes and me by the hand, and seemed to introduce us to the Numidian, who then desired us all to come down, and he would conduct us to a place where we should see something not unworthy of being seen. About to follow these directions, I felt my gown seized from behind, and looking round, observed that it was my faithful Briton, who, from the heat and confusion of his aspect, appeared not to have come thither without a considerable struggle. Sabinus seeing him, said, "Ah! my old friend Boto, how have you come to this part of the Amphitheatre? We must not leave you behind us, however: Of a surety, you have never seen a lion—you shall descend along with your master; and who knows but we may persuade Xerophrastes that you also are a brother philosopher?"—"Most noble Centurion," replied the grateful slave, "I saw you and my master from the very topmost bench, where I have been sitting for these three hours with Dromo, and I was determined to draw near to you, if it were possible. To go from this place up to yonder quarter would perhaps be impossible; but it is never a very difficult matter to go down in this world; so, saving your reverence, I trundled myself over the benches, and when heads were in my way, I trundled myself over them too."—"It is well, good Briton," quoth the Centurion—by this time we had crossed the arena—"and now prepare to exercise your eyes as well as you already have exercised your limbs; for know, that very near to you is the abode of nobler animals than even your lord hath ever observed."

With this the African opened one of the iron doors edging the arena, and having received some money, admitted us to the sight of a long flight of marble steps, which appeared to descend into the bowels of the earth, far below the foundation of the Amphitheatre. "Come along, masters," quoth he; "we had better go down this way, for we shall have a better view of the animals so, than on the other side. My master, Sabinus, will tell you all, that old Aspar knows as much about these things as any Numidian in the place."—"Indeed, since friend Bisbal is gone," quoth the Centurion, "there is not another of these that is to be compared to you."—"Ah!" replied Aspar, "Bisbal was a great man; there is not a feeder in Rome that is worthy to tie the latchet of his sandals, if he were alive."—"Why, as to that," said the other, "old Bisbal was very seldom worth a pair of sandals worth the tying, when he was alive; but, come on, we have no great leisure for talking now, and Aspar shall shew a lion with any Bisbal that ever wielded whip.—Come on."

We soon reached a large vaulted place, apparently below the Amphitheatre, the sides of which were almost entirely covered with iron-gratings,—while up and down the open space were strolling many strange groupes of men, connected in different capacities with the bloody spectacles of the arena. On one hand, we saw some of the gladiators, who had already been combating, walking to and fro with restless and agitated steps, as if they had not yet been able to recover themselves from the excitement into which their combats had thrown them. Even of such as had been victorious, I observed that not a few partook in all these symptoms of uneasiness; and the contrast thus exhibited to the haughty mien of calmness they had so lately been displaying, affected me with a strange sense of the irrational and inhuman life these unhappy persons were condemned by folly or necessity to lead. The blood had forsaken the lips and cheeks of others, and from the fixed stare of their eyes, it appeared that their minds were entirely withdrawn from every thing passing around them. Their limbs, so recently nerved to the utmost show of vigour, were now relaxed and unstrung, and they trod the marble floor with heavy and straggling feet. But they that appeared to me to be in the most wretched state, were such as, they told us, expected to be led forth shortly to contend with the wild beasts, in whose immediate vicinity they were now walking. The summons to battle with a human opponent calls into action the fierceness and the pride of man; but he that has to fight with a beast, how should he not be weighed down with the sense of mortal degradation; how should the Reason that is in him not fill him, in such a prospect, with dispiriting and humbling, rather than with strengthening and stimulating thoughts? Howbeit, the Centurion, although the most good-natured of mankind, being rendered from custom quite callous to these things, immediately entered into conversation with some of those unfortunates, in a tone of coolness and unconcern that shocked me the more, because it did not seem in the smallest degree to shock them. Among other topics, he enlarged at much length to one of them upon the best method of evading the attack of a tiger.

"Look ye now," said he, "there are some that are always for taking things, as they call it, in good time,—these will be pointing their swords before the creature makes his spring; but I have seen what comes of that, and so has old Aspar here, if he would be honest enough to confess it. The true way is to watch his eye when he is setting; let him fairly fix upon his mark, and spring; but at the moment when he is taking his leap, then is the time for the gladiator to start aside, and have at him with a side-thrust. Your side-thrust is the only one I would lay an *as* upon."—"Yea," quoth the grinning Aspar,—"it was always on your cool steady side-thrust, the moment he had sprung, that the great Bisbal used to stake himself. Ha! ha! I was fond of the side-thrust in my day myself; but I got a scratch once—witness my poor leg, masters,—and since then I am a poor feeder."—"I was always clear for the side-thrust," quoth Sabinus. "I never saw it fail but twice, and then, to be sure, the men died; but they could have had no chance at all with the frontguard; and it is always something," continued he, clapping one of the poor expecting gladiators on the back,—"it is always something to have a chance. Be sure you try him with the side-thrust, if it come to your turn to-day."

The poor creature—he also was an African—lifted up his head on being so addressed, and shewed all his white teeth in a melancholy attempt at a smile; but said not a word in reply, and forthwith became as downcast as before. But the Centurion took little or no heed of the manner in which his advice had been received. He contemplated the man's figure for a moment, as if to form some judgment concerning the measure of his strength; and after doing the like in regard to some of his companions, commanded Aspar to shew us where the prime lions of the day were reposing.

The Numidian seized a long pole that was leaning against one of the pillars of the vault, and led us to a certain part of the grated wall, behind which was the den, wherein six monstrous Atlantic lions were kept. I looked in upon them with wonder, and not without dread, through the iron net-work of the doors. An imperfect gleam of light descended from above upon their tawny hides and glaring eyes. They, like the gladiators, seemed also to be preparing for the combat; but not like them in fear, nor in cold dewy tremors; for the deprivation of food, which they had been made to suffer in prospect of the exhibition, had roused all the energies of their savage natures; insomuch, that a sulky and yearning rage seemed to spread through every nerve and sinew of their gigantic frames, and to make them paw their quadrangular prison with long and pliant strides. They moved, however, as yet in total silence; so that Boto having fixed his eyes upon them, took courage to approach the grate,—slowly, nevertheless, and with a face that appeared to lengthen an inch for every inch he advanced. But when he had almost touched the bars, one of the huge lions came forward towards him, with something between a growl and a sigh, which made Boto spring backward with great and surprising agility, and with such force, that both he and Xerophrastes, who happened unfortunately to have been standing a little way behind him, were overthrown at all their length upon the floor.

The Centurion, and the limping old keeper, burst into laughter; but Xerophrastes rising, and shaking his garment, said, with some warmth, "Think not, O Sabinus, that any sudden start of fear has thus ridiculously stretched me upon the floor; but attribute the mischance only to this rude offspring of British earth, whose unreclaimed natural feelings are still shamefully affected by natural causes."—"Castor and Pollux," quoth the Centurion,—"you take every thing too seriously, my friend."—"I take it not seriously," replied he, with admirable gravity. "My philosophy forbids me to do so; it has steeled me against externals."—"Has it so, in faith!" rejoined the Centurion. "I think some of your equanimity is, in fact, owing to the trifling circumstance, that you have in reality received no injury whatever from your tumble. And as to steeling, let me tell you, I think the iron in the grated door there is much better placed, than in the bosom of a philosopher; for, in the door, it serves the purpose of preventing all harm; but if these animals were once out, all the mental steel of which you boast would not save every bone in your body from being cracked in the twanging of a bow-string."—"You speak," replied Xerophrastes, "as if you had embraced the tenets of a sect not worthy of the lovers of wisdom—You speak as if the artificial contrivances of human workmen were all in all. An iron cage may confine wild beasts; but can cages be made for all those misfortunes to which mankind are liable, and against which the force of the mind is their only means of defence? Can you cage the Eumenides, when they come to avenge a life spent in ignoble indolence and degrading luxury?"—"In truth," replied the Centurion with a smile, "I have never seen the Eumenides except once, and that was in the theatre of Athens. But Boto, perhaps, has been more fortunate. Did you ever see the Eumenides, good Boto?" "No, master," replied, stupidly, the perplexed Boto, "I never was at the theatre."

"Ye gods!" exclaimed the Stoic, "of a surety this Britain must have been the last spot rescued from the dominion of Chaos!"

But while we were yet contemplating those enormous animals, and amused with the awkward gestures of Boto, the trumpets were blown in the Amphitheatre, and no sooner did the sound of them penetrate into the vaults, than it was evident, from the bustle which ensued, that the Emperor had returned to his place. With all speed, therefore, did we reascend to the upper air, leaving the gladiators in the act of mustering in their respective quarters of the gloomy vault; and the feeders not less busied in preparing their beasts for the expected combat. Had we not been under the protection of Sabinus, we should have attempted in vain to regain our places; but he being an acknowledged and current authority, known in every department of the Amphitheatre, the door-keepers, and other functionaries, durst refuse him nothing; room was made for us where no room appeared; and, in a word, we shortly found ourselves once more seated by the side of Rubellia and Sextus.

CHAPTER XII.

The day was by this time considerably advanced; and, in spite of the awnings spread all over head, the rays of the sun were so powerful, that the marble benches felt hot to the touch, wherever they were exposed to them; and altogether there was such a glare and fervour throughout the place, that my eyes began to be weary of gazing; and very gladly would I have retired, rather than remain to see out the rest of the exhibition. Nevertheless, there was no appearance of any one having gone away in weariness; but, on the contrary, the seats, and even the passages, seemed to be more crowded than they had been in the anterior part of the morning.

The arena was vacant, when I looked down upon it; but in a short time, a single old man, who, as Rubellia told me, had, without doubt, been found guilty of some atrocious wickedness, was led forth from a small wicket on the one side, and presently his fetters being struck off, those that conducted him retired, leaving him alone upon the sand. The eyes of this malefactor refused at first to look steadfastly on the objects around him, and it seemed to me that he had probably been long confined in some dark place, so grievously did the dazzling splendour, reflected from the floor and walls, appear to bewilder and confound him. Nevertheless, after a brief space, he seemed in some measure to recover himself, and assumed a posture of resignation, leaning with one hand against the parapet, as if he needed support to uphold himself. Pallid and extenuated were the outlines of the old man's visage, and his hair and beard exhibited not a little of the squalidness attendant on long confinement; yet there was something in the attitude, and even in the countenance, which made me harbour the suspicion that he had not, at some former period, been altogether unacquainted with the luxuries and refinements of social life. The beauty, indeed, of the mould in which his form had originally been cast, might, perhaps, have been the sole cause of these casual demonstrations of elegance; yet it was impossible not to regard the man with greater interest, by reason of the contrast suggested between what he once perhaps had been, and what he now was.

A feeling of the same sort seemed to pervade many more in the assembly; and I heard a continual whispering among those around me, as if there was a general anxiety to learn something of the history of the man. No one, however, appearing to be able to say any thing concerning this, I kept my eyes fixed upon himself, awaiting the issue in silence. Judge then, what was my surprise, when one of the heralds of Trajan, having commanded that there should be silence in the amphitheatre, said, "Let Tisias of Antioch come forth, and answer to the things that shall be alleged against him." To which the old man, that was alone in the arena, immediately made reply,—"Here am I—my name is Tisias of Antioch."—In vain, however, even after hearing

- 69 -

the well-remembered voice, did I attempt to persuade myself that the face was such as I had pictured within myself; for, as to seeing it, I have already told you that utter darkness prevailed in the dungeon all the time I was there with him.

Then arose the Prefect of the city, who had his place immediately under the chair of Cæsar, and said in a voice, which, although not loud, was heard distinctly all through the Amphitheatre,—"Tisias of Antioch, being accused of blasphemy and contempt for the Gods, has been brought hither, either to refute this charge, by doing homage at the altar of Jupiter Best and Greatest; or, persisting in his rebellion, to suffer openly the punishment which the laws have affixed to such perversity. Let him remain where he is until the Flamens invite all to join in the sacrifice."

Tisias, hearing these words, stept forth into the middle of the arena, and folding his arms upon his breast, stood there composedly, without once lifting up his eyes, either to the place from which the Prefect had spoken, or to any other region of the Amphitheatre. The situation in which he stood was such, that I commanded, where I sate, a full and distinct view of every movement of the old man's countenance, and assuredly my eyes were in no danger of being directed away from him. For a few moments there was perfect silence throughout the assembly, until at length the same herald made proclamation for the doors to be thrown open, that the priests of Jupiter might have access. There was heard forthwith a noise, as of the turning of some heavy machinery, and a part of the ground-work of the arena itself appeared to be giving way, right over against that quarter in which Tisias had his station. But of this the purpose was soon manifested, when there arose from underneath into the space thus vacated, a wooden stage, or platform, covered all over with rich carpetings, whereof the centre was occupied by a marble altar, set forth already with all the usual appurtenances of sacrifice, and surmounted on one side by a gigantic statue of bronze, in which it was easy to recognize the features of the great Phidian Jupiter. Neither had the altar any sooner made its appearance there, and the sound of the machinery, by which its great weight had been lifted, ceased to be heard, than even as the herald had given command, the main gates of the Amphitheatre were expanded, and thereby a free passage prepared for the procession of the Flamens. With that, all those that were present in the Amphitheatre, arose from their seats and stood up, and a sweet symphony of lutes and clarions ushered in the sacred band to the place appointed for them. And, first of all, there marched a train of fifty beautiful boys, and then an equal number of very young maidens, all, both boys and maidens, arrayed in white tunics, and having their heads crowned with oaken garlands, and bearing in their hands fresh branches of the oak tree, which, above all the other trees of the forest, is, as you have heard and well know, held dear and sacred to Jupiter. Then these youthful bands were separated, and they arranged themselves, the boys on the right, and the girls on the left hand of the altar, some of them standing on the arena itself, and others on either side, upon the steps of the platform whereon the altar was fixed; and beautiful, indeed, was their array, and comely and guiltless were their looks; and much modesty was apparent, both in the downcast eyes and closed lips, with which some of them stood there to await the issue of their coming, and in the juvenile admiration wherewith others of them were regarding the wide and splendid assemblage around them; insomuch, that I could not but feel within myself a certain dread and fearfulness, when I saw the feet of so many tender and innocent ones placed there upon the same hot and guilty sand, which had so often drunk the blood of fierce beasts and cruel malefactors—alas!—which had drunk the blood of the innocent also—and which was yet to drink thereof abundantly.

And after them there came in the priests themselves of Jupiter, arrayed in the white garments of sacrifice, walking two by two, the oldest and principal of them coming last. And behind them again, were certain younger assistants, clothed also in white, who led by a cord of silk inwrought with threads of silver, a milk-white steer, without spot or blemish, whose horns were already gilt, and his broad brows crowned with oak leaves and roses. And last of all entered the Vestal Virgins, none of whom had ever before been seen by me, and they also walked two by two; and no one could contemplate without veneration the majesty of their demeanour. With broad fillets were they bound around the forehead, and deep flowing veils hung down to their feet, entirely covering their faces and their hands; nevertheless, their dignity was apparent; and it was not the less impressive, by reason of the great mystery in which all things about them appeared to be enveloped.

Imagine, therefore, to yourselves, how magnificent was the appearance of all things, when youths and damsels, and priests and vestals, had taken their places, according to the custom of their sacred observances; and all that innumerable company of spectators yet standing up in the amphitheatre, the choral-hymn was begun, in which every voice there was united, except only that of Tisias the Christian. Now, it was the soft low voices of the young maidens that sounded, and then these would pause, and give place to the clearer and more piercing notes of the boys that stood on the other side of the altar; then again the priestesses of Vesta would break in from afar with their equable harmony; and anon these in their turn ceasing, the Flamens of Jupiter would lift up their strong deep chanting, until, at the appointed signal from him that stood on the highest step of the altar, with the cup of libation in his hand, the whole people that were present burst in and joined in the rushing stream of the burden, "Jupiter,—Jupiter, hear us!—hear us, Father of Gods and men!" while the wine was poured out, gushing red upon the marble, and the incense flung on high from fifty censers, rolled its waves of smoke all over the surface of the arena, and quite up to the gorgeous canopy of that resounding Amphitheatre. Magnificent, indeed, was the spectacle, and majestic the music; yet in the midst of it, how could I take away my eyes from the pale and solitary old man, by reason of whose presence alone all these things were so? With calm eyes did he regard all the pageantry of those imperial rites,—with closed lips did he stand amidst all the shouting multitudes. He bowed not his head; he lifted not up his hand; neither would he bend his knee, when the victim was slain before the horns of the altar; neither would he in any thing give semblance of being a partaker in the worship.

At length the song ceased, and there was a proclamation again for deep silence; and the Prefect of the city, addressing himself once more to Tisias, spoke thus:—"Impious and unhappy man, with great clemency have all things been conducted as concerning thee. When, after long imprisonment, and innumerable exhortations in private and in public, thou hadst always rejected every means of safety, and spurned from thee the pardon of those in whose hands thy being is placed, yet, notwithstanding of all thine obstinacy and continual rebellion, was it determined, that, in the face of all the people, thou shouldst once more have free grace offered to thee, provided only thou shouldst, when all the assembly worshipped, join thy voice with them, and bow thy head also toward the altar of Jupiter. Nevertheless all that now hear me shall bear witness, that, with open and visible contumacy, thou hast rejected this opportunity also of being reconciled unto the prince and the empire,—that, when every knee bent, and every voice was lifted up, thou alone hast stood upright, and thy lips alone have been closed. If it be so, that, from some inflicted, rather than voluntary perversion of mind, thou hast never yet been able to understand the danger in which thou art placed, know now, that there remains no hope at all for thee, except for a moment; and let the strong fear of death open thine eyes, that thou mayst see where thou art, and for what purpose thou hast been brought hither. Thou art a born subject of Rome, and thy life can only be held by thee, in virtue of obedience to the laws. These are clearer upon nothing, than the necessity that all men should acknowledge the deities of Rome; and of good reason, since, if they be despised, and their authority set at nought, by what means shall an oath be ratified, or a pledge given; or how may the head, which counsels and protects, be assured that the members shall not be lifted up against it? Let silence remain in the assembly, and let Tisias of Antioch make his election, whether he will give obedience, or suffer the penalty of transgression."

Then the Prefect, and all those round about Trajan, sat down, and there was a deep silence throughout the lower region, where, for the most part, they of condition were placed; but when the rabble, that sat above, beheld the stern and resolute countenance with which the old man stood there upon the arena, it seemed as if they were enraged beyond measure, and there arose among them a fierce uproar, and a shouting of hatred; and, amidst groans and hisses, there was a cry from innumerable voices of—"Christian! Christian!—Blasphemer! Blasphemer!—Atheist! Atheist!—A tiger! A tiger!—Let loose a tiger upon the Christian!"

Nevertheless, the old man preserved unmoved the steadfastness of his demeanour, and lifting up his eyes to the place from whence the tumult proceeded, regarded the ferocious multitude with a visage, not of anger or of scornfulness, but rather of pity and calmness; insomuch, that I perceived the nobles and senators were somewhat ashamed of the outcry, and the Prefect of the city arose from his place, and beckoned with his hand, until the people were weary of shouting, and order was, in some measure, re-established in the Amphitheatre.

Then Tisias, perceiving that silence once more prevailed, lifted up his hand, and bowed himself before Trajan, and the great men of authority that were near to his chair, and said, with a firm clear voice, in the Roman tongue, "My name, O Trajan, is Tisias—the son of Androboulos. I am a native of Antioch, in Syria, and have in all things, except only in what pertains to this cause, observed throughout all the years of my life the statutes of the empire, as they, by whose accusation I have been led hither, shall themselves be constrained to bear witness for me this day. My father was a Greek of Macedonian extraction, being descended from one of those that came into Syria beneath the banners of the great King Seleucus; but he took to wife a maiden of the Hebrew nation, and in process of time became a proselyte to the faith of her fathers. Nevertheless, he lived in trust and honour beneath the governors appointed by those that were before you in the empire, and brought up me and all his children to reverence, in all things that are lawful, the authority of Cæsar. But as to the faith of the true God, whose worshippers ye blindly and foolishly call atheists and blasphemers, from that he neither swerved himself, nor would permit any of those that were in his household to depart. Now, when he had been a dweller for some time in Jerusalem, the great city of the Jews, he began to examine into those things which were reported publicly concerning Jesus of Nazareth, who is also called the Christ, of which things not a few that had been eye-witnesses were then living in that city. And when he had been satisfied from their testimony, that those miracles, of which you have all heard, were in truth performed in the sight of the people by Jesus, and had listened unto the words of their teachers, and saw how they proved that the old prophets of the Hebrews had foretold those wonderful works, he perceived that Jesus of Nazareth was indeed the Christ of God, and the great Deliverer that had been promised to that people, even from the beginning of their nation. And he believed on him with all his household; and I also, from a stripling, have, although unworthy, been a Christian; for by that name were they first called in Antioch, the city of my birth.

"But being brought into trouble by reason of his religion, which the rulers of the Jews abhorred, my father departed, after a time, from Jerusalem, and dwelt with my mother in one of the villages of Palestine, until his death. Not long after which time, the Jews rebelled against Cæsar, and the great war began, which terminated in the overthrow of Jerusalem, and the utter ruin of their nation. Now, when Vespasian first came with his army into those regions, I, being without employment in the place where we had our habitation, and having, moreover, taken up a great, and perhaps a sinful, wrath against the Jews, on account of the sufferings which my father had undergone among them, and of the evils which, at their hands, our whole household had sustained, joined myself to one of the bands of Syrian auxiliaries; and although my mother entreated me, could not be persuaded to refrain from following the camp of Cæsar with them. Of which thing it has often since then repented me, and in which, it may be, I still hold myself not to have done altogether as was right; for if the Jews had offended Cæsar, it was, indeed, a reasonable thing that Cæsar should visit them with his vengeance; but, peradventure, it behoved not any of them that were descended from the fathers of that people, to take part in the warfare. Nevertheless, being then young, and, as I have said, irritated by the sense of domestic injuries, I scrupled not to fulfil in all things the duty of a soldier, and followed the eagles of Vespasian and his son, even to the day when the lines were drawn around the Holy City; and it was manifest, that the war could have no end, but in the eternal overthrow of the power of the Jews. Neither did the length of the siege weary me, or produce within me any sort of unwillingness; but, on the contrary, so long as the city was beleaguered, I remained with the band in which I had numbered myself, and did in all labours such service as my strength would permit. Even among the soldiers that have guarded my prison, since I was led into Rome for the sake of that accusation which has been brought against me in the matter of my belief,— even among them, I have seen the faces of some that were my comrades in that fierce war, and that long beleaguerment, who also, if they be commanded, will not refuse to bear testimony before you, that all these things are true, even as I have said, and that I was a faithful soldier, both of Vespasian and of Titus, unto the last. Neither, indeed, did I lay down arms immediately when Jerusalem had been sacked, and the Temple burnt, according to the prediction of Christ, but went with Cæsar along the sea-coast, and was present with him all through the journeyings he made in Egypt, even to the day when he made his great festival at Alexandria, and crowned the Ox Apis with his own hands, in the presence of all that people. On which day it was, that, for the first time, I also was accused of being a

Christian, and at the command of Titus himself, was interrogated by one of the rulers of the army.

"Now with shame and confusion of face must I acknowledge, that on that day I, from desire of life, forgot myself utterly, and being deserted of all steadfastness, went up to the altar in presence of my judge, and offered gifts there, whereon I was declared free of all blame; and even received honour and commendation thereafter from them, on account of my services in the war. But, from that day, my spirit sunk within me, and I knew not what to do; I grew weary of all things, and determined to leave the band in which I was serving, that I might seek out, if it were possible, the habitation of my mother, and make atonement in secret for the wickedness of which I, unhappy and fearful man, had been guilty at Alexandria. Being absolved, therefore, from my oath of service, on account of the length of time I had remained with the army, I departed from Egypt, and, after a time, found out my mother where she was dwelling in the mountainous country of Palestine, to the north of Jerusalem. In going thither, however, I was constrained to pass by the place where I had so long lain in your camp, O Romans! and to look with my own eyes on the sorrowful desolation of that ancient city, where so many holy prophets of the Hebrews had ministered, and so many great kings reigned in the days of the old time, when their nation flourished, and was chosen and favoured of the Almighty. And it was then, indeed, that I first began to repent me of having been present in the host of Titus, and of having had a part in that terrible destruction; to which, when I added the recollection of my own miserable timorousness at Alexandria, great was my perplexity, and I fled across the mountains with much speed, seeking in vain to fly from the stings and unceasing torment of my own meditations, which nevertheless continued ever more and more to sink into my spirit; insomuch, that when I came into the place where my mother was dwelling, scarcely could she recognize me, wasted and worn as I was with that perpetual misery of shame and repentance. Without reproaches, however, and indeed with great kindness, did she receive me into her habitation, even although, as I have said, she had been much offended with me because of my going up to the beleaguerment of the city of her fathers. But when I, being humbled, made confession to her and her household, and to all the faithful that were in that place, of the grievous sin whereof I had been guilty in Egypt, both she and all the rest of them busied themselves continually to comfort me, and to assure me that there was yet hope, if my repentance were sincere, and my resolution immovable never again to yield myself to any similar temptation. One of them also, that had been set apart to minister in holy things among the scattered believers that dwelt up and down in that region, came not many days after to the same place, and having publicly heard my confession, admitted me once more to be a partaker with them in the mysteries of the sanctuary. From which day, O Trajan! I have never again been so far deserted of myself, as to fall back into that miserable error, or by any cowardly word of mine, to deny the faith that is in me, which is the faith of the True God that made heaven and earth, and of his Son Jesus Christ, whom he sent into the world to teach loving-kindness, and long-suffering, and patience, among all kindreds, and tongues, and nations of mankind; and to make expiation, by the accursed death of the cross, for the evil and the wickedness that is in the world. From which faith, should I now depart, out of terror for that which, by your command, may befal me in this place, of a surety no comfort could ever again come to me in my mind, for I should be bowed down, and utterly miserable, out of grief and shame; which as you yourself, O Cæsar, will admit and acknowledge, is far worse than death itself, or any evil which the body of man can sustain. Neither could I have any hope of being reconciled unto the True God, whom I should have so, once and again, denied; insomuch, that neither in life nor in death should I be able to have any happiness;—for in life, what happiness is there to him that is ashamed of himself?—and, in departing from life, what comfort can be given to him, that, knowing the truth, hath openly abjured the truth for the sake of a few, at the utmost, and these most miserable and unhappy years? I am an old man, and my near kindred and my friends are already dead, so that poor after all, and not worthy to be mentioned, is the sacrifice on which I have this day resolved. And as for you, O Romans, should I now make shipwreck of my faith, and tell a lie to save my life before you, with what contempt would yourselves be constrained forthwith to look upon me? Whosoever is wise among you, according to the philosophy of the earth, would utterly despise me; and whosoever is brave and steadfast of spirit, would think foul scorn that a soldier of Titus should be so much afraid to die. Therefore, O Trajan, am I resolved to endure all things rather than sacrifice to your gods; and if such be your will, I will not refuse to die for this cause, to which witness has already been borne in Rome by the blood of holy Apostles, and other noble martyrs of Christ."

The old man, having said these words, bowed himself once more reverently before Trajan, and then folding his arms in his cloak, appeared to await whatever might be appointed. Steadfastly did I look upon his face at that moment, to see whether it might exhibit no trace of wavering, or at least, if pride barred irresolution, whether, nevertheless, there might not appear some token of natural sorrow, and human unwillingness to die; yet in vain did I scrutinize and seek for any such symptoms of spiritual weakness; for although it was visible that, with the exertion of so long standing and speaking, to say nothing of thought and anxiety, his bodily strength was much spent, still his eye preserved firmness, and his brow remained serene; and the parched lips of the old man did not once betray the least shadow of trembling. Methinks I see him even now, as he then stood—his deep calm eyes sometimes turned upwards to Trajan, but for the most part bent to the ground, beneath those gray brows of his, whose dark shade rested upon his large solemn eyelids. Upon his broad front, as he stooped, no hair appeared, but long hoary ringlets, clustered down on either side, mingling with the venerable, although dishevelled beard, that lay upon his bosom. Heroic meekness was enthroned visibly upon all his lineaments, and a murmur began to run through the assembly, as if—even in a Christian—it were not possible to contemplate such things without admiration.

But as they afterwards related to me—for I myself was not indeed sufficiently attentive to it—Trajan, who had as yet, during all the occurrences of the day, preserved unmoved the majestic serenity of his countenance, when he observed this last movement in the spirit of the assembly, began all at once to be very indignant, that such things should occur in such a place, in consequence of the appearance merely, and the language, of a culprit and a Christian. I confess it, that I was too much occupied with gazing on Tisias, to have any leisure for remarking the particulars of the deportment of any other person present—no, not even of Cæsar; yet such had been the effect produced on me by the history which the old man delivered of himself, that I indeed was not prepared at the moment to find the strong arm of power directed ruthlessly, and immediately against him. At least, said I to myself, the Prince will institute an inquiry among all those now present in the capital, who are likely to be able either to contradict essentially, or to confirm, the narrative in which this man has thought fit to embody his only defence. Many years indeed have elapsed since the walls of Jerusalem were shattered by the engines of Rome, and the golden gate of its antique temple refused to be any protection against the furious soldiery of Titus. Yet surely not a few of such as were present in that proud host, must be still in life; yea, not a few of them must be now present in the capital of the world. The old spearman, with whom I talked in the guard-room, and beside the ramparts underneath which this Christian was imprisoned, he surely cannot be the only witness that remains to give testimony. He at least there is, and we shall forthwith have him at least confronted with Tisias.

Such were my thoughts within me; judge, therefore, what was my astonishment when I heard the trumpet sound, and perceived that its note, without any word being spoken, was at once received as a sufficient warning by the priests and the vestals, and the youths and the damsels, and all those that had in any way been connected with the service of the altar, to retire from the place whereon they stood, and leave the old man there alone, to await the issue of his destiny. Immediately on the signal being given by the trumpet, did all these begin to move away; but although in silence they had at first marched into the Amphitheatre, they did not retire from it in silence. Another hymn, on the contrary, in which also, as it seemed, different parts were allotted for each different order of singers, was begun to be sung by them even before they had moved from the arena; and after the last of their procession had disappeared behind the wide folding-doors of the Amphitheatre, we still heard their voices chanting solemnly until they had entered the great Temple of Isis and Serapis, which, as I have already said, stands over against it, on the brink of the Esquiline. And while all were yet listening to their singing, and to the harmony of lutes and other sweet-sounding instruments that accompanied their voices, the slaves and other attendants removed every thing from the arena, except only the altar and statue of Jupiter, which were still left where they had been placed; insomuch, that ere they had made an end of singing, and we of listening, the old man was left alone there as at the beginning, when he first came forth.

But just when deep silence once more prevailed, and expectation was most intense concerning what should be at length commanded by Trajan, it fell out so, that a little bald ape escaped through the bars of one of the grated doors, which were along the boundary-wall of the arena, and leaping forth upon the sand, began to skip up and down, challenging, by all manner of foolish gestures, the attention of those that sate over against it, leaning down from the parapet. And immediately certain painted courtezans, that were sitting not far from thence, with gilded breasts and bright-coloured garlands, and all other gorgeous trappings of the degradation of harlotry, began to throw down apples and nuts to the obscene creature, and to testify much delight in the grimaces with which it received them, hopping to and fro, and casting them away, and then catching them up again, with continual gibbering and prating; and no sooner did the rabble that were above perceive these things, than they all, as with one consent, began to applaud; so that the vaulted vomitories and wide arches of entrance, and all the marble walls, re-echoed with every wild sound of carelessness and merriment. While, in the meantime, the African feeders and naked gladiators, and all those hangers-on of the Amphitheatre, whom we had seen in the dark places below, hearing now the sounds that had arisen among the assembly, began to shew themselves in crowds from behind the same grated doors through one of which the monkey had escaped, and to partake in the mirth of the spectators, and to whistle upon the creature, and to excite it to new caperings, by their outcries and jeerings. It seemed as if the minds of all present were entirely occupied with the pranks of this brute; and that almost it was forgotten amidst the tumult, not only for what purpose all that solemn and stately pageantry had just been exhibited before them; but even that Tisias was still standing there upon the same arena.

For myself, who had never before looked upon any creature of this disgusting tribe, and had gathered only some general notion of its appearance from the treatises of the physiologists and the narratives of travellers,—I could not, indeed, refuse to contemplate at first its motions with some curiosity; but I knew not, after the scene had lasted for a little space, whether to be more humbled within myself by the monkey's filthy mimickings of the form and attitudes of mankind, or by the display of brutish heartlessness, which burst forth from all that countless multitude, while gazing on that spectacle of humiliation.

But it was not until my eye fell again on Tisias, who stood all this time solitary and silent amidst the hub-bub, that my sorrow and indignation were the greatest. There stood the old man even as before, with his arms folded in his gown, and his eyes resting on the sand before him, pale, calm, and unmoved in his meekness, even as if his ears had not once received any sound of all the shoutings and the joyous laughters of that unpitying rabble, that had come there to behold him die. Once, indeed—it was but once—I thought I could perceive that a slight emotion of contempt wreathed for an instant his thin and bloodless lips; but it seemed as if that were but the involuntary and momentary passing over him of one proud thought, which he cast from him immediately, as a thing unworthy of the resolute mind of his integrity, choosing rather to array himself in the divine armour of patience, than to oppose, with any weapon of human passion, the insults heaped upon his head by the cruel callousness of that degenerate congregation of men. And, whether it were that the sight of all this did not affect me alone with such reflections, or only that they in authority were afraid too much of the day might be occupied with what formed so unseemly an addition to the ordained business of the assembly, while the uproar of mirth was yet at its height, certain of the lictors that were about the consular chairs leapt down into the arena, and beat the monkey back again among the feeders, and other base hirelings, that stood behind the grated doors of which I have spoken. Whereupon there was at once an end of the tumult, and the lictors having reascended to their places, the eyes of all began once more to fix themselves upon the Christian.

And he also, when he perceived that it was so, and was sensible of the silence that once more prevailed, it seemed as if he, too, were aware that at last his appointed hour had come, and that he must needs prepare himself in good earnest for the abiding of the issue. For, instead of continuing steadfast in his place, as he had done during all the time he had as yet been exposed there, it appeared as if now at length, being swallowed up in the contemplation of the approaching fate, he had quite forgotten all the rules he had laid down to himself concerning his behaviour. Not that he now lost remembrance of the courage which hitherto he had manifested, or even, that any the least symptom of changeableness was made visible upon his countenance. But it seemed to me, of a truth, that of such things as he had determined upon within himself before he came thither, touching the mere external demeanour of his bodily frame, the memory now, in this final moment of expectation, had somewhat passed away; for Tisias stood still no longer on the centre of the arena; but retaining his arms folded as they had been, and his eyes fixed upon the sand, he began to pace rapidly to and fro, traversing the open space whereon he alone now was, from side to side, without once looking up, or exhibiting any token that he was conscious of the presence of any man. By and by, nevertheless, in the deeper knittings of his brows, and in the closer pressure of his extenuated lips, and then again in the quivering of the nerves and muscles upon the arms and legs of the old man, as he moved before us, it was testified how keenly the spirit was at work within; the strong soul wrestling, it may be, with some last stirring temptations of the flesh, and the mind itself not altogether refusing to betray its sympathy with the natural shudderings of the body. But the moment that the herald of Trajan commanded attention in the assembly, and that the Prefect of the city began again to prepare himself for speaking, that moment did the old man appear to return at once again entirely to himself; and he fixed his eyes upon the Prefect with even the same steadfastness as when he made his oration to Cæsar.

"By all the gods," whispered Sabinus at that moment, "this is a true soldier of Vespasian and Titus. He will die for this superstition with the constancy of a Roman."—"With all the constancy of a philosopher, say rather," quoth Xerophrastes, who had overheard his whisper—"yea, with all the constancy of a philosopher. Of a surety, there must be some lessons of nobility in this faith of the Jews."—"Now, speak not, but look at the old man," interrupted Rubellia; "the signal is given for the executioner."

And I looked, and saw that the Prefect was standing up in his place, immediately below the chair of Trajan, and immediately he began to speak; and he said, first looking towards the people,—"Let there be silence, and let no man stir in this place until this matter be ended." And then addressing himself, as it seemed, to Tisias,—"With all patience," proceeded he, "have the words which this man chose to utter in his defence, been listened to; but it must be manifest to all men, that they contain no shadow of apology, but rather afford the strongest confirmation of all that had before been alleged. Instead of departing from his error, or offering any extenuation of its magnitude, his words have tended only to shew what was already well known to all that have had any dealings with the adherents of this blasphemous sect; that their obstinacy is as great as their atheism is perverse; and that no clemency can, without blame, be extended to their wilfulness, and to the scorn wherewith they are resolved to regard all things sacred. Nevertheless, inquiry has been made, and confirmation has been given, by those who were present in the wars of the Divine Titus, as to that which this man hath said concerning his own service throughout the glorious campaign of Palestine, and the siege of the city of the Jews. For which service, it hath seemed right unto Cæsar, Ever-Merciful, that no circumstance of needless shame be added to the death by which this Christian must now expiate before all them who have seen his contempt of the sacrifice of Jupiter, and heard his words of blasphemy against all the gods, the guilt of which, it is manifest to all, he hath been justly and necessarily accused. Let those, therefore, who had been commanded to bring forth a tiger, depart now with their beast, and let this man be beheaded before the Altar of Jupiter; after which, for this day, the assembly will disperse; for, until the morrow, the spectacle of the wild animals, which the Prince hath prepared, must be deferred."

The Prefect made his obeisance again to Cæsar, and sate down in his place, and immediately one of the doors of the arena was flung open, and there entered some slaves, bearing a wooden block upon their shoulders, behind whom followed also certain ill-favoured blacks, out of the company of African gladiators, one of whom carried bare in his hand a long and heavy sword, the surface of which glittered brightly as he moved, as if newly sharpened and burnished for the occasion. Seeing all which fatal preparations, Tisias immediately flung aside the long cloak in which hitherto his arms and all his body had been wrapped; and after regarding those that had come in for a moment with a steadfast eye, he turned himself to the place where the Prefect was sitting, as if he had yet one word to say before he should submit himself to the sword; whereupon the Prefect said,—"If the prisoner has yet any thing to offer, it is not too late for mercy—Let him speak."

"I have nothing more to offer, O Romans!" answered the old man, "as concerning that of which I have spoken. But since already some favour has been extended to me by reason of my services in the army of Cæsar, perhaps so neither will this be refused, that my body may be given to such as shall ask for it, that it may be treated without indignity after my soul is released."

"It is granted," replied the Prefect.—"Is there any thing more?"

The old man was silent.

With that, the block being already fixed upon the sand immediately in front of the Altar of Jupiter, one of the Africans moved towards Tisias, as if to conduct him to the place where it behoved him to kneel; but he, observing what was his intention, forthwith prevented him, and walked of himself steadily close up to him in whose hand the sword was unsheathed. Being come thither, he immediately took his station over against the block, and having for a moment placed his hand upon his eyes, and moved his lips, as it seemed, in fervent supplication, dropped his one knee on the ground, and stretched forth his neck towards the block; but suddenly, after he had done so, he sprung again upon his feet, and began to gaze with a keen eye all around the assembly, as if he were in search of some one to whom he had something yet to say. In vain, however, as it appeared, did he make this endeavour; for after a little space, he shook his head despairingly, and gave over the steadfastness of his look. Nevertheless, he lifted up his voice, and, surveying once more the whole face of the Amphitheatre round about, from side to side, said audibly,—"There is one here who made last night a promise to me in my dungeon. I cannot see him where he is; but I conjure him to take good heed, and execute, as he is a man and a Roman, all those things which he said to me he would do." Now, when I heard him say so, I well knew within myself that it was for me only his eye had been searching, and half did I arise from my seat, that he might see I was there, and observe my resolution to keep the faith I had plighted voluntarily to him in his prison. But Sabinus, having watched my earnestness in contemplating Tisias, and comprehending something of that which was meant, held me firm upon the bench, whispering, "As you regard me, Valerius, and as you regard your own safety, be still."

Being thus constrained, I neither rose up, nor made any attempt to attract the attention of Tisias—for which forbearance, I confess to you, I have since that day undergone the visitation of not a few bitter thoughts—but remained steadily in my place, while the old man once more addressed himself to kneel down upon the block that was before him. Calmly now at length did he kneel, and with much composure did he place himself. Yet, before the gladiator was ready to strike, he lifted his head once again, and gazed upwards for a moment towards heaven, with such a countenance of faith and hope, that there went through all the assembly a murmur, as it were, and a stirring breath of admiration. Then bowed he for the last time his gray hairs, and almost before he had rested his neck upon the tree, the strong sword of the African smote with merciful fierceness, and the headless trunk falling backwards upon the sand, the blood spouted forth in a gushing stream, and sprinkled all over with red drops the base of the statue of Jupiter Capitolinus, and the surface of the marble altar, whereupon the sacrifice of the Flamens had been offered.

The executioner having made an end of his duty, wiped his sword from the blood of the Christian, and advancing towards the seats of the magistrates, claimed the largess that was due to him,—which when he had received, as is the custom, he and all his attendants withdrew immediately from the arena; the Emperor, at the same moment, and the Consulars, and all they that were about him, departing also from the assembly; and the whole Amphitheatre speedily being filled with the clamours of an universal upbreaking and dispersion.

BOOK II.

CHAPTER I.

I saw, my friends, that you listened with not less of indignation, than of astonishment, to the account which I yesterday gave you of a day spent in the Amphitheatre of Vespasian. Neither did I expect that it should be otherwise with young persons of ingenuous minds, whose feelings have never been hardened by any experience of the life of Rome.

And yet, when you reflect a little more upon the matter, I think you will abate something of the wonder you manifested on hearing of the fondness of the Roman people for some of those cruel, ruthful spectacles. You will admit, at least, that there is a certain natural principle, on an exaggerated and morbid obedience to which, rather than on any total and absolute departure from the laws of our mind, much of that which excited so much of your astonishment and indignation also may be supposed to depend. In and by myself, I maintain it must always be a most interesting thing for a man to witness, in whatever shape, the last moments of any human creature. I mean not those merely corporeal struggles, in which there must always be every thing to revolt, and nothing to interest, because in them, it is evident, the nobler part of our nature can have no share—the soul being already swallowed up, and its divinity absorbed in the intense convulsions of animal suffering. These are things on which no eyes can gaze willingly, without indicating degradation of spirit. But before that curtain falls, beyond which every one must shudder to penetrate, there is a last terrible act of the real tragedy, which must ever have power to fix the eyes with an earnestness not the less deep, because of its being preceded by some struggles of reluctance. We live in a state in which, however we may clothe ourselves in the armour of levity, or with the more effectual armour of occupation, it is impossible that the one fearful idea of dissolution should not ever and anon come to scare us with its terrors. We feel that we are walking over a soil, on the most level and the most rugged parts of which it is equally possible we may meet with the dark pit wherein it is our destiny to stumble. How sudden, or how gradual soever the inevitable fall may be, we well know we shall have little enough space to prepare ourselves for the last leap, when we shall be fairly on the declivity; and I maintain, once more, that it is a rational, no less than a natural, curiosity, which leads us to seek to supply, in some measure, this necessary defect, and to gather, if possible, from witnessing the last moments of others, some hints which may be of use to us when our own dark hour shall come. We see a being standing on the edge of a precipice, to which the only thing we know certainly, is, that we ourselves shall one day be brought; and shall it be possible to feel no curiosity concerning the manner in which he conducts himself on that giddy brink? That which is denied to us in our own person, may, in part, be supplied in his; and the eyes which dwell upon his features, while they are filled with the overwhelming expectation of near approaching death, make the closest approximation of which our nature admits to penetrating the actual mysteries of the unseen region. For myself, both wiser and better did I come away from all that mournful spectacle. But perhaps I am joining together things which, after all, had no necessary connection, when I ascribe to my contemplation of the death of Tisias, and the other cruel sights which, as it seemed, were regarded with indifference by the great multitudes around me, so much of the change which, about this period, my own spirit underwent.

The slumbers which followed that busy day of novelties and terrors, were long and heavy; for utterly worn out were both mind and body, and youth hastened to repair the waste of its energies, by drinking deeply at the great fountain of natural refreshment. Nevertheless, although the hand of sleep had lain steadily upon me, when I awoke in the already-confirmed light of morning, I found myself yet filled with a confused and tremulous sense of excitation, as if the spirit had disdained to be idle after having received so much food for activity, and Fancy had still been garnishing the passive sphere of the night with aerial representations of all the gorgeous and solemn realities of the by-past day. I lay there ruminating amidst the dispersing shadows of the mysterious world of dreams, and scarcely as yet aware that a whole night had passed since I had returned from the Amphitheatre, when I was at length roused to a sudden and complete recollection of all things by the entrance of Boto.

"My dear master," said he, making a sort of start after he had come in, "I was afraid you would be angry with me for not coming to you sooner, but now I perceive you have been as lazy as the rest of us. Why, surely, you are not aware what time of day it is! What would my dear old lady over the water say, if she heard of my young master lying in bed till within three hours of noon? Oh, what a place is this you have brought me to! Why, when I awake in the morning, the first thought that comes into my head always is, What, Boto, and is it really possible that all that wide roaring sea lies between you and the green banks of quiet Anton? Is it truth, good truth, and neither dream nor witching, that you, *Boto*, are in *Rome*? But I sometimes have to jump up, and take a look out of the window before I am quite convinced; and then, to be sure, I know well enough that I, who used always to dream about driving cattle to Venta, and perhaps kissing a Brigian lass by the way, could never dream of so many fine things unless I were really among them. Good heavens! what a heap of stories I shall have to tell, when we get safe back to Old Britain!"—"Indeed, Boto," said I, "you will be quite a travelled man. Be sure you do not give yourself too many airs on the occasion."—"Travelled man, in faith," replied the clown. "I should like to know, who it is that will be able to hold up his head with me, when I am once fairly back again? Oh, how the old smith will be humbled! He thought himself such a mighty person, because my old master, your father, had taken him with him as far as Camolodunum, and how he used to brag of what he had seen there; but now, I trow, Master Pernorix will be fain to talk quietly about his journeys.—O Rome, Rome! what fine things shall I have to tell them all about Rome,— and the lions, and the monkeys, and Cæsar, and the elephants, and the fighting men, and the Christian, and all the wonderful sights we saw yesterday. But the worst of it is, that nobody will ever be able to believe one half of what I shall tell them.—And when does my dear Master Valerius think we shall be returning to my old lady, and all the rest of them in Britain?"

"Of a truth, good Boto," said I, "that is more than I can pretend to give you any notion of; but I dare say, you shall have both time and opportunity to pick up a few more marvels still before we go. In the meantime, you are comfortable, I hope, in your quarters, and Dromo takes good heed of you."—"Dromo," quoth he, looking as arch as his massive features would admit of,—"Dromo, indeed!—If I had nobody to trust to but him, I should be very ill off. Dromo is a great man; the young lord of the house has him up in his chamber every day to talk with him by himself; and when he comes down again, or returns from any of the errands he is sent out upon, there is no bearing with him in the court-yard, where we are all huddled together. As for the overseer, old Sarcalus, the freed-man, he has quite given him up. Nobody dare speak about whipping him; he looks upon himself as almost as important a person as his master, I believe, if the truth were known; and yet I should not complain, for, after all, it was Dromo that carried me yesterday to the Amphitheatre."—"Ay, that was very kind of Dromo—I should have thought of it myself. And did he not see that you got your supper snugly, when you came back?"—"Ah! now, master, don't make them whip me—I see they have told you all."—"All!" said I—"I do assure you they have told me nothing about you; but come, speak out. It must be something very bad that would make me think of having you whipt. You have only been three days in Rome—I shall make allowance for a few vagaries, provided they be not very extravagant."—"Well, then, Master Caius," quoth he, "since they have told you nothing beforehand, and you seem inclined to be so good-natured with me, I shall e'en tell you all myself, and I hope you won't think me, after all, very much to blame."—"Speak out, my honest Boto, and remember there is Dromo also to be examined, in case you keep any thing back from me."—"Ah! master, but Dromo would not be so easily caught as poor Boto. Dromo is a cunning man, and a close; and besides, they say he was born in a city they call Crete, and the people of that place can't speak a word of truth, even although they were willing. Do not think any thing at all about Dromo; but trust entirely to your own poor Boto, and he will tell you every thing. Dromo is a sad dog."

I know not what more he might have proceeded to say concerning Dromo, had not that crafty Cretan, who, without question, had been listening all the while behind the door, just at that moment glided in on very delicate tiptoe, and coming close up behind the British slave, as he stood in the act of haranguing me, smote him a smart fillip upon the cheek with the back of his fingers, mimicking, at the same time, the outlandish accent of the man, and repeating after him into his tinkling ears, the words, *Dromo is a sad dog—Dromo is a cunning man, and a close—Dromo would not be so easily caught as poor Boto.—* "Ha, ha! Master Valerius," then said he to me, "and so you would really take the trouble to ask questions of this worthy man, when you had it in your power to send for me? I thought it had not been for nothing that three persons I could name entered upon a certain alliance—but 'tis all one to the Cretan.—Both Sextus, and you, may manage your own affairs for yourselves, if such be your pleasure."

I knew not on this whether to be more amazed with the impudence of the Cretan, or the confusion of poor Boto, who stood rubbing his cheek with a strangely mingled aspect of sheepishness and sulkiness; but Dromo soon put an end to the affair, by turning round with a face of admirably feigned astonishment to my Briton, and saying, "Good heavens! Boto, are you still there? Do you not perceive that your master and I have something to say to each other in private? Begone, my good man—shall I never be able to render you susceptible of the smallest polish?"

These last words being accompanied with a gentle push on the back, soon expelled poor Boto, who, nevertheless, did not depart without casting towards me a look of woful appeal over his shoulder. But I perceiving plainly, in the midst of all his frolicsome behaviour, that Dromo had really something to say to me; and suspecting, of course, that the interest of Sextus might be concerned in what he had to say, suffered my slave to withdraw in good earnest. Dromo, after the door was shut, laid his finger upon his lip, and stood still for a moment in an attitude of close attention; but the heavy heels of the reluctant Briton were heard with great distinctness, lumbering along the marble floor of the gallery; so, being satisfied that there was no eavesdropping in the case, the varlet seated himself forthwith in a posture of great familiarity on the nether end of my couch, and, to judge from the expression of his countenance, seemed evidently to be preparing himself for a disclosure of some importance. At length, after not a few winks of much intelligence, it was thus he began:—"You may hear Boto's story, sir, at any time you please, and I dare say it will amuse you; but, in the meantime, I must really have you attend to me, for, without jesting, things are by no means in so fair a train as I had thought for my young master; and if something effectual be not speedily discovered, I am really at a loss to think how we shall be able to get out of our difficulties, in such a manner as may be either satisfactory to him, or creditable to my management. But you had better get up and dress yourself, and while you are doing so, I will tell you every thing."

I did as he bade me, and then the Cretan proceeded:—"As I was coming out of the Amphitheatre yesterday, I happened to find myself rubbing shoulders with a certain old fat Calabrian, whom I had seen before about Rubellia's house in the Suburra, and thinking that no harm could possibly come of being civil to him, I began immediately to ask his opinion of the spectacles. I wish you had been there to see how much he was delighted with the attention I paid him, and how he plumed himself on being admitted to talk on such subjects with such a person as me; for the man himself is but an ignorant fellow, and seems never to have kept company but with the grooms and hinds. From less to more, we began to be the greatest friends in the world; and by the time we got to the Arch, it was evident that we could not possibly part, without having a cup together to cement the acquaintance. Well, we were just about to dive into one of the wine-cellars there, below the gate-way, when I saw your friend Boto standing by himself in the middle of the street, apparently quite a-gaze and bewildered, and not able to form the smallest guess which way he ought to take in order to reach home; and being a good-natured fellow, in spite of all that has been said, I immediately shouted out his name till he was compelled to hear me, and then beckoned to him to come along with us, which indeed he did without much coaxing."

"Well, Dromo," said I, "and so all your great news is, that you have been leading my Briton into one of your debauches? In truth, I think you need not have made such an affectation of mystery withal."—"Stop now," quoth he, cutting me short; "if the slave be too slow, I am sure the master's quickness will make up for it.—Hear me out before you begin commenting; such interruptions would bring the Stagyrite himself to a stand. We were soon, all three of us, seated in one of those snug little places, which if you have not yet seen, you are ignorant of the most comfortable sight within all the four walls of Rome,—a quiet cleanly little place,—three good hassocks upon the floor, a handful of sausages, a plate of dried fish as broad as the shield of Ajax, and a good old fashioned round-bellied jolly jug of Surrentine in the midst of us. I dare say, there were a hundred besides employed in the same way in the house; but we shut the door, and were as private as behind the altar of Vesta."—"A tempting scene, Dromo; and what use did you make of your privacy?"—"All in good time, Master Valerius; you would have the apple before the egg. We had scarcely emptied our first jug, ere the conversation between the Calabrian and me took a turn that was not quite unnatural; for slaves, however little you may trust them, will always be smelling out something of the truth; and you may be sure, all this visiting, and feasting, and riding about in chariots, and sitting together at the Amphitheatre, has not been going on, without causing a good deal of talk both in this house and the rich widow's. The courtship was of course the subject of our conversation, and I, pretending to know nothing of it myself, except from the common report of the slaves about our house, affected to consider it as highly probable, that the fat Calabrian might have had much better opportunities than mine of being informed how the affair really stood."

"And did he really seem to have any knowledge about it?" said I.—"Not much—not much; but still the man did tell me something that I think may turn out to be well worth the knowing. 'I am sure,' said I, (by this time Boto was fast asleep,)—'I am sure, if Rubellia won't have my young master, it won't be for want of presents; for we all know he has already given her a whole casket of rings and bracelets that belonged to his mother, and he is sitting for his picture, which, they say, he is to give her besides.'—'And *I* am sure,' quoth the Calabrian in return, 'that if your young master don't have my lady, it won't be for want of presents neither; for she is the most generous open-handed lady in the world, and that her worst enemies will allow, although her father be an old rogue, and an usurer, as all the town says he is. No, Dromo,' continued he, 'nor will it be for want of philtres, nor of charms, nor of any thing that soothsaying can procure; for, between ourselves, my lady keeps up a constant traffic of late with all that sort of gentry; and what the issue of it all may be, Hecate only knows.' Now, Master Valerius, when I heard him speak of philtres and charms, you may be sure I began to quicken up my ears more keenly than ever."

"Dromo!" said I; "you are not serious. You do not mean surely to make me think that you believe in the efficacy of love-potions, or any such quackeries?" "Quackeries! do you call philtres quackeries? Why, there was a girl once gave myself a philtre that kept me raving for six months."—"What sort of a looking girl was she, good Dromo?"—"Bah!" quoth he; "don't expect to jeer me out of memory as well as judgment. Heavens and earth! when did any body ever hear of any body denying the efficacy of philtres? What an atheistical sort of barbarians those Britons must be. I wonder you are not afraid of some evil coming upon you. Remember Dian's handful; remember the fate of Actæon!"—"Good Dromo," said I, "I suppose you also suffered from peeping. But talk seriously; are you yourself a dealer in philtres, that you are so anxious I should believe in their power? Or what is your meaning?"

"My meaning is this," quoth he, with great vehemence,—"it is, that if Rubellia gives Sextus such another philtre as a certain cunning damsel gave me, before I left pleasant Crete, to be a drudge and a packhorse here in Rome, where a man may sweat all his life in another's service without being once thanked for his pains, and perhaps be laid out, look ye, for a supper to the vultures at last, because no body will treat his carcase to a blaze of old sticks,—I say, that if the Lady Rubellia contrives to give Sextus such another philtre as that, the game's up, Master Valerius; and we may as well set about painting the dead, as try to save him from her clutches. The man's gone—he's as lost as Troy."—"Well, Dromo," said I, for I perceived there was no use in fighting it with him, "and have you not been able to hit upon any feasible scheme?"—"Ay, have you come to that at last? that is just what I have been cudgelling my brains about for the last twelve hours. But if I do hit upon any thing, I shall need assistance. In such cases, the best judgment can do nothing by itself."—"Fear not, Dromo," quoth I; "if my assistance can do you any good, you well know you can command it to the utmost."—"Then prepare," replied the Cretan, rising up with an air of much solemnity—"then prepare in good earnest; for, may Cerberus growl upon me, if I don't find out some scheme before another day goes over, and shew you all what stuff I am made of. To think of entrapping Sextus without consulting Dromo!—No, by Cretan Jove, she shall not accomplish it—no, not even with a sea of philtres."

"And, in the meantime," said I, "what must Sextus do with himself?"—"He must not go near the Suburra; he must remain closely at home; and as for tasting any thing at her house, or any thing that comes from her—by heavens, if he does not take his oath against that—we may as well leave him to his destiny. If he will but take good care for this one day, I think there is every chance something may be hit upon ere the morning. I have got my cue, and shall not be idle, I promise you; but I undertake nothing, unless you swear to keep Sextus safe, and at a distance from her, till night-fall."—"Good Dromo," said I, "make yourself easy on that score; it will be a new circumstance indeed, if we find any difficulty in persuading Sextus to stay a single day away from the Suburra."

"Persuading!" quoth the slave; "who ever heard of such a word as persuasion at such a crisis as this? I tell you he *must* be kept away; and if no other plan can be fallen on, I have a great mind to turn the key on him and his pedagogue both together. I heard them hammering at their lessons already as I came along—and that puts me in mind that I have a very shrewd notion there is more between that bearded goat of ours and this Rubellia, than any of us had been suspecting. Unless that Calabrian lies—and I think lying is above his sphere—this old rogue has been oftener in the Suburra of late than we had any thought of. So help me Hermes! I believe Licinius has been employing him to go his private messages to Rubellia—but that is only one insult more, and I shall have my revenge all in a lump."

"I think it very likely," answered I, quietly, "that Licinius may have been employing Xerophrastes in some such embassies; and, if I mistake not the matter, he would feel himself quite as much in his element, trotting along the Sacred Way, and so forth, on such delicate errands for the father, as in expounding musty parchments to the son."—"No matter for all that," quoth Dromo, rubbing his hands; "the more enemies the more glory. Would Miltiades have been pleased had the Spartans arrived?—Leave all to me—take you care only of Sextus, and I am not afraid for any reinforcement that rascally rhetorician may bring against me."—While he was saying so, the face of the Cretan exhibited symptoms of incipient glee; and he concluded with snapping his fingers, and uttering a short keen whistle, such as you have heard from the lips of a hunter, when the dogs begin to bay around a thicket.

Seeing his eyes dance with the expectation of some bustling scene, I could not help participating, in some measure, in the feelings of the Cretan; and, "Dear Dromo," said I, "I beseech you, if it be possible, let me have a share in whatever you resolve upon."—"Watch well," replied he, "during the day, and you shall see what you shall see, when the moon mounts above the Cœlian, and the hour for grubbing among herbs and bones is come.—But now I hear some one coming—it is Licinius."—Dromo, finger on lip, glided from the room. Nor had his well-practised ears deceived him, for he scarcely vanished, before my kinsman entered.

"Valerius," said he, saluting me affectionately, "I thought you were probably much fatigued with your spectacles, so I desired that nobody should call you this morning; but I met Boto in the hall, and hearing that you were astir, I have come up, for I wish a little private conversation. Shall we walk in the eastern portico, till Xerophrastes leaves Sextus at liberty?"

He led the way along the gallery, and in passing, we also heard the deep voice of the rhetorician resounding among the pillars, and could even catch a few of the magniloquent phrases with which he was feeding the ears of his pupil. "Ay, ay," says Licinius, "I wish, indeed, it were possible to inspire the youth with some sense of what is due to the dignity of principle, and how absurd it is to think of gratifying whims at the expense of duty. But I fear the boy is incorrigible; and, Caius, I am sorry to say, I suspect you have been looking on his errors with a countenance rather of favour and of confirmation, than, as I should have expected, of rebuke."

"Licinius," said I, "you know not how much you distress me. I could rather die than encourage Sextus in any thing I thought evil; but, indeed, I have seen nothing to make me imagine him capable of such conduct."

"Come, by Hercules," returned he, "there is no occasion for so many words. I thought it very odd that you went away so soon from the Forum the other day, considering that you had never been there before; but I thought it doubly and trebly remarkable that Sextus should have accompanied you, when the case in hand affected the affairs of Rubellia. But I have since found out that it was not the society of old Capito which attracted him—no, my friend, nor yet the alarm of a thunder storm that detained you at the villa. In a word, Valerius, I strongly suspect that Sextus is carrying on an intrigue with a young lady whom I never saw, but who, I am quite sure, will never be mistress of a dozen lizards, and that this is the true cause of his reluctance concerning a match, which, to say nothing of the pleasure it would give to me, is the only means by which I can see any prospect of the young man's fortune being made, and the dignity of his family kept up, after another effigy shall have been added to our hall. Infatuated and headstrong boy! if he owes nothing to himself or to me, is it possible that he can look upon that venerable line of sages and heroes, without feeling shame in the degradation of his own earth-stooping desires?"

"Without question," said I, "you allude to the Lady Rubellia, whom, as I have heard from various quarters, you are desirous of seeing wedded to Sextus."

"Yes, Caius Valerius, it is indeed to her I allude; and it is of the obstacle which—unwittingly, I doubt not—you yourself have been throwing in the way of that union, that I have now to make my complaint. Not such the service that I had expected from my kinsman. Rubellia is descended from a noble family, and, both in possession and expectation, her wealth is great. Two heavy fines laid upon me by Domitian, and the expense at which I have maintained my rank among the great patrons of Rome—these things together have impoverished me, and to an extent not altogether convenient. In this boy my hopes were placed; and see now how they are all likely to be blasted for a dimpled cheek and a pair of wanton eyes!—or rather, indeed, I should say, for the sake of the malignant pleasure that is derived from thwarting my purposes; for, if beauty were what the boy wanted, where should he find beauty beyond Rubellia? Perhaps, Caius, I should, before this time, have made you acquainted with my intentions from my own lips. But it is my own foolish indulgence which has made my degenerate boy quite forget, not only what is the duty of a son, but what is the power of a father."

"I trust," said I, "there is no need for all this seriousness. Sextus has only laid aside the garb of a stripling; it is too much to be despairing of his success in life, only because he is unwilling, at a period so early, to enter upon a permanent connection. Is it possible, that, if he really dislike Rubellia, you would wish to see him marry her—only to divorce her, without question, as soon as he should find it possible to do so without inconvenience?"—"Handsome, rich, noble, and almost as young as himself, why, in the name of all the gods, for what cause should he divorce Rubellia?"—"Sir," said I, "he loves not Rubellia, nor will ever love her; and if you cause your son to marry this woman, look you well to it, that the unhappiness of both rest not on your head. Handsome, rich, noble, and young she may be; but I am sure, she has neither such a heart, nor such a mind, as should belong to the wife of your Sextus. A luxurious woman is Rubellia, and I have seen her find luxury in the contemplation of blood. Wed not Rubellia to your son."—"Peace, Valerius," he answered; "what boyish nonsense is this?—I *will* wed Rubellia to my son; and let him see to it, that he tempts me not farther with his disobedience."

Licinius said these last words in a voice of so much earnestness, that I knew not well what answer to make to him; but while I was hesitating, one of the little boys about the house, (I mean the children of the domestic slaves,) said, "If it please my lord, the same senator that was here in the morning is waiting in the hall."—"Pontius Mamurra!" said the orator, leaving me.

I, for my part, when I heard the name of the visiter, began to understand somewhat of the channel through which my kinsman had been informed about what had passed at the Suburban. I had no leisure, however, to reflect long upon this hint; for I found Sextus waiting for me. "Come," he said, "I was afraid I must set off without you. My father has been looking on me this morning with such an aspect of displeasure as I rarely before witnessed in him, and if I defer going to the painter about this likeness, he will be altogether enraged at supper-time. I know very well he means the ring, in which it is to be placed, for another present to Rubellia; but notwithstanding, what can I do? Any opposition to him in lesser matters would only tend to bring on some final explanation about the great affair itself, and that, whether it be weakness in me or not, I as yet have no courage to encounter. The man must be expecting me; and I am sure you will accompany me, for I have much need of you to keep up my heart. Xerophrastes, indeed, has been desired to go with me; but he will be no comfort, for I see plainly, from the drift of his harangues, that he is enlisted against me. Dear Caius, I have nobody in the whole world I can trust to but Dromo and yourself."

He had scarcely said so, when we heard Xerophrastes pacing up and down with solemn strides in the gallery; so I knew not how to excuse myself, although I was very anxious to have staid at home for another purpose. Sextus had taken my gown from the nail; he threw it over my shoulders before I had time to say any thing, and we were soon on our way to his ungrateful destination.

CHAPTER II.

We had to traverse a considerable part of the city; for this painter was one of those who exercise their art during the public hours of the day in the baths of the Palatine, where, as you have heard, in the wide circuit of the princely residence, abundant accommodation is set forth for all such ingenious persons. We proceeded along the edge of the river, and by the west of the Capitol, following the line of that great Triumphal Way which has been witness of so many glorious pageants; for so, they told me, we should most easily ascend into the Cæsarian courts. But when we had come thither, we found the whole open space, in front of the portico and stairs of Trajan, occupied by a detachment of the Prætorian cohorts, drawn up in splendid array to receive some promised donative; while the music, and the clamours of their mustering, had collected enough of spectators to render the passage onwards in some measure difficult. We were constrained to form part of their attendance, and stood gazing among the multitude. Even Xerophrastes caught some animation from the brilliancy of the spectacle; and the enamoured and perplexed Sextus himself, beating time on my shoulder, seemed to have forgotten, for a moment, the anxieties of his situation.

Some horsemen, however, riding along to keep the ground open in front of the soldiery, compelled us to shift to the eastward, where many chariots were drawn up—and in one of these Rubellia. The lady looked paler than I had before seen her, and had not the air of being in the smallest degree occupied with what was passing. I did not think it necessary to take any notice of her being there to my companions, and was willing, indeed, to keep myself turned away from the place where she sat, in order to avoid our being recognized. Yet there was something in her aspect and attitude, that, as by a sort of fascination, drew my eyes to the spot I wished to avoid. From time to time, therefore, I felt myself constrained to regard the melancholy lady; and by and by, Sextus perceived what it was that attracted my attention:—so I discovered, although he said not a word, from a fervent pressure upon my arm as I stood before him. At that moment there drew near a little ugly old woman, with no covering upon her head but long coarse gray clusters of hair hanging matted and twisted down upon her shoulders, who lifted up a basket of trinkets, and presented it; but Rubellia started on her seat, and, looking in the face of the old creature, manifested signs of no trivial emotion; for her colour returned with a sudden flush, and her eyes recovered all their animation, and it was evident she had something to say which could not regard the gaudy ornaments offered to her view. Whatever it was, however, she did not occupy much time in saying it; for scarcely a minute elapsed before the basket was lowered again, and the old woman began to move towards another part of the crowd; on which Rubellia sunk back in her chariot, and appeared to relapse into pensive abstraction.

Presently a low voice croaking out, "Rings, rings—amulets and rings!" amongst the crowd that stood immediately behind me; and I perceived the same woman pushing her basket between Xerophrastes and Sextus.— "Noble youth," quoth the hag, leering, "lovely young gentleman—sweet Adonis, my charming lord, do now look into old Pona's basket—do take a look at Ponula's rings and amulets—her amulets and rings. Here is one that I could have sold a hundred times, but I was determined to keep it till I should see the prettiest young gentleman in Rome, and I will never go back to Naples without selling it, after this day; for this little amulet must be nobody's but yours. You will break my heart, my prince, if you buy not my beautiful amulet."

"And what," said Sextus, blushing and laughing, "may be the virtues of your amulet?"

Then laying her yellow hand upon his shoulder, till she had made him stoop down so that she might get close to his ear, she began to pour out, with much mysterious volubility, all the story of its marvellous potencies; but what she said even I could not know, only I heard the words, "Æthiopian, Æthiopian," and "Memnon, Memnon," and something about "not a pretty lady in Rome." But just as the woman was most earnest in her whisper, and Sextus, apparently at least, in listening, I found my gown plucked from behind, and behold, there was Dromo, with a countenance tremulously agitated, and white as a piece of dead parchment, pointing to his young master and the old hag, and beseeching me to separate them, by motions in nowise to be mistaken. How he had come thither, or what was the cause of this anxiety, I had no time to conjecture, for before I could say a word, he began to bellow out,—"The horses, the horses—make room for the horses;" and immediately those that stood near him began to move a little, and then, the cry being repeated, those that stood farther off mistaking the noise of their feet for the approach of some new squadron, there arose a sort of rushing among the crowd; and, in a twinkling, the voice of Pona was heard grumbling and croaking at a distance from the place to which our party were borne. Close, nevertheless, did the faithful Cretan stick to us; and no sooner was quiet in some measure restored, and the false alarm he had created at an end, than he whispered into my ear, "For the sake of all that is sacred, let not that foul hag speak another word to my young master—I will tell you more anon. Meantime, haste ye, haste ye. Make the best of your speed to the Palatine; it will be much easier for you to push your way thither, than it was for me to reach you."

My friend being already weary of the heat and the pressure, we were ready to take advantage of an opening pointed out by the Cretan. It so happened, however, that in the same commotion the chariot of Rubellia also had changed its situation; for just as we had escaped, as I thought, and were about to place our feet on the magnificent flight of stairs that leads from the New Way to the Augustan Towers, there came to us a lad of that lady's household, who told us she was near at hand, and desirous, if it so pleased us, of our company. Aware that we were in sight, how could we disobey? We found the lady in her chariot, but not such as we had seen her before. On the contrary, the liveliness of her aspect seemed now to be restored, and she received us with her usual gaiety of address. "Careless men," said she, as we drew near; "I suppose I might have sat here till the Greek Kalends, before any one of you would have observed me."

"Most noble lady," quoth Xerophrastes, "bear it not indignantly, that amidst all the confusion of men and horses, and trumpets and shoutings, our attention was abstracted from that which was most worthy of notice. My young friends deserve to be excused, since even I, who am not in the habit of being much troubled by such vanities, was so bewildered that I scarcely knew my right hand from my left, in this human chaos.—Pardon, noble Rubellia; we have been unwitting offenders."

"And was it so?" said the lady, not looking at the Stoic.—"But I did not call for you to hear useless apologies. What new sight is it that attracts you to the Palatine?—or is it only that you are desirous of exhibiting to Valerius the old-established wonders of the place? In either case, I have half a mind to accompany you. In spite of all they tell us about the Golden House, I can scarcely think the Palatine shewed more splendidly than it does now, even in the days of Nero."

"Indeed," said I, as we began to mount together the broad slabbed steps which rise up, tier above tier, from the portico on the street, to that which hangs on the brow—"Indeed, it is not easy for me to doubt that Rubellia is in the right."—For now, on one side, were all the pillars and arches of the Forum stretched out below us, and, on the other, lay the great Circus, topped with its obelisk; while before rose the gray cliffs of the Capitoline, with their domes and proud pinnacles in the glow of noontide—the space between, radiant with arms and banners. Even Xerophrastes did not refrain from some ejaculations.—"Illustrious Rome! how great is thy sublimity!" And then, after a pause, he repeated, in a voice of much majesty, those verses from the Fury of Ajax:

"Oh! might I be where o'er the living deep

Lies the broad shadow of the Sounian cliff,

Waving with all its glorious garniture,

Of rock-sprung foliage: from old Ocean's side,

That I might look on Athens once again!"

Some of the hints which had reached me concerning his nativity recurring to my recollection, I could not help echoing his quotation with another from the Æneid, about the wide tracts ploughed by the Thracians; of which impertinence the sage took no notice.

Nor was admiration diminished when, having gained the top of that massive staircase, or rather, as I should say, hill of marble, we passed beneath the sounding portal, the sole remnant of the original pile of Augustus, and found ourselves within the first of those great imperial quadrangles, by which the whole summit of that once so variously and multitudinously peopled region is now occupied. The light and airy porticoes—the domes—the princely towers—the universal profusion of marble, brass, ivory, flaming gold, lavished on arch, metope, and architrave—all conspired to dazzle the sight, and I stood still to gaze.

"Observe," said Sextus, "those two equestrian statues of bronze on the left hand. I have heard my father say that they mark the sites of two houses, which, before Augustus began to enclose the whole Palatine in his walls, were inhabited, the one by Cicero, the other by Clodius; these are the only traces of their mansions."

"What grim-looking figures!" said the lady; "yet, I dare say, they don't cast half such fierce looks on each other, as the predecessors you mention. I should like to have seen the countenance of old Tully, the morning he went down the hill to deliver his harangue for Milo."

"I am glad," said I, "that Sextus has told me this; for in reading those famous philippics in time to come, I shall possess a new key to the bitterness of their phraseology, knowing, as I do, that the two lived just over the way from each other, and that the orator, when his spirits were flagging, could derive a new reinforcement of spleen from merely putting his head out of the window."—"To hear you," says Rubellia, "one would think you were studying the art of making philippics—I am afraid, that if it be so, my joining your party may prove to have been but an ill-judged thing; for if any of you be preparing to abuse me, my presence will serve to sharpen your weapons."—"In that case, however," interrupted the smiling Xerophrastes, "my noble lady will admit, that the converse also will hold good, and that if praise be in meditation, it will not be the feebler because the subject of the intended panegyric has passed before our eyes."—"Most courteous of men," replied the lady, "who talks of the stiffness of the Porch? To-day and yesterday you have paid me as many compliments as might give a lesson to the gayest trifler about these baths. If all," she continued, (gazing as she spoke, with all her eyes upon Sextus,)—"if all were as profuse, I should be unable to sustain the weight of their civilities."—"Nay, Oh! generous lady," quoth the sage again, "it must be remembered, that, as the poet has expressed it, there are two kinds of shame—there is the wicked shame and the good shame. Why should it be doubted, that a modest Verecundity, not unsuitable to their age, has laid her finger on the lips of our young friends? I swear by the Victrix of Ida, that your presence itself is that which occasions their silence;—bear it not ill— bear it not harshly—the young will learn—not every one has seen Corinth."—"No, truly," answered the laughing lady; "but I doubt whether they that have been so fortunate, have ever seen any thing half so fine as what now awaits Valerius."

She pointed to the solemn Doric columns which sustain the portico of the famous Temple of Apollo, whose shade lay far out upon the court before us; and, passing between those brazen horsemen, we soon began to ascend the steps that lead up to the shrine. Nor can I tell you how delightful was the fragrant coolness, which reigned beneath the influence of that massive canopy of marble, to us whose eyes had been so long supporting the meridian blaze. We entered with slow steps within the vestibule of the Temple, and stood there for some space, enjoying in silence the soft breath of air that played around the flowing fountains. Then passing on, the airy hall received us; and I saw the statue of Phœbus presiding, like a pillar of tender light, over the surrounding darkness of the vaulted place; for, to the lofty shrine of the God of day no light of day had access, and there lay only a small creeping flame burning thin upon his altar; but a dim and sweet radiance, like that of the stars in autumn, was diffused all upon the statue, and the altar, and the warlike trophies suspended in the inner recesses, from the sacred tree of silver that stands in the centre; amidst the trembling enamelled leaves and drooping boughs of which hung many lamps, after the shape and fashion of pomegranates: and out of every pomegranate flowed a separate gleam of that soft light, supplied mysteriously through the stem of the silver tree.

There appeared presently from behind the statue, a majestic woman, arrayed in long white garments, and having a fillet of laurel leaves twined above her veil. Venerable and stately was her mien, but haughty, rather than serene, the aspect of her countenance. Without looking towards us, she went up to the altar, and began to busy herself in trimming the sacred fire, which, as I have said, exhibited only a lambent flame. When, with many kneelings and other ceremonies, she had accomplished this service, the priestess turned again, as if to depart; and then first, as it seemed, observing the presence of strangers, she stood still before the altar, and regarding us attentively, began to recognize the Lady Rubellia; whom, forthwith advancing, she saluted courteously, and invited to come with the rest of us into her privacy, behind the shrine of the God.

She led the way, Rubellia and the rest of us in her train, through several folding-doors, and along many narrow passages all inlaid, on roof, wall, and floor, with snow-white alabaster and rich mosaic work; until at length we came to a little airy chamber, where three young maidens were sitting with their embroidering cushions, while one, taller than the rest, whose back was placed towards us, knelt on the floor, touching, with slow fingers, the strings of a Dorian lyre. Hearing the sound of her music as we entered, we stood still in the door-way, and the priestess, willing apparently that our approach should remain unknown, advancing a step or two before us, said, "Sing on— I have trimmed the flame; but remember, I pray you, that the precincts of Phœbus are not those of Pluto, and let not your chant be of such funereal solemnity. We solitaries have little need of depressing numbers."

"Dear friend," replied she that had been thus addressed, without changing her attitude, "you must bear with my numbers such as they are; for if you bid me sing only merry strains, I am afraid neither voice nor fingers may be able well to obey you."

These words were spoken in a low and melancholy voice, which I well recognized. Sextus, also, perceived who spoke; but when he looked at me to signify this, I motioned to keep silence.

"Then please yourself," said the priestess, laying her hand on Athanasia's shoulders; "but do sing, for I should fain have my maidens to hear something truly of your music." With that she again applied her fingers to the lyre, and stooping over it, began to play some notes of prelude, less sorrowful than what we had at first heard. "Ay, my dear girl," says the priestess, "you could not have chosen better. Heavens! how many lordly choirs have I heard singing to that old Delian air. There are a hundred hymns that may be sung to it—give us whichsoever of them pleases your fancy the best."—"I will try," replied the maiden, "to sing the words you have heard before. If I remember, you liked them." Then boldly at once, yet gently, did her voice rush into the current of that ancient strain that you have heard so often; but it was then that I myself for the first time heard it.

The moon, the moon is thine, O night,

Not altogether dark art thou;

Her trembling crescent sheds its light,

Trembling and pale, upon thine ancient brow.

The moon is thine, and round her orb

A thousand sweet stars minister,

Whose twinkling rays dark wells absorb,

And all the wide seas drink them far and near.

They kiss the wide sea, and swift smiles

Of gladness o'er the waters creep;

Old hoary rocks rejoice, and isles,

And there is glory on the slumbering deep

Afar. Along the black hill's side,

Right blithe of heart the wanderers go,

While that soft radiance, far and wide,

Gleams on the winding streams and woods below.

And gaily for the fragile bark,

Through the green waves its path is shorn,

When all the murmurs of the dark

Cold sea lie calm'd beneath that gliding horn.

Yet hail, ye glittering streaks, that lie

The eastern mountain tops upon!

Hail, ye deep blushes of the sky,

That speak the coming of the bridegroom sun!

Hail to the healing beam of day,

That rouses every living thing!

The forest gulphs confess thy sway,

And upon freshening branches glad birds sing.

And loathsome forms, that crept unseen

Beneath the star-light faint and wan,

Cower in their brakes the thorns between,

Dreading that fervid eye, and its sure scan

Triumphant. Welcome life and light!

Sing rocks and mountains, plain and sea;

Fearful though lovely was the night;

Hail to more perfect beauty—hail to THEE!

"Why stop you, Athanasia?" said the priestess, finding that here she paused,—"why do you rise up, and take your fingers from the lyre, before you sing out the chorus?"—"No more, dear aunt—excuse me—no more. I have already sung all that I can," replied Athanasia.—"Nay, then," says she, "if you be fatigued, sing not; but join me, maidens, in the close—perhaps it rises too high for Athanasia."

And with that the ancient lady herself, joined by the three damsels that had been embroidering, took up the strain, which, indeed, rose higher towards its end

Hail to thee Phœbus, son of Jove,

Glorious Apollo, Lord of Light,

Hail, lovely in thy Delian grove,

And terrible on Delphos' haunted height!

Hail to thee here beneath the dome,

Great Phœbus, of thy Latian shrine;

All hail from Cæsar and from Rome;

Hail by thy dearest name, God Palatine!

But as they were singing the last verse of all, Rubellia also aided their melody with a rich strong gushing voice, which rose far above all the others; and the silent Athanasia turning round quickly, perceived, not without manifestation of alarm, by how many strangers her song had been overheard. On seeing who we were, she saluted Sextus and myself with modest courtesy, amidst her confusion; and it may be that my companion, as well as myself, blushed at the same moment; for he could not see Athanasia without thinking of Sempronia.

It seemed as if her confusion were not unconnected with some suspicion of having been recognized near the Prætorian guard-house; for, after the first glance, I in vain endeavoured to meet her eye; while on the contrary, to Sextus she directed both looks and words, enough to provoke visibly some not altogether benign movements in our Rubellia. Such, at least, was my interpretation of the fair widow's aspect, and the tone of impatience in which she, after a minute or two had passed, began to urge the propriety of our proceeding to the part of the imperial edifice in which the painter was expecting us.

The priestess of Apollo hearing her say so, courteously offered to guide us beyond the precincts of the temple, and our whole party were again in motion; but Athanasia remained behind with the three young damsels, and I, who walked last, saw her, ere the portal received me, preparing again to handle the lyre, with fingers visibly trembling, and a pale countenance, not as I thought unstained with some yet more distinct traces of keen emotion. The sight of her agitation fixed my footstep for a moment, and it was then that, on her casting a sudden glance round to the place where I stood, I perceived truly that I had not been mistaken, and that the tears were gathered within her eyelids. It was no more, however, than one glance, for immediately she stooped again, and, dashing her fingers along the chords of the instrument, appeared to bury her thoughts in its harmony. I stood for a moment, and then ashamed of myself, and troubled with her troubles and with my own, I followed the rest into the great library which Augustus placed beneath the protection of the Palatine Apollo. The priestess parted from us at its entrance, after pointing out a low and massive door of bronze on the right hand, within which, as she told me, the remains of the Sybilline prophecies are preserved, unseen by profane eyes, watched over perpetually by the guardians of the place.

CHAPTER III.

I had walked by the side of my young friend, and behind the Stoic, (who, I think, was expressing, in his pompous fashion, much admiration of the singing of Rubellia,) along one or two of the great halls in which the library is contained, before the novelty of the objects surrounding me made any impression even on my eyes; and even after these were in some measure engaged, my mind still continued to dwell on that troubled aspect, and on the notes of the uncompleted song. At length, however, the levity of youth, and natural curiosity revived; and I began to be present, not in body merely, in a place where there was much that might well interest the mind. Far-receding rows of columns conducted my eyes into the interminable recesses of that wide range of chambers, in which the records of the thought and spirit of all past ages are piled up together; and gazing on the loaded shelves which every where ascended into the galleries, I could not but be affected with many new emotions. I perused glorious names on the busts that seemed to preside over the different compartments. The high filletted front of Homer detained for the first time my contemplation; the eyes of the divine old man, even in sculpture, distinctly and visibly blind, while the serenity and sanctity of the towering forehead, revealed how the intense perception at once of the lovely and the great could compensate for visions of earthly beauty shut out. The mild Plato, and the imperious Stagyrite—Pindar—Simonides—Alcæus—and I know not how many more, succeeded as we passed along—each in his own sphere, reigning by himself; yet all connected together by a certain common air of greatness, like so many successive princes, or contemporary heroes of the same mighty empire.

From this main range, there diverged many lesser chambers, in which we saw studious persons engaged, each seated by himself, and having his eyes fixed on the parchment before him. Of these, some deigned not to intimate by the smallest movement their perception that any one had approached; but with others Xerophrastes exchanged, as he walked, lofty salutation, and one or two even entered, for a moment, into conversation with him. With one of these, indeed, (an ancient of bitter aspect,) to such a length did the colloquy extend, that we began to think we should never be able to get our Stoic away from him; till, as our fortune would have it, it became necessary for them to have a certain book for the purpose of reference, and then Xerophrastes began to make inquiries concerning Parmeno, who, as I gathered, must needs be one of those intrusted with the care of the library.

"I am afraid," said the other, "if we must wait for him, we shall not be able to get that work either to-day or to-morrow; for his pupil, the son of Fabricius, is dead, and I suppose he will now change his quarters, and be no longer seen so often about these haunts of the muses."

"Alas!" interrupted Sextus, "I met Fabricius in the Forum a few days ago, and he told me his son was ill; but little did I imagine my dear companion was so near his end! Is it indeed so?"

"Even so," rejoined the other. "Rapid have been the shears of Atropos! It is but a few moments since Agaso, the painter passed; and, he told me he had been receiving orders to take a likeness, as well as he could, from the corpse."

"If Agaso be so engaged," replied Xerophrastes, "I am afraid we need not expect to find him neither in his usual place. Perhaps we had better make inquiry for him at the dwelling of Fabricius."

To this Sextus assented; or rather, being lost in reflection concerning the death of his friend, he suffered himself to be conducted by the Stoic. Passing, therefore, through one or two more apartments, we issued forth, and drew near to the vestibule of Fabricius' house, who, as they told me, was a noble Roman, having the chief superintendance of the whole library, and an intimate friend of Licinius—one whose domestic calamity could not fail to spread much affliction through a wide circle of patrician kindred.

At the vestibule, we found assembled not a few of the young man's relations; but Xerophrastes immediately said, "Behold Parmeno, he is the most afflicted; and what wonder that it should be so?"

"Alas!" said Sextus, "the bier is set forth; the last rites are to be performed this evening."

This Parmeno was a striking figure. Seated close by the bier, his head was involved in his cloak, so that only his eyes and his nose could be seen, but these of themselves expressed a decorous affliction; and the folds of the cloak fell down over the rest of his person in great order and dignity. On the pavement beside him was seen lying, half-unfolded, a book inscribed with the name of Heraclitus, which he appeared to have been reading. When Xerophrastes approached, this mourner stretched forth his hand, and shook his head, but he did not say any thing, nor even look towards the rest of us; and indeed to have done so, would have disturbed the attitude in which he had placed himself. Xerophrastes, on his part, received the proffered hand, and shaking his head in response, said, "Yes, my Ionian friend, I may still bid thee hail and live; but I must say farewell to the plant thou wast rearing. Farewell to the youthful promise of Fabricius!"

On hearing these words, the sitting philosopher drew his mantle quite over his face, and leant himself heavily against one of the fluted columns of the vestibule, for he seemed to be much shaken. In the meantime Sextus approached the bier, and contemplated his companion as he lay there wreathed with melancholy garlands; his countenance bearing a natural mixture of sadness and astonishment. Nor could I, who had never before seen the young man, behold the spectacle without similar emotions; for his age, as it seemed, could not have been much different from my own, and the pale features were interesting, their expression not less amiable than solemn.

"Alas!" said Sextus, "the last time I saw him, how differently did he appear! We rode out together with some others to Tibur, and spent all the day there; and as we returned by the moonlight, how joyous his conversation! Methinks I yet hear him laughing and speaking. We parted at the foot of the Capitoline, and never did I see him again till now."

"Oh, fate of man!" quoth Xerophrastes; "how uncertain is life, how certain death! Without doubt, young Fabricius had as little thought of dying as any of your company; and yet, see now, he is arrayed for the last time, and this juvenile gown, which he should so soon have laid aside for the manly, is destined to be consumed with him."

"A fine lad he was," cries one of the standers by,—"a fine lad, and an excellent horseman. The Martian Field did not often behold such a rider in these degenerate days of the Roman youth."

But while the rest were still contemplating the bier, Xerophrastes, turning to his brother philosopher, said, "Tell me now, my learned friend, do you still, after this mournful event, continue to reside with the elder Fabricius? Has that excellent man any more sons to be educated, or will he retain you only for the sake of the library, with which assuredly he will find few so conversant as yourself?"

To which Parmeno replied, "Your question, O Xerophrastes, shews that clear judgment concerning the affairs of men, for which you have always been celebrated. No, my friend, the gray-haired Fabricius no longer requires my residence here; for he is about to retire into one of his villas on the Campanian shore, and to bury for ever his affliction in the privacy of his woods. We are about to part, not without mutual tears; and several Patricians have already been applying to him for his influence with me, whom, although unworthy of so much research, they earnestly covet, and wish to engage as the instructor of their young men. I have been sitting here not unseen, beside this my former charge, and each is impatient to solicit me into his service."

"Your reputation I well know is high," replied Xerophrastes, "and deservedly so; more particularly, for that fine talent you have for giving metaphysical interpretations of mythology, and for explaining the obscure allegories of ancient poets. But for my own part, Parmeno, I find not so much delight in abstract ideas, or in the passive contemplation of the universe; but incline rather to study, as heretofore, that part of philosophy which relates to action, and the morality of duty."

"Yes, worthy Xerophrastes," returned he, with a most languid serenity; "and so far as I understand, you sort well in this with the stirring disposition of your friend Licinius."

To which Xerophrastes made answer:—"My patron Licinius is fond of action, and I of the rules of action. He says, it is only in war, or in civil functions of a public nature, that a person can prove himself a man. The rest, he says, is visionary, and comes to nothing, or is a slumber of the mind in sensuality, without thought."

"Does he think, then," quoth Parmeno, his wobegone countenance relaxing into a smile,—"Does Licinius think, then, there is no sensuality in perpetual action, and declamation and noise? To me such things appear almost as trivial as the lazy enjoyments of Epicureans, besides being harsh and disagreeable, and not unfrequently ridiculous. But observe, O Xerophrastes! that I speak these things as it were abstractly, and not by any means in disparagement of Licinius, your excellent patron and friend."

To which the stoic replied in astonishment—"What is this you have said? Do you assert that action is sensual?"

Then Parmeno, lifting from the pavement the book which he had been reading, or appearing to read, said, "It is even so, most erudite Xerophrastes. Indeed, I have always delighted in the most primitive and remote doctrines handed down from antiquity; and among others, in the riddles of this obscure Ephesian. Following the scope of his philosophy, I am led to believe, that, so often as the mind impels, or is impelled by other causes, it begins to lose sight of pure knowledge, and becomes in danger of thinking that every thing is vain, light, and evanescent, except what is perceived by the senses. Heraclitus well says, that Love and Hatred govern all things. Now, when the principle of Discord prevails, it subjects all things to the dominion of action, and to the gross perceptions of sense. But when that of Love is prevalent, it emancipates the struggling chaos of things from the yearning of compulsion, and from the darkness of sensual proximity; for, between things that struggle immediately against each other, light has no room to enter in and shine; and therefore it is, that, when Love gains the ascendency, a new arrangement is produced—an arrangement which, if I may so express it, is more serene, transparent, orderly and divine, and wherein things exist in safety from the danger of mutual destruction."

After a preliminary cough:—"My opinion," replied Xerophrastes, "coincides rather with that of Empedocles. The immortal Sicilian thinks that Discord is the only separating and arranging principle which marks the boundaries between things, and enables them mutually to act and repel, in such a way as to preserve order."—"Nay, nay," interrupted Parmeno, his hands being by this quite disentangled from his cloak, and his countenance lighted up,—

"Nay, nay, to such doctrine I never shall assent. From Empedocles—even from Xerophrastes, I must differ for ever on this head. The order of which you and the Sicilian speak, is the order of darkness only, and of blind force,—a kind of order in which fierceness and cruelty always reign." But Xerophrastes continued:—"And I farther concur with Empedocles in thinking, that Love is a principle of which the predominance is more fit to turn order into a chaos, than to produce the effects you have described."—"Nay, speak not against Love," quoth Parmeno—"Speak not against Love, nor believe that any respect is due to the dictates of Empedocles, who taught the worst that can be taught by any man—that is to say, the alternation of order and confusion succeeding each other throughout all time. To seek for truth in conceptions like these, is no better than to seek repose in the bosom of Ætna."—"In reference to that point," resumed Xerophrastes, "I agree with you in your disapprobation of Empedocles. But when you say, that Love is the source of knowledge, you much astonish me; for I have always thought rather that its tendency is to bring confusion upon the mind."

"Once more," said Parmeno—"once more, let me beseech you to say nothing against love. You are thinking of the love of particular objects. You speak of Cupid, and not of that heavenly Eros, who, so far from enchaining, or tyrannizing over the mind, rather enables it to escape into the tranquil freedom of far extended contemplation. But what is contemplation without the knowledge of permanent forms, on which the mind may find repose, and so keep itself from being perplexed by the shifting aspects of the many-coloured universe? And therefore it is, O Xerophrastes, that, sometimes laying aside Heraclitus, I study the ancient verses of the poet, Xenophanes, who shews, by the nature of abstract forms, that a certain unity pervades all things. Xenophanes mused of old at Colophon, looking through the blue ether of my native Ionia.—But why should I speak thus at length? Alas! what is the occasion of our being here!—I perceive the approach of the poet, who was to compose an inscription for the urn of my dear Fabricius. Yonder also is the architect, who comes with a design for the tomb. Oh! day of wo, that I should sit in judgment concerning the epitaph and tomb of my ingenuous youth!"

"It is, indeed, true," replied Xerophrastes, "that even I, in the repercussions of our talk, had well-nigh forgotten this unhappy occurrence; but, perhaps, there is something not after all entirely excusable in our giving so much superiority to the affairs of philosophical discussion. Now, however, it is evident, that we must suspend our colloquy—And who, I beseech you, above all things, is he that now draws near to the place of this mournful assembly, holding a horse in his hand. Methinks I have seen his face before."

"That you have indeed, Master," quoth he that had come up,—"that you have; and no longer ago than yesterday neither, if you will be pleased to give yourself the trouble of recollecting. My name is Aspar—I am well known. If but my excellent friend, the noble Centurion Sabinus, were here, poor old Aspar would have no reason to complain of the want of a good word."

"Good morrow to you, Aspar," said Sextus; "but what is it that brings you hither just at this moment? And for what purpose have you brought your horse with you? for people of your sort do not in general ride in the courts of the Palatine."

"Alas!" quoth Aspar, "and is it you, who seem to have been one of the contemporaries of that peerless youth—is it you that ask such a question as this? I did not, in truth, imagine that there was any friend of young Fabricius, who did not know his affection for little Sora. There is not such another within twenty miles of the Capitol; but I brought her hither merely out of regard for the family. As for myself, I should never bear to look on her again with pleasure, after knowing the sudden manner of his death. I wish to Heaven the filly were fairly lodged in one of the paddocks of the Lord Fabricius himself."

"Lead the animal round into the stables," says Parmeno, "and I doubt not care will be taken of her.—Yonder comes one of the buffoons of the theatre;—he, I doubt not, is here to disgrace, if he be permitted, this solemn scene, with ranting quotations from the tragic poets. Alas! alas! I cannot bear all this: There also advance the officiators from the Temple of Libitina; they have their cypress boughs ready in their hands. Oh, my learned friend, I cannot sustain these things; let me be gone into the mansion."

The admirer of Heraclitus, picking up his scroll, and gathering together the folds of his mantle, moved slowly into the house, Xerophrastes following with similar gestures. Sextus and I also were about to take our departure; and he, having procured from one of the slaves of the house a myrtle garland, had already placed it upon the bier of the young Fabricius, as the last testimonial of his concern; when there drew near two young men, clad in long mantles of black, who, solemnly embracing my friend, began to exchange with him many expressions of grief.

While they were thus engaged, Rubellia, who had been standing all this while a little apart, sent a boy to inform us that the painter we were in search of had at last made his appearance, and was anxious to proceed with his portrait. I drew Sextus away, therefore, and soon joined the lady and the artist; but as we were moving off thus, one of the bystanding slaves, an old gray-headed man, came up and whispered to Sextus, "Sir, be not deceived; these two nephews of my bereaved master are to me the most disagreeable part of all this preparation. You have heard their lamentation, and seen their sweeping raiment of mourning; but, be sure, a principal subject of their reflection is the probability that one or other of them must be adopted by Fabricius. Alas!

alas! so goes all between Lucina and Libitina. There was never a birth nor a marriage that did not create some sorrow, nor a funeral procession that did not give rise to some joy. Your rhetoricians talk, but what avails it all? Slaves and masters are alike subjected to the evils of the world, and of these death is both the last and the least."

CHAPTER IV.

Agaso, the painter, was a smart dapper little bandy-legged man of Verona, dressed in a Grecian mantle, and endeavouring to look as much as possible like a Greek. Had Xerophrastes not gone off with his brother of Ionia, I have no doubt this man would have made his presence a sufficient excuse for speaking nothing but Greek to us; but, even as it was, his conversation was interlarded with an abundant intermixture of that noble tongue. Nothing could be spoken of which Agaso did not think fit to illustrate, either by the narration of something he himself had seen or heard during his residence at Athens, or, at least, by some quotation from the Grecian poets. To judge from the square, and somewhat ponderous formation of the man's features, Nature had not designed him for any of the most mercurial specimens of her workmanship; but he contrived, notwithstanding, by perpetual shrugging and grimacing, and, above all, by keeping his eyes and eyebrows continually in motion, to give himself an air of no inconsiderable life and vivacity.

Hopping before us with much alacrity, this artist conducted our steps through eight or ten galleries, until at length a curtain being withdrawn, which had covered the space between two pilasters, we found ourselves in a spacious apartment, which, from the courteousness wherewith he bowed us into it, there could be no difficulty in perceiving to be the customary sphere of his own exertions. It was not altogether deserted even when we entered, but the removal of the curtain attracted more of the loungers of the baths, and ere Sextus was fairly fixed before the table of the painter, the modest youth had the mortification to find himself surrounded with a very crowd of knowing and curious physiognomies. The presence of these, however, appeared not unwelcome to the master. On the contrary, there arose between the little man, as he was preparing his brushes, and those who had come to survey him at his work, such a gabble of compliments, remarks, and disquisitions, that it seemed to me as if he would have been disappointed had he not been favoured with their attendance.

"How noble," cries one, "is that portrait you have just been finishing of Rupilius!—Heavens! with what felicity you have caught the air! Methinks I see him about to enter the Basilica, when he knows that some great cause is awaiting his decision. What solemnity in his aspect! what grandeur in the gown!—How finely the purple of the laticlave is made to harmonize with the colouring of the cheeks and chin! What beautiful handling about the fingers with which he grasps his tablets!—As for the head of the stylus, it is the very eye of the picture."—"Exquisite indeed," quoth another; "but who can look at it, or at any thing else, in the same room with this little jewel?—Heavens! what a beauty! who can it be? for I never saw her either at the Circus or the Amphitheatre. What an inimitable modesty!"

The painter heard this last piece of eulogy with an air of some embarrassment, and at the same time looked very cunningly towards the person who had uttered it. But the Lady Rubellia tossed her head, and whispered to me, "Pretty she may be, though I cannot say that style of dressing the hair is at all adapted for such features; but for modesty! hem. I asked Agaso two or three days ago who it was, and he told me—guess!—it is a little Spanish girl, whom that august-looking person, with the grand laticlave, and the purple cheeks and chin, and the glittering stylus, thought fit to bring home with him when he was relieved from the hard duties of the Pro-prætorship. I dare say, he takes care she shall not be seen either at Circus or Amphitheatre; and, indeed, I think it is sufficient impudence to shew her likeness in the company of so many portraits of respectability."

"My dear lady," quoth the painter, who overheard somewhat, "for the sake of all that is sacred, no word of this again! Wait, at least, till the canvass for the Augurship be over. There are always so many to exaggerate and misrepresent."—"Exaggerate, indeed! I think Rupilius ought to be ashamed of himself; and at his time of life too. I think you said he was just the same age with my uncle?"—"Yes," says the painter, "he must be of that standing; and I think he went to Spain just about the period of your marriage."—"Filthy old fellow," quoth she, very quickly; "and this is the treasure he has brought home with him! I have a great mind to tell his wife."—"Hush, hush," said Agaso, "this is the very day Rupilius spoke of bringing her to see his own portrait; and, indeed, I am sure that is the Senator's cough. I rely on your prudence."

And the portly original of the laticlaved portrait walked into the room, having his gown and every part of his dress arranged as represented in the picture; although in the living countenance it was easy to discover a few lines and spots which had been omitted in the copy. By his side moved a short woman, arrayed in the extremity of costly attire, whose swarthy complexion did not, in spite of cosmeticism, harmonize very well with the bright golden ringlets of her Sicambrian peruque; while behind the pair came a thin damsel, whose lineaments exhibited a sort of faint shadow of the same visage, the rudiments of which had been so abundantly filled up in that of the rubicund magistrate. The ex-pro-prætor, after saluting Agaso, stood still with dignity in the midst of the apartment, while the fond daughter, rushing close up to his picture, could with difficulty affix any limits to her expressions of satisfaction:—"O Jupiter! look at the ring. It is the very ring he wears!—the very images are engraved upon it; one can see the three Graces. I never saw such a picture—when will it be brought home?"—"Hush, hush, now, Primula," quoth the mother. "It is certainly a likeness; but why will artists, now-a-days, always paint people older than they are? And besides, it wants something of his expression. Don't you think so yourself, sir?" (turning to the painter) "Rupilius has surely been looking very gloomily when he sat."

On this the painter, leaving Sextus, advanced to her side, and after a pause of some moments, spent in contemplating alternately his own work and the original, said, with a courteous simper, "How much am I indebted to you, most noble lady, for this visit, and these judicious remarks! I only wish you had accompanied the senator, for then, without question, his countenance would have worn the look you desiderate; and I perhaps might have more easily succeeded in catching it, being aided by your suggestions. I hope it may yet be amended."—"How modest he is!" ejaculated the spouse. "A single sitting will suffice, I am sure. We shall come some day when you are quite alone, and I will sit by you, and talk to Rupilius all the while."—"Delightful!" replied the artist; "how happy shall I be in such an opportunity of improving both the picture and myself! We must positively prevail on the senator to give us this one sitting more."—"Never ask his consent," quoth the matron, smiling upon her lord; "leave the whole matter to me. The picture is for me. And besides, if he were to refuse, I know how I should be certain to overcome him; for he has asked me to sit to you myself, and you know if I were to persist in sitting with my gloomy face, as he has with his, we should soon bring him to his right reason."—"*Your* gloomy face, noble lady!" replied the artist, strutting back a pace or two. "I am afraid, if that is the charm by which alone he is to be softened, we must give up all our hopes."—"I protest," says the lady, "I believe you will keep me laughing all the time I sit. And pray now, what dress do you think I should wear? Prima says, I ought certainly to be in green; but I was thinking, that perhaps a yellow byssine would suit me better. But I shall send over half a dozen robes, and then we can choose whichever seems to be the best. One thing only I am quite resolved upon, and that is, that I shall have my golden chain, with the miniature of the Pro-prætor—the Senator, I mean—at the end of it."— "Nothing could be in finer taste," he made answer; "and if my lady should think of green, or purple, or any dark colour for the gown, the rings of the chain and the setting of the miniature would have the richest effect."—"And do, my dear mother," interrupted Prima; "and do have on the sapphire tiara when you sit to Agaso. Or what would you think of having your own hair simply like this lady here? What a beauty!"—"A smart little girl, indeed," quoth the mother. "I think I should know that face. Is she Roman, Agaso?"—"No, not a Roman," answered the artist; "nor do I think my lady can ever have met with her. But perhaps my Lord Rupilius may, for she is a Spaniard."

Agaso turned with a smile to the Senator; but he, scarcely appearing to look at the picture, answered, with great gravity, "I think I have seen the countenance before; and perhaps it was in my province. The face is certainly a pretty one; but nothing so very extraordinary."—"They may say what they like," observed the spouse, drawing herself up; "but there is no such thing as a really urbane air to be got out of Rome."

Meantime, in another part of the room, some other picture appeared to be exciting a scarcely inferior measure of curiosity. On approaching the party, I perceived that this was a sketch, in chalk only, of the head and shoulders of an old man; and when I had gained an opportunity of more nearly surveying it, I recognized without difficulty the features of Tisias of Antioch. The greater number of those who were looking on it, seemed also to have been present at his death; for I heard pointed out by them with exactness the parts in which the resemblance had been most successfully taken. The beauty of the old man's lineaments, and the serenity of his aspect, they all admired; and while they were loud in praising these, Agaso himself also joined them, saying, "Oh, so you have found out my old Christian! How did you get hold of him? for I meant it not to be seen till I had lain on a little of the colour. But is it not a fine study?—is it not a noble head? I think I shall introduce it in the picture I am painting for Pliny. The subject is the sacrifice of Iphigenia. I went to the Amphitheatre," he continued, "rather late, without expecting any thing particular; but it immediately struck me that he might be turned to some account. I made several little sketches of him, for it was a long time ere it was over; and this is from the one I took just after he had made his oration. His hands and feet were singularly fine, I thought. Here," said he, turning over the leaves of his tablets—"here you have him in a variety of shapes!— the muscles shewed powerfully when he knelt;—there, again, you have his fingers as they were folded on his breast—not much flesh, but the lines good—veins well expressed."

But about this time the great bell rung in the tower above the Baths, and the greater part of the young loungers soon dispersed themselves; some to fence or wrestle—others to play in the tennis-court—others to ride in the Hippodrome, in preparation for the bath. So Agaso, being left alone with Sextus, Rubellia, and myself, had at length leisure to proceed with his portrait of the youth.

Much did the lady and the painter discourse, and many merry things were said by them both; but all they said could not entirely remove the embarrassment fixed on the countenance of Sextus; nor, of a truth, did he present himself with much advantage before the artist. Rubellia, nevertheless, sate over against him with looks of no severe criticism; and I doubt not she would have remained to the end of the sitting, had not one of her household come with a message, which, as it seemed, rendered necessary her departure. It struck me, that the messenger answered very well to Dromo's description of the fat Calabrian with whom he and Boto had been drinking; but of this I said nothing to Sextus.

It was near the hour of supper before we were dismissed, and we found Licinius already about to enter his eating chamber.

CHAPTER V.

The orator received us with less coldness than I could have expected. I suppose his knowledge that our morning had been spent in Rubellia's company, had in some measure softened his feelings of jealousy towards his son; and perhaps he had given me credit for advice, to the merit of which I had no claim. But he remained not long at table after supper was concluded, being summoned to discourse in private with a client:—so that Sextus and I were left to spend the evening as it might please ourselves; for as to Xerophrastes, he had not as yet made his appearance, and we took it for granted he had remained at the mansion of Fabricius, for the purpose of consoling with philosophical controversies his bereaved brother of Ionia.

We retired, therefore, into the apartment of my young friend; but he could not read a page without coming upon some verse which made him throw down the scroll to ruminate on the charms of his Sempronia. When he took up his lute, his fingers seemed to evoke only the most melancholy sounds. It was only in the exercise of the foil, that he succeeded in banishing from his thoughts the troubles of his situation; but both of us having contended till we were breathless, were soon compelled to sit down, and then the unhappy boy's exhausted body seemed to communicate a new debility to his mind. We sat for the most part in silence, (for I soon found that I could not say any thing capable of interesting him,) until the shades of evening had quite darkened the chamber, and then we walked together, not less silently, in the adjoining open gallery, until the moon had arisen from above the tall poplars around the Pantheon and Baths of Agrippa, and diffused her radiance over all the beautiful gardens and noble edifices that lay beneath us down to the brink of the river. Lassitude of spirit then, if not expectation of sleep, rendered Sextus desirous of retiring to his couch; so, having exhorted the youth to wrestle with his grief, and to call hope to his aid, I at length left him to himself. But as for me, I had as yet no feeling of weariness, and, besides, I remembered the promise I had made to Dromo in the morning.

I was very much surprised, indeed, that the Cretan had not as yet come to me, and made inquiry concerning him of Boto; but hearing that the man was absent from the house, I thought from this there was the more likelihood of his being engaged in some scheme, the result of which I should by and by learn from his own lips. I dismissed my Briton, therefore, and prepared to read by my watch-light, and while I was considering what I should read, I remembered the scroll I had received from Tisias, which forthwith I took from the place in which I had locked it up on the morning of the preceding day. There fell from out of it, as I unfolded it, a letter sealed, but without any superscription. This I of course considered as meant only for the eye of

Athanasia; so I kissed the parchment her fingers were destined to touch, and, before I began to read, restored it to its receptacle.

More than one of you, my young friends, have already heard me speak, on another occasion, of the impression which that night's reading made upon my mind, and been told, from my own lips, what book it was that was contained in the scroll of Tisias; the rest of you will judge for yourselves with what astonishment it was that I, who had at the best expected to unfold some obscure treatise of Asiatic lore, some semi-barbarous exposition of mystical riddles, found myself engaged in the perusal of a plain and perspicuous narrative of facts, written evidently by a man of accomplishment and learning, and in Greek of which the most elegant penman of these times could have had no occasion to be ashamed. In a word, it was the Gospel of the holy physician St Luke which had been put into my hands; and at this day I am still grateful that this was the first of the Christian books which I had an opportunity of seeing; for such had been my education, that I am afraid others, not less worthy of the true faith, might have repelled me by the peculiarities of their composition, as well as by the acquaintance with many things, to me then entirely unknown, which they take for granted in the style of their commencement. Here, however, there was enough only of mystery, the more effectually to stimulate my curiosity, while the eagerness with which I engaged myself in its gratification, was abundantly repaid from the beginning, both by the beauty of the simple narrative itself, and the sublimity of the conceptions embodied and evolved in its course.

Considering the book which I was reading, as one merely of human origin and invention, I could not help regarding it with such admiration, that it appeared to me above all things wonderful, I had never seen it mentioned by any of the writers of the age, or heard it spoken of by any of those who, in my presence, since I came to Rome, had talked concerning the faith and doctrines of the persecuted Christians. But this was not all. At least, said I to myself, there is something here which deserves to be inquired into and examined. Of things such as these, if told falsely, it must needs have been— nay, it must still be, easy to prove the falsehood. It is impossible that, in the days of Tiberius, any such events should have occurred in Palestine, without being more or less submitted to the inspection of Roman eyes. This is no wild tale, handed down from the dark ages of a barbarous race. Here I have a Roman Centurion described as among the witnesses of this man's miraculous power, and acknowledging the divinity of his benevolence. Here, at least, must have been one spectator without prejudices, otherwise than against this Prophet of Nazareth. Of a surety, the legends of Rome herself contain many tales which demand a much greater measure of indulgence; since the wonders they narrate appear to have been oftentimes attended with no beneficial consequences, either to individuals or to the state; whereas here the occasion seems always to have been such as might justify the interference of supernatural might. The power of this person seems to have been exerted only for good; and his precepts are full of such godlike loftiness as neither Socrates, nor Plato, nor any of those Greek sages, who bowed in reverence to the hoary wisdom of Egypt and India, would have disdained to admire.

The doubts, suspicions, and distrusts, with which such thoughts were mingled,—the under-current of reluctance with which I felt myself all along contending,—were such as you may more easily imagine than I can describe.

As the narrative went on, however, you will have no difficulty in supposing that my attention became more and more rivetted, and that, occupied with the strange events and sublime scenes it unfolds—and agitated by turns with the pity, the wonder, the terror, and the admiration that matchless story must ever awaken,—I had forgotten every thing beyond the page of the volume on which my finger was fixed.

It was only the rustling of Dromo's cloak against the edge of my chair, that made me aware my privacy was disturbed. His hands seemed to be busied in tightening his girdle even before he was able to speak, and the first words he uttered, were—"Come, sir—this is no time for study. I have acquaintance with some of the soldiers at the Capene Gate, and they will let us pass through; but they are relieved at the next watch, and then we shall have no chance."—"And why," said I, hastily thrusting the scroll into my bosom— "why, Dromo, or for what purpose should we desire to pass through the Capene Gate at the dead hour of night?"—"Come," said he; "there is no time for explanation. It is simply because it is the dead hour of night that we must pass through the gate; for it would do nobody any good to pass through at any other time. Come—or abandon Sextus to his fate."

Thus adjured, I could not oppose any obstacle to his zeal. The chained porter was lying asleep across the threshold; but Dromo had already found means to have the door opened, so he leaped lightly over the man, and I imitated his agility. The Cretan then locked the gate on the outside, by means of a key which he carried in his bosom; and I followed his rapid steps without farther question.

This cunning varlet, (who seemed, indeed, to move as if he had a natural aversion to every open place,) threaded one obscure lane after another, keeping always, where the moonlight had any access, to the dark side of the way; a person better skilled than myself might well have been somewhat puzzled; as for me, I had not the least conception whither I was going. Close, however, did I adhere to him; and we reached the Capene Port, which is on the south side of the city, not many bow-shots from the Anio, before I could have imagined it possible to traverse so great a space.

Here Dromo told me to wait for him a single moment, and stepped down into a cellar, in which a light was burning; but he staid not long, and when he returned to me, I observed that his style of walking was more clumsy than usual, which, indeed, was not to be wondered at, considering that he had now to carry, not only himself, but two huge skins of wine, intended, as I at once suspected, for the purpose of facilitating our passage. I told him my suspicion in a whisper; but he made no answer, except by handing to me one of his burdens. So laden, we crept on as well as we could to the portal, beneath the shadow of which two Prætorians were pacing, their armour ringing audibly upon them amidst the silence of the night.—Silently did the well-oiled hinges turn, and very silently stooping did we step beneath the lintel of the Capene Gate, which as silently was again made fast.

As we advanced among the funereal monuments which line the Appian Way on either side, Dromo stood still every now and then for a moment, as if to listen; but whatever he might have heard, or expected to hear, I perceived nothing, except here and there the howl of a dog, or the lazy hooting of the night-owl, from the top of some of the old cypresses that rose between us and the moon.

At last he seemed to catch the sound he had been expecting, for he started suddenly; and laying his finger on his lip, crept to the parapet.

The ground behind was more desolate of aspect than any part of that which we had traversed—stoney and hard, with here and there tufts of withered fern; and immediately below the wall two human figures were visible. The one was sitting on the ground, wrapped in a dark cloak which entirely concealed the countenance: the other was a half-naked boy, holding in a string a little new-shorn lamb, which with one of his hands he continually caressed. But forthwith the sitter arose, and throwing away the cloak, displayed the gray tangled tresses of an old woman, and two strong boney arms, one of which was stretched forth with an impatient gesture towards the stripling, while the other was pointed upwards to the visible moon. "Strike," said she, "strike deeply—beware lest the blood tinge your feet or your hands;"—and I recognized at once the voice of the same Pona that had attracted my notice in the morning, at the foot of the Palatine.

The boy drew forth instantly a knife from his bosom, whose glittering blade was buried in the throat of the yearling, and it was then first that I perceived a small ditch dug between the boy and the woman, into which, the lamb's throat being held over it, the blood was made to drop from the wound. So surely had the blow been given, that not one bleat escaped from the animal, and so deeply, that the blood flowed in a strong stream, dashing audibly upon the bottom of the trench. And while it was dropping, the old woman muttering a sort of chant to Hecate, as I gathered, showered from her girdle I know not what of bones or sticks, mingled with leaves and roots, which afterwards she seemed to be stirring about in the blood with one of the tall strong stems of the fern that grew there. The wildness of her gestures was such, that I could not doubt she had herself some faith in the efficacy of the foul charms to which she had resorted; nor could I see her stirring that trench of innocent blood, without remembering the still more ruthless charms, whose practice the poets of Italy have ascribed to such hoary enchantresses. The dreariness of the midnight wind, too, as it whistled along the bare and steril soil around us, and the perpetual variations in the light, by reason of the careering of those innumerable clouds, and the remembrance of the funereal purposes for which, as it seemed, all this region was set apart—the whole of this together produced, I know not how, a certain pressure upon my spirits, and I confess to you, I felt, kneeling there by the side of my now trembling Cretan, as if I owed him no great thanks for having brought me that night beyond the Capene Gate.

It seemed as if the goddess, to whom the witch's song had been addressed, did not listen to it with favourable ear; for the clouds gathered themselves more thickly than ever, while the wind howled only more loudly among the tombs, and the half-scared owl sent up a feebler hooting. Notwithstanding, the old woman continued fixed in the same attitude of expectation, and the stripling still held the well-nigh drained throat of his lamb above the trench. By degrees, however, the patience of both seemed to be exhausted; and there arose between them an angry altercation. "Infernal brat of Hades!" quoth the witch, "look ye, if you have not stained your filthy hands, and if the thirsty shadows be not incensed, because you have deprived them of some of the sweet blood which they love!"—"Curse not me, mother," replied the boy—"Did you think, in truth, that the blood of a stolen lamb would ever propitiate Hecate?"—"Imp!" quoth she, "Hold thy peace, or I will try whether no other blood may make the charm work better!"—"Beware!" quoth the boy, leaping backwards—"beware what you do! I am no longer so weak that I must bear all your blows."

"Stop," cried I, "for there are eyes that you think not of, to take note of your wickedness;" and in my vehemence I shook one of the great loose stones that were on the top of the wall, which rolled down and bounded into the ditch beside them; and the woman, huddling her cloak over her head, began to run swiftly away from us, along the wall over which we were leaning. The boy only stood still for a moment, and looked upwards towards the place where we were, and then he also fled, but in the opposite direction; and Dromo said to me in a very piteous whisper, but not till both were out of sight,—"Heaven and earth! was ever such madness as to scare the witch from her incantation? Alas! for you and for me, sir—and, most of all, alas for Sextus—for I fear me after this we shall have no luck in counteracting the designs of Rubellia."

"Rubellia! what? can you possibly imagine Rubellia to have any thing to do with this madness?"

"Imagine?" quoth he; "do you need to be told, that if things had gone well with that woman and her ditch, we should never have been able to preserve Sextus from her clutches?"

"By the rod of Hermes, good Dromo!" said I, "this will never do. I shall believe much on your credit, but not things quite so extravagant as this."

He made no reply save a long, incredulous, and, I think, contemptuous whistle, which seemed to reach the ears of every owl between us and the Appian; with such a hooting and screeching did they echo its note from every cypress. And when Dromo heard that doleful concert, his dread redoubled within him, for he shook from head to foot, while I held his arm in mine; until, at last, he seemed to make one violent effort, and springing on his feet, said—"Come, Master Valerius, let us behave after all like men!"—I smiled when he said so—"The hour has not yet come, if my Calabrian friend is to be trusted, at which the lady was to visit Pona in her dwelling. It is but daring a little more. If she has seen and known us already, then nothing can endanger us farther; and if she hath not, we may escape again."—"Well spoken," said I, "most shrewd Dromo, and like yourself; but what is it that you would have us to do?"—"The first thing," he replied, "is what has already been too long delayed."

The Cretan produced from under his cloak a long fictitious beard, which he immediately proceeded to fix upon his own face with a string. A thin tall cap of black cloth was next brought forth, which he fastened in like manner around his brows; and a little piece of chalk, with which he once or twice rubbed over his black bushy eye-brows, completed a disguise beneath which I should certainly have sought in vain to discover any trace of the natural countenance of Dromo. In short, after a few changes in the folding of his cloak, there stood before me a figure so venerably mysterious, that had I met it unawares at midnight, in the neighbourhood of so many tombs, I am not sure, although of no superstitious temper, that I could have regarded it without awe.

"Come now, good Master," quoth he, "you are taller than I, pluck me a branch from the nearest tree, and I think you shall confess I make a decent Soothsayer." In this it was easy to gratify him; for there was an old willow just a few yards off, and its boughs were so dry with age, that I soon abstracted a very proper wand for him. After receiving which, he stood for a moment leaning on it in a dignified fashion, as if to rehearse an attitude worthy of his new vocation; and then said—"Well, sir, I think if the Lady Rubellia comes now, we shall be tolerably prepared for her. But I have no disguise for you; therefore, the moment you hear a footstep, be sure you wrap your face in your gown, and stand behind me, for so shall you best consult both your own concealment, and the dignity of this Assyrian. There is no other way by which she can come from the Suburra, therefore we might stay very well where we are; but I think it might be still better to await her coming where there are either tombs or larger trees to cast a shade over our equipage, in case the moon should take it into her head to be more kind to us than she was to Pona."—"By all means," said I, "most venerable man— and besides, the wind is rather chilly, therefore I shall be well pleased to have shelter as well as shade."

"You shall have both," quoth he; "there is a thick grove of pines only a little way on. I believe there is a very grand tomb in the midst of them, in case you should prefer to sit under it.—By the bye," he continued, after some little pause, "it is odd enough that it should be so; but I believe it is the very place where all that race of the Sempronii, to which a certain young damsel belongs, have been burnt and buried ever since Rome was a city. You cannot see their tomb yet; but that is only from the thickness of the trees, some of which are, I suppose, even older than itself. Now I remember me, it was just there that they set up two winters ago the funeral pile of old Caius—I mean the father of the Lady Athanasia, whom you saw at Capito's villa. They are a very noble race, and although none of the richest now-a-days, there is not a prouder in Rome. I saw the procession at that old man's funeral myself, and I think the images of his ancestors that they carried before him, would have reached half way from hence to the Great Road. Grim, dusty figures, I trow they were; but I doubt not there had been many a haughty captain among them when they were alive."

These words were spoken as we were moving onwards towards this same grove of pines, and before he had made an end of speaking, we could clearly hear the wind sighing among their branches, and along the dry underground. And on coming to them I found that he had said truly there was a tomb in the midst of them, for a very noble, high, circular tower was indeed there, which, from the grayness of its walls, and luxuriance of ivy, had the appearance of being at least as ancient as any of the surrounding trees. The only method of access to the inside, seemed to be by means of a winding stair, which rose on the exterior from the ground to the summit—a method not unusual in Roman sepulchres—and it was on one of the steps of this stair that I seated myself, where, between the shaded wall on the one side, and the pine branches on the other, I was effectually concealed. As for Dromo, I know not whether it was that he coveted not exactly such close proximity to the stones of such an edifice; but instead of ascending with me, he took up a position beside one of the largest pines over against me.

Although the moon had got rid of her clouds, and the sky, where any of it could be seen, was abundantly brilliant, the natural darkness of that funereal grove was such, that very little difference could be produced in the midst of it by any variation on the face of any nightly luminary. The tower itself received some of the moonbeams on its carved surface; but its contemporary trees participated not in any such illumination,—one solemn shade covering all things beneath the influence of their growth. "I can scarcely see you, Dromo," said I; "but I think that speck must be your beard, and if so, I beg you would tell me what it is you really have in view by all this preparation? Do you expect me to stay here on a tomb-stone all night, merely because you wish to have an opportunity of terrifying poor Rubellia by some ghost-like howl or other when she passes you?—which, by the way, it seems by no means certain she will do at all. Or what is your purpose?"—"Hush!" was his answer; "ask no questions, but hem thrice if you hear a footstep—for young ears are the keenest." Accordingly silence was kept so strictly, that, in spite of the chillness of the stone on which I sate, I presently fell into a sort of dozing slumber.

By degrees, however,—nor, considering the hour and the fatigue I had undergone, is it wonderful that it should have been so,—my sleep must have become sufficiently profound, for I did not at first, on waking from it, very well remember either where I was, or for what purpose I had come thither. And, indeed, I have little doubt my slumbers might have continued till day-break, but for the interruption I am now to mention.

And yet it seemed as if even in my sleep I had been prepared for this by some strange anticipation, for although it was a near sound of singing voices that dispelled my slumbers, and made me start from the stone on which I had placed myself, I could not help feeling as if that sound were not altogether new to me;—whether it were that the half-sensible ear had been already ministering indistinctly to the dreaming spirit, or that some purely fantastic prelude had been vouchsafed to the real music. I started up suddenly, that much is certain, and listened with astonishment, yet not altogether with such surprise as might have been expected to attend a transition so hasty from sleep to waking, and from silence to the near neighbourhood of sounds at once so strange and so sweet. With breathless curiosity, nevertheless, with awe, and not entirely I think without terror, did I listen to the notes which seemed to ascend out of the habitation of the noble dead into the nightly air—wild, yet solemn, as if breathed from the bosom of a stately repose and a pensive felicity; insomuch, that almost I persuaded myself I was hearing the forbidden sounds of another world, and the thought came over me,—yet almost I think at that moment without farther disturbing me,—what fearful interpretations the old poets have affixed to such untimely communion, and how the superstition of all antiquity has shrunk from its omen.

My first impulse, after a moment had elapsed, was to call on Dromo, and I did so, at first in a low whisper, and then two or three times more loudly— but all equally in vain, for no answer was returned; and though I strained my eyes in gazing on the place where I had last seen him, yet there I could perceive no trace whatever of any human figure. The moonlight indeed shewed with more distinctness than before the tall stem of the old pine-tree against which he had been leaning; but no motion, nor the least appearance of whiteness, could either my eyes or my imagination discover there. I might easily, you will say, have stept across the road, and entirely satisfied myself; but I know not well what it was that nailed me to the place where I stood, and prevented me even from once thinking of doing so. The calm sepulchral music, my friends, still continued to stream from the recess of the mausoleum, and painless awe held me there, as if by a charm incontrollable. I gazed upwards, and beheld the moon riding above the black pine tops, in a now serene and cloudless heaven. The wind also had passed away, as it appeared, with the clouds it had agitated. The bird of night was asleep on her unseen bough; and all was silent as death, except only the dwelling of the departed; and a certain indescribable delight was beginning, as I gazed and listened, to be mixed with the perturbation wherewith at first I had been inspired.

And I know not how long I might have stood so, but while I was yet listening to this mysterious music, there was mingled with its expiring cadence the sound of a heavy footstep on the staircase above me, and looking up, I perceived in the moonlight the figure of a man, clad in a white gown, but having a naked sword stretched forth in his hand, immediately over the place whereon I was standing. I obeyed the first natural impulse, and leaped downwards swiftly on seeing him; but this availed me nothing, for he also leaped, and almost before my feet had touched the ground, I felt the grasp of his hand upon my shoulder, and that so strongly, that I perceived plainly there was as little possibility of escape as of resistance. I made therefore no farther effort, but suffered him to do with me as he pleased; and he, on his part, said not a single word, but still retaining his hold, pointed with his sword to the same steps from which I had descended, and compelled me to mount them before him, up to the very summit of the round tower.

"Why is this, sir?" said I; "and whither do you conduct me?"

"Peace," was all his answer; and, in like manner as he had made me climb the exterior, so also he compelled me to begin the descent of a similar flight of steps, which led down from an aperture above, into the interior of the edifice. And although I must confess to you that I obeyed not this silent guidance without considerable fear, yet I strove as well as I could to control myself. I moved with a step in which I think not there could be perceived any trembling.

Yet you will admit that even had I been master at that moment of less firmness, I might have been excusable; for looking down, I perceived that a lamp was burning in the midst of the sepulchral tower far below me, and saw sitting around it a company of eight or ten persons, at whose mercy, it was quite visible, I must be placed. Neither, if I might judge from the demeanour of the person that was bringing me into their assembly, did there appear to be any great room for dependance on them; for, as to themselves, not one of them looked up towards me as I was stepping down, and being wrapped in their cloaks, I had no means of discovering what manner of persons they were. The way in which I had been treated, however, by one of their number, was a sufficient evidence, either that they conceived themselves to have been injured by my being there, or that they were capable of taking some undue advantage of my helpless condition. The calmness of their attitudes, and the recollection of the sounds that I had heard, inclined me to the former of these suppositions; and when I perceived that not one of them stirred, even till I had reached the lowmost step of the interior staircase, in this, without question, I already felt myself considerably strengthened.

"Behold," said my guide, as I at length touched the marble floor of the mausoleum itself—"Behold proof, and that living, that my suspicions were not quite so groundless as you were pleased to imagine. Here is a man whom I found listening, even on the very steps of this tower. It is for you to decide what shall be done with the eaves-dropper."

With this the whole company sprung at once to their feet, and I perceived evidently, from the surprise expressed in their looks and attitudes, that until that moment not one of them had been aware of my approach. I was about to speak, and declare my innocence of any treachery, or even of any knowledge concerning the purpose of their meeting; but before I could do so, one of them, and I think the oldest of all that were present, having in an instant recovered the tranquillity which my arrival had disturbed, said to me in a voice of the utmost gentleness, "Young man, what has brought thee hither, or who sent thee? Art thou indeed a spy, and was it thy purpose to betray our assembly?"

"Sir," said I, "I know nothing of your assembly, or of its purpose; I fell asleep by accident on the outside of this tower, and, when I awoke, the music that I heard detained me."

"Examine the stripling," quoth he that had conducted me—"examine his person."—"His looks belie him," replied the senior, "if you have cause for suspicion. But if you will it so, search the young man." And with that my guide, laying his unsheathed sword upon a table, or altar of black marble, proceeded to search my garments, and finding in my bosom the scroll which I had received from Tisias, he glanced on it for a moment, and then handing it to the senior, said, "Now, sirs, doubt ye if ye will."—"Before heaven—it is the book of the holy Luke!" said the other; "this is indeed suspicious. How came this scroll into thy hands, young man? Art thou aware that one of the books of the Christians has been found in thy bosom?"—"I know it," said I; "it is one of the books of their faith, and I have read in it this evening for the first time."—"Then thou art not thyself a Christian?"—"I received the book from one Christian," said I, waiving the question; "and I made promise to deliver it into the hands of another?"—"Name the Christian who gave thee this book!" said my stern guide.—"Tisias of Antioch," I replied; "the same who died yesterday in the Amphitheatre."—"Yes," quoth he, again; "and I suppose it was there he gave it to you. Every one knows the name of Tisias. Name, if you please, the person to whom you are to deliver the book."—"You shall pardon me," said I, "that I will not. You may call me an eaves-dropper, if you will; but you shall find I am no traitor. It is a Roman— a noble Roman lady to whom I must give this book; and I would not tell you her name although you should slaughter me here in this tomb, which I have entered living and without guilt." And having said this, I folded my arms, and stood still, abiding their will.

But scarcely had I finished these words, ere I felt a small trembling hand laid upon my shoulder, and looking round, I perceived Athanasia herself, who whispered into my ear,—"Valerius, was the book for me? If so, you may say it boldly, and I will vouch for your word."—"For you, lady," I answered in the same tone, "and for none other. You well know that I was present in his prison the night before his death; so far at least you can confirm what I have said."

"Sir," said she, addressing the old man that had before questioned me, "I know this young man: and I believe what he has said, and will be answerable for his fidelity. It was he that went in to our friend the other night in his prison, and the book was intrusted to him by the old man, that it might be given into my hands. His name is Valerius—Caius Valerius—and he is by birth a noble Roman."

"Say you so, lady?" interrupted my original conductor; "then I ask his pardon. I have wronged Caius Valerius; but both you and he must forgive me, for it must be confessed he was found in a very extraordinary situation."

"Even so," I replied, "I have nothing to complain of. I perceive that I am present in an assembly of Christians; but he shall do me much wrong that thinks I bear any enmity to them,—or, from all that I have yet seen or read, to the faith which they profess. I have read part of that book," I continued, "for I made promise to Tisias that I should do so before giving it to Athanasia; and I trust I shall still be permitted by her to read more of it before it is finally demanded from me."—"Oh, read it!" said Athanasia, gently again whispering to me. "Oh yes, read the book, Valerius, and may God enlighten the reader." And so saying, she herself took up the scroll from the table on which it was lying, and gave it again into my hands.—"There was also a letter for you," said I, receiving it, "but that I left at home."—"No matter," said Athanasia, "you shall give me the letter and the book both together hereafter."

"In the meantime," said I, "I suppose it were better I should retire."

"Young sir," said the senior, "that is as you please; in a little while we shall all be moving towards the city. Stay with us till then, if such be your will; that which you may hear, can at least do you no harm. Already, I doubt not, you have seen enough to despise the ignorant calumnies of our enemies."

When he had said so, the old man walked to the side of the sepulchre, and took out from behind one of the urns that stood there, (ranged in their niches,) a small casquet, which, returning, he placed before him on the marble table. Then, opening the casquet, he brought forth a silver goblet, and a salver containing some little pieces of bread; and, untying from his neck a massive cross of gold, he set that also on the table, between the cup and the salver. In brief, the Christian priest, (for such, as you already see, he was,) had finished his preparation, and was about to commence the administration of the blessed Eucharist. And when all the rest were kneeling before the table, Athanasia, laying her hand upon my arm, beckoned to me to kneel by her side; and so indeed I would have done in my ignorance, had not the priest himself pointed to a station a few yards behind the lady, to which, accordingly, I drew back—apart from those who were to be privileged with the participation of those holy symbols.

Scarcely had they composed themselves in their places, and listened to the first words of the appointed service, when I, standing there by myself, thought, unless my ears deceived me, there must be some one on the outer stair-case of the tower; and my eyes instinctively, I suppose, were fixed upon the aperture, which, as I have told you, was in the high roof above the circle of the niched walls. Here, however, when I first looked, there was nothing to be seen, but the round spot of the sky, far up in the midst of the marble roof; but while I was looking steadfastly, that space was suddenly diminished; and a dog bayed, and at the same moment a voice which I well knew, screamed, "I have them—I hold them—let them burst the net if they can."

The cry of Pona disturbed effectually the Christian priest, and the whole of those that were with him. Rising up hastily from their knees, they stood all together around the table, while the old man, having kissed both the cup and the cross, restored them as quickly as he could to the casket from which they had been taken. But while the priest was doing this, he that found me on the stair appearing to revert into his suspicion, and looking sternly upon me where I stood, said, "Is this then the innocence which we spared! Is this the noble Roman for whom Athanasia pledged herself? Speak, brethren, what shall be done to this traitor, by whom, even more than by those dogs of the tombs, it is a shame for us that we have been hunted?" Saying so, the man lifted up his sword again, and it seemed as if he would have smitten me to the ground without farther question. But Athanasia threw herself swiftly between him and me. "For shame, Cotilius," said she; "such suspiciousness is unworthy of a Roman knight."—"You say well, noble damsel," quoth the old priest, interrupting her; "but you might say also that such cruelty is unworthy of a soldier of Christ. Peace, peace, children; there is no evil in the youth, nor, if there were, would it be our part to avenge it."

While he was saying this, three or four blazing torches were thrust down into the place from above, and Athanasia, laying her hand upon my arm, said, "Look up, Caius, I see helmets.—Alas! am I not already here? why, if they will slay me, should they drag me away now from the tomb of my fathers?" I felt the trembling of her hands, and she leaned upon my shoulder. I know not, I will confess to you, whether at that moment I tasted more of pleasure or of pain.

But by this time several of the soldiers had already begun to descend into the tower, and before another minute had elapsed, we found ourselves surrounded by the flame of their torches. And he that seemed to lead the party, after counting us one by one, said, turning to his companions, "Well, an old woman has told the truth for once—here are even more I think than she warned us of.—Come along, worthy people, you must not keep the Tribune waiting for you all night, and our watch is well-nigh expired already. Come, mount the stair—it will take a good half hour yet, I believe, to lodge you all safely in the Tullian—And do you," he added, laying his hand on the hilt of Cotilius' sword—"do you, brave sir, allow me to save you the trouble of carrying this bauble." Nor was the stern knight so foolish as to dispute the command; but having yielded up his sword, he forthwith began to ascend, one or two spearmen preceding him with their torches. The priest followed, and so did the rest; the last being Athanasia and myself.

On every side around the old tower, when I looked from the summit of it, I perceived foot soldiers drawn up in a double line, while the road along which I had come with Dromo, was occupied by a band of horsemen, one of whom moved forward when he saw us descending, as if to take cognizance of the number and quality of the surprised assembly. His long cloak being muffled about his ears as he sate, and the shadow of his helmet falling deeply, I did not at first suspect who it was; but he had not counted half the party to the superior Officer behind him, ere I recognized him from the sound of his voice; and who, think ye, should it be but my good friend Sabinus?

The Centurion, when his eye detected me, checked his horse so sharply that the animal bounded into the air; and, "Valerius!" quoth he, "ha! by the life of Cæsar, what is the meaning of this? Valerius in a Christian synagogue! By all the gods, there must be some mistake." But before I, in my confusion, could make any answer to these exclamations, his eye chanced to glance on Athanasia, who, trembling, still retained the support of my arm; whereupon, "Ha! ha!" said he, in a quite different tone of voice, "there is a lady in the case." And then, stooping in his seat, he whispered, half laughing, into my ear, "My most hypocritical smooth-face, you shall see what is the consequence of bringing these transatlantic pranks of yours to Rome. By Hercules, you wild dog, it may cost you some little trouble to get out of this scrape."

Having said so, he turned his horse, and rejoining the troop, appeared to enter into close conversation with him who sate at the head of the line. Of what my friend said, I could catch nothing more than certain vehement oaths, while, all the time, the Tribune (for such he was) continued to shake his head, in a way significant at once of doubt and determination. The end was, that he pointed with his sword; and Sabinus forced his horse backwards, at one plunge, into the place from which he had advanced.

Our party were immediately separated one from another. I saw the priest lifted on a mule and hurried away towards the city, with a horseman on each hand of him. The fiery Cotilius, and one or two more, were compelled to follow, with similar attendance, in the same direction; others, again, had their horses' heads turned more to the westward—but all departed at speed, and were soon lost to my view among the projections of the tombs. The last that remained to be disposed of were Athanasia and myself, and for a moment I had some hope that we might perhaps be intrusted to the same guards; but this hope was in vain, and after I perceived that it was so, scarcely even was time permitted to me for bidding her farewell. To kiss her hand, and to whisper a single word of parting hope into her ear, was all I could do. A tear rolled from her cheek and fell upon my hand; yet she smiled faintly upon me, and "Hope," said she—"yes, dear Valerius, Hope and Faith both go with me." And with that the pale maiden was separated from the arm to which she had trusted, and I saw her also mounted and borne away rapidly. A moment after, I found myself, in like manner, seized and lifted upon a horse, and almost before I could look around me, we had escaped from the flare of the torches, and the crowd of the soldiery, and were stretching at a rapid pace, I knew not whither, although I suspected, from the width of the road, that we had regained the Appian.

But I have forgotten to mention to you, that just at the moment when they were lifting Athanasia upon the mule that was to bear her from my sight, my eye caught a glimpse of the witch Pona, who was sitting at the root of one of the pine-trees, close to the tower. And behind her stood, leaning against the tree, a figure wrapped in a rich red cloak, which I suspected to be a female also, but could not be certain, because the countenance was concealed in the folds of the garment. To this person, whoever it might be, the witch turned round eagerly, while the soldiers were carrying off Athanasia. I saw no more, for, as I have told you, immediately afterwards I also was carried away.

CHAPTER VI.

Our hasty pace had not borne us to any great distance from the place where all these things occurred, ere the sky, which, as ye have heard, had all that night been sufficiently variable, began to exhibit appearances which my two companions interpreted as significant of the approach of one of those nocturnal storms, to which, at that season of the year, the fair heaven of Italy is peculiarly subject. That they apprehended somewhat of this sort, I perceived from their looks, as they stopped for a moment to draw the hoods of their mantles over their brazen helmets; for words they uttered none, either to me or to each other, until our journey drew near its close. For me, however, the numberless agitations through which I had passed in the course of the few preceding hours, had, I suppose, communicated an unnatural measure of ardour to my boyish blood; for neither did I feel the night-breeze chill me as we rushed through it, nor partook, in any sort, of the desire my companions testified to cover themselves from the rain, which seemed to be about to discharge itself out of all those black and lowering clouds now gathered above our heads from every region of the heavens. When, on the contrary, the first heavy drops fell, I bared my forehead with the eagerness of one who, in a parched region, comes suddenly upon the margin of a well-spring. Nor did this sensation subside even after the storm had thickened to the utmost, and the dusty roads had drunk abundantly of the plashing rain. The strong wind blew with redoubled coolness upon my moistened neck— the rain-drops dashed on my hot hands; and I perceived, that, as is the nature of those animals, the thunder which was mustering in the air, filled my horse one moment with dread, and the next with a blind fierceness. At last the thunder shouted over-head, and its echoes spread wide and far on either side, until they seemed to be absorbed to the left in the remote depths of the Appenine, and on the right hand in the measureless bosom of the Western Sea—of which, as we galloped along the hill side, the broad lightning (unless my fancy deceived me) revealed ever and anon a distant and melancholy glimpse.

We had passed a hill covered with towns, villages, and stately mansions, (which I afterwards learned was no other than the famous Alban,) ere the storm subsided beneath the influence of the reddening dawn. Yet even then we slackened not our pace, although the horses were by this time not a little exhausted with the swiftness of their motion, and the weight of their wet riders. On rode we in the growing light of the morning; but I perceived ere long that we had left the wide and magnificent Appian Way, and were pursuing the line of a narrower road, which seemed to carry us more and more westward.

We halted for a moment on the brow of a declivity, where three paths separated; and I perceived that among my guides there was some little uncertainty as to which of these it behoved them to follow. While they were muttering together, I looked and beheld at length the wide sea heaving far below, over what appeared to me to be a forest as mighty as I had ever seen in my native island.

Old hoary oaks leaned on either hand quite over the narrow path-way, into which (after their brief pause of consultation) my conductors directed our course. Here and there, such a shield had those huge leafy boughs extended over the road, that the dust rose from amongst the feet of our horses as if all that night not one drop of rain had fallen there; although elsewhere, in the absence of such mighty trees, the water lying across the path in pools testified abundantly that the tempest had not spared the forest any more than the champaign. Vast waving gulfs of bay and ilex, with here and there some solitary pine raising itself proudly in the midst, seemed to stretch away on either hand between the groves of those gigantic oaks.

The path we followed carried us ever deeper and deeper into the bosom of the woods; and, at length, so buried were we in the windings of their stifling shade, that I had lost all notion of the direction in which I was moving; until, after two or three hot hours, weary man and jaded horse were, I believe, equally delighted with snuffing once more the open current of the air. We reached not the edge of the forest, however, before I could hear distinctly the dashing of the Mediterranean waves; and the last ascent we climbed laid open to my view a long sweep of the rolling waters, and their rocky coast garnished every where with the richness of superincumbent woods. Far, very far, in the distant north, I thought I could recognize some of the stately towers of Ostium, bosomed apparently within the billows over which they presided. All between was one wide waste of wood and rock, save here and there a watch-tower perched on the margin, and whitened half-way up with the foam of the yet uncalmed sea.

Then, nor ever could I look upon the waters of the great deep, without something of that filial yearning which seems so natural to every native of our sea-girt island. But neither could I contrast the condition in which I now approached it, with the gay and hopeful mood in which I had so lately left it behind me, without many thoughts more sad and serious than as yet had frequently visited my bosom. What a strange brood of visions had passed before my eyes, since, but a few days before, I stept for the first time, light of heart, beneath the shadow of those far-off bulwarks! What new emotions had arisen, in the interval! How had every sense been gratified! how had every dream of imagination been exceeded! Yet what a void had been revealed within!—Alas! said I to myself, why is it that I have been subjected to all these novelties? Had I not done better to have remained, after all, where life flowed ever calmly—where affection hung over me like a protecting buckler, and my soul could sleep in the security of unbroken faith! But this was only for a moment. The thoughts of Athanasia haunted me more deeply and more firmly. I thought over every word she had spoken—every look of hers rose up in succession, with all the vividness of a beautiful and a troubled dream. I seemed to feel, as if she were yet present beside me, the trembling of her pale fingers upon my shoulder—I kissed the hand on which her parting tear had fallen, as if it were yet wet with the dear moisture. When I thought of the perils in which she must now be enveloped—of the pains she must have suffered—must at that moment be suffering,—it was as if I could have burst bands of iron, like flax, from off my hands. When a glimpse of the darker future opened before me, I shuddered, and, urging my poor horse onwards in the recklessness of total abstraction, I perceived that even my guides pitied the agony of my despair.

CHAPTER VII.

We stopped before one of the watch-towers which, as I have told you, I had seen scattered along the edge of the sea. But this, when we came up to it, appeared larger than I had expected to find any of them. The narrow way, alongst which we had been riding, brought us close to its gate, on the side towards the land; but the rock shelving rapidly on the other side, gave it the semblance, at a little distance, of being suspended over the waves.

It was a building of rude, and apparently very antique structure, the under part square, but the upper circular; as is, for the most part, the old Roman fashion in such erections. And this, indeed, I doubt not, might have stood there long enough to have shewn a beacon, when some fleet of Syracuse or Carthage darkened the blue sea over against the Lestrigonian bay renowned in old song, or the snow-white promontory of Gaieta.

One of the soldiers dismounted, and began to knock rather violently at the door; but some little time elapsed ere any sound from within responded to the clamour he raised. At last a hard and withered face made its appearance at a little opening above the door, and then the helmets passed, I suppose, for a sufficient warrant, for in a twinkling we heard the bolts creaking; the old postern was soon set ajar, and forth stepped the venerable keeper. Imagine a tall, skinny man of threescore years, with a face as dry and yellow as ye have seen on the outside of a pye, and hair as white as ever the skill of a confectioner could represent, and legs bearing the same proportion to the feet, which the shaft of Saturn's scythe usually does to its blade. Clothe the nether part of this figure in Dacian, or Gaulish breeches, throw a somewhat threadbare cloak over his shoulders, and to finish the outfit, deck his head with a casque of the Macedonian cut, that is to say, sitting close above the ears, and topped with a bristling plume of horse hair. The Warder stood with dignity, and listened with gravity, while one of my Prætorians whispered his message. On its conclusion, he shrugged his shoulders, and regarding me with a glance made up, I think, in pretty equal proportions, of surprise and contempt, signified by the motion of his hand that we might all three enter. He whistled at the same moment, and there came forth a comely damsel, who, with many blushes and smiles, took possession of the reins of our horses.—"Stand there," quoth he, "stand there, little Cestia, and see if there be never a handful of corn to be got for the prince's cattle,—stand there, and we shall be with you again anon." And then he also whispered something into the maiden's ear, and I saw her looking at me from under her eyelids with an expression of very uncommon curiosity. Two or three curly-pated urchins, of different sizes, joined her at the same moment, and to them, in her turn, the maiden whispered; whereupon the eldest of the children retreating behind her, eyed me earnestly along the skirt of her tunic, while the younger ones continued to gaze where they were, with looks of open stupidity and wonder. Of all this I could make nothing at the moment, but when we had got fairly into the inside of the tower, I heard the children whispering to each other, "A Christian! A Christian! A Jew! A Jew!"

The lower part of the tower, into which I had now been conducted, seemed to form nothing more than one huge, bare, and quadrangular apartment, serving, I supposed (and rightly) at once as hall and vestibule to the upper chambers contained within the walls. A small flight of steps, in one of the corners, seemed to afford the only means of access to what was above; but from the position of a door immediately below these, it was we inferred that there were vaults under ground. Close beside this door there stood, upon a very rude pedestal, a still more rude bust, either of Jupiter, of Apollo, or of Hercules. The workmanship was such, that I could not be very certain which of the family it was intended to represent, nor whether the principal appendage was a club, a lyre, a bow, or a thunder-bolt; but it did not escape my observation, that the old keeper crept as close as he could to the sacred stone, as soon as I stepped over the threshold.

One of the little boys that had come out to the door on our arrival, busied himself in setting forth a wooden board, whereon he placed in great order a huge piece of yellow cheese, and a heap of crisp white cakes of rye. A large jug of water also garnished the mess; but there seemed to be a little less of diligence, or more of difficulty, about the wine. After some pause, however, the mistress of the garrison appeared. A string of amber beads floated to and fro on the ocean of her bosom. She had fine golden bracelets on her arms too, but they were only half seen, being almost buried in fat; and she wore a flaxen wig, which did not entirely conceal the dark bristles below. At the girdle of the amazon hung, on the right side, the much desiderated bunch of keys, being balanced on the left by a dagger and toothpick case, almost of equal dimensions.

"Will *you* drink to Cæsar, young man?" cried the matron, ere the sitting had been much prolonged; "will you drink honestly to the Emperor, in case you also have a full cup given you? and, by the by, I think you must have almost as much need of it as the rest." And, with this courteous invitation, I heard her whisper to one of my guards,—"By Jove, 'tis a proper lad, after all; is this true that they have told me of him? Why, I believe, the young man has a red edge to his gown. What is his name? who is he?"—I heard him answer,— "By the life of Cæsar, you know as much about him as any of us. There was a whole cluster taken last night a little way beyond the Capene-Gate, and he was one; but what they were about, or who he is, I know not, only he is certainly somebody, for I saw our Centurion salute him."—"I saw him with Sabinus," whispered the other—"I am quite sure of it, the last day the Amphitheatre was open; they sate together, and appeared familiar."—"I pray you, sir," quoth the lady, raising her voice,—"I pray you fill your cup, and here I pledge you to our better acquaintance. You shake your head—well. But what must be, must; and while you are with us, we may at least be good friends."—"Thanks," said I, complying with her command; "Here, then, is health to all present; and fair health to the great Trajan, says no one here more heartily than I."—I drank off the wine, and setting down the goblet, I believe I said, "Excellent, by Jove," or something of that sort; for they all started when they heard what I said, and the old woman called out lustily, "Fill him another cup to the brim, whether he be Christian or not. The young man at least swears by the gods, and drinks to Cæsar."

"The old man," observed one of the soldiers,—"he that was killed the other day in the Amphitheatre—he might have saved his head, even at the last moment, if he would have done as much."—"Well, well," quoth she again; "let every one mind his own matters. Husband, bring down your book, and let the new-comer enter his name with his own hand."

Having drained his cup, the keeper rose, and ere long returned with a musty scroll of parchment, which, having blown away the dust from it, he presented to me. I glanced over the record, and found in it the names of various persons, all apparently entered in their own handwriting; and most of them, as I could perceive, bearing date in the troublous reign of Domitian. The last was that of Marcus Protius Lamontanus, who, as it seemed, had been set free from his confinement immediately on the accession of Nerva; and immediately under this I wrote my own name, with that of my birthplace. The keeper read, and said, "So preserve me the power of Jove! A Valerius! and born in Britain! Can you be the son of the same Valerius who was Centurion in the ninth legion under Agricola?"—"You have guessed rightly—I am the same."—"Then the more is the pity," he replied, in a grave voice, "that you should have entered, in such a case as this, the dwelling of one that was a true soldier beneath the eagle of your father. But forgive me if in any thing we have been disrespectful."—"There is no occasion," said I, "for any such apology. I am here as a prisoner, and have been treated with all courtesy beyond what a prisoner could expect."

"By Hercules!" interrupted the spouse, "I thought I had some knowledge of the face—Well, I hope ten years hence he will be as fine a man as his father was the day he slew the Caledonian giant, and tumbled him from his chariot in front of all the line—yes, in sight of Galgacus himself. It was the same day," said she, turning to her lord, "that you were taken prisoner, and driven away into the woods."—"As witness these marks," quoth the man; and with that he stripped open his tunic, and displayed part of his breast, stamped with various figures of blue and yellow, after the northern fashion, and bearing withal the traces of two formidable wounds.

The woman redoubled her kindness; but not wishing to interrupt festivity, I soon requested her to shew me the place where I was to be confined. And, indeed, as you may imagine, I had by this time not a little need of repose.

Both she and her husband accordingly rose to usher me to my prison. I gave money to the soldiers, and requested them to inform Sabinus of the place to which I had been conveyed; but did not choose to write any thing, either to him or to Licinius, until I should have had a little time for reflection.

CHAPTER VIII.

My fatigue brought speedy sleep; and so profound, that before I again unclosed my eyes, the calm sea was already purple below me, and the sun about to set. But neither purple sea, nor golden sky, nor all the divine tranquillity of the evening air, could sooth my mind into repose, after I had once awaked to a sense of the situation into which I had been brought—I should say rather of the situation in which Athanasia was placed. For myself, I could not in seriousness fear any calamity worthy of the name,—if such should come, it must be my business to wrestle with it as I might. But to think of her, young, beautiful, innocent; and of all to which she might be exposed amidst the rude hands in which I had left her!

Some time had passed before my attention was attracted by a conversation carried on in the chamber below me, in which you will not be surprised that I should have felt myself interested, even although the distance was such that I could not distinguish one word that was said. I knew from the first moment that it was impossible I should be mistaken—I was perfectly certain it was Sabinus himself, who was talking with the old woman; and I at once suspected that the worthy Centurion, having learned from the soldiers who carried me off, to what place they had conveyed me, had undertaken this speedy journey, for the purpose of comforting me in my confinement. The kindness with which he had treated me from the beginning of our acquaintance had been such, that I could have no occasion to wonder at his exerting himself to discover me; but I confess this alacrity was more than I had been prepared for, and I waited only for the moment when he should enter my apartment to throw myself upon his bosom, and intrust all my troubles to him, as to a friend and a brother. There was something, however, which I could not at all comprehend in the merriment which seemed to be reigning below on his arrival. Peals of female laughter interrupted the uniform hearty tone of the Centurion's voice; and the feeble treble of the old Warder himself was stretched ever and anon in attempt at a chuckle.

At last in they came, and Sabinus, embracing me affectionately, thrust into my hand a piece of parchment, which I perceived to be nothing less than an order for my immediate release. Then taking off his riding-cap, and rubbing with his handkerchief his most audacious and soldier-looking brows, "My dear boy," quoth he, "I see you are going to thank me—but wound not modesty by fine speeches. There was war before Helen—have a better care another time, and don't pay Rome such a poor compliment, as to say that you can find nobody to charm you but a Christian damsel, and no place for flirtation but a gloomy tomb lined with urns and lachrymatories. My honest friend here was quite frightened with the idea of having such an unbelieving reprobate as they said you were, under the same roof with her children. But now her fears are dispelled, for good souls are always tolerant to the little vagaries of young blood; so thank your hostess, my lad, kiss her hand, take one cup to the hearth of the old tower, and tighten your girdle."

"Well!" quoth the woman; "who should have thought when the soldiers brought him in with such mystery, that it was all for kissing by moonlight! I protest to Venus, they would have made me believe he had been caught eating an infant; but still I cannot quite pardon him. Well—well—we must e'en take good hope he will mend ere he dies."

"Die?" cried the Centurion; "do you talk of dying to one that has scarcely yet begun to live!—Come, come, Caius, I hope, after all, you may never get into a worse scrape."

"And if I do," said I, "I hope I shall always be equally fortunate in my jailers."

"By the beard of Jove!" quoth Sabinus, "it needs no great skill to see that you have been fortunate in that respect. I swear that, if the truth were known, you are almost as unwilling to leave this tower now, as you were last night to be torn away from another."

"Oh, Master Kæso," quoth she again, "when will you have done with your joking? Well, your father loved a jest in his time himself; but now he, I suppose, is quiet enough. And he, good old man, how does he wear?—Can he still sit in his porch of a fine morning, and listen to the news, as he used to do, with his cup at his knee?"

"I trust the old grasshopper can still chirp when the sun shines. But to tell you the truth, it is long since I have seen him; and if this young blade has no objection, I mean to pay him a visit this very night. I am only just come home from Britain, and have not yet had leisure to salute my Lares."

I said something about being anxious to return as soon as possible to Rome; but the Centurion answered me with another shout, "Come, come; she's safe enough. I suppose you think every one gets out of jail as easily as yourself."

I found it was out of the question to disapprove of any of the schemes of Sabinus; so, having saluted the hostess, and flung my purse to her children, (who, by the way, still regarded me with looks of apprehension,) I accompanied him with a good grace to the gate. I made inquiry before I went forth concerning the old jailer likewise; but I could easily gather from the expression of face with which his wife accompanied her indistinct reply, that he had, long before that time, reached a state in which she felt little desire to exhibit him. The Centurion whistled as he stepped across the threshold, and there forthwith drew near a soldier, wearing the Prætorian helmet, (now sufficiently familiar to my sight,) and leading in his hand three horses. In the rear, I recognized, not without satisfaction, the busy countenance of my friend Dromo, whose ass did not appear quite so eager to join the party as its rider. A few sturdy thumps, however, at last brought the Cretan close to us, who saluted me with great appearance of joy, and then whispered into my ear, "Great Jove! we must keep silence for the present. What a story I have to tell; and I suppose there is one to hear likewise—but all in good season. We must not crack nuts before monkeys. I have a letter for you," he added, "from Sextus, and another from Licinius."

The Centurion sprung on his trusty war-horse, who seemed to rejoice in the feeling of his weight; and we were soon in motion. I asked no questions either about the course or distance, but rode by his side so silently, that he bestowed on me many good-natured rebukes, for suffering a little affair of love to distress me so greatly. "Cheer up now," quoth he, "and do not make me repent of carrying you to my father's house, by shewing the old man, who has had enough of troubles, such a countenance as must make him think of Orcus, even although he did not know himself to be near its gates. It is more than a year since I have seen him."

This sort of speech he repeated so often, that I thought the best way would be to tell him frankly the true history of the adventure, from whose immediate consequences he had delivered me. I told him, therefore, every thing about both Tisias and Athanasia, and, indeed, kept nothing from him in the whole matter, except only what referred to the impression made on my own mind by what I had read of the Christian book,—for, as to this subject, it was one which I totally despaired of being able to make him in any measure comprehend,—and besides, the state of my own mind was still so uncertain in regard to it, and my information so imperfect, that I could not trust myself with speaking of it to any one, until I should have had leisure for more both of reading and of reflection.

He preserved silence for some minutes, and then said, "In truth, Caius, you have distressed me. I thought it was merely some little frolic born of an hour, to be forgotten in a day; but I cannot refuse you my sympathy. Would I had more to offer!"—"Dear Sabinus," said I, "I know not how to thank you. You saw me but a few days ago the merriest young fellow that ever trod the pavement of Rome—happy in the moments that passed, and full of glad hopes for all that were to come; but now I feel myself quite changed. Almost I wish I had never left my British fields; and yet I should never have seen Athanasia."—"Poor fellow!" quoth he, laying his hand on the mane of my horse, "I perceive there is, indeed, no trifling in your case. Compose yourself; whatever chances there may be in your favour will never be bettered by despondence." He paused a little, and proceeded—"The worst of the whole is this new bitterness against these Christians. Except during Nerva's time, there was always some punishment to be feared by them, in case of being detected; but there was a way of managing things in almost every case, and people were well enough disposed to grant immunities which were always attended with some good to the Fisk. Nero and Domitian, to be sure, acted otherwise—but these were madmen; and even they did so only by fits and starts. But now, when a prince like Trajan has taken up the matter, it is no wonder that one should consider it more seriously. One cannot help fancying he must have had some good reason before he began—that is one thing; and having once begun, he is not the man to drop it lightly—which is a more weighty consideration. Do you think there is positively no chance of her giving up this dream, when she finds what it has exposed her to?"

"No," said I; "I am sure she will not, nor can I wish it would be otherwise with her."

"Well," he resumed, "I enter into your feelings so far, my friend, even on that point. I cannot imagine you to have been so deeply smitten with a girl of a flighty unsteady character. But then this is not a case to be judged of on common principles. It is no light thing to be exposed to such examinations as are now set afoot for these people; and if she behaves herself so resolutely as you seem to expect, what is the end of it? I consider it highly probable— for there is no friendship in uncandid speaking—that, in spite of all her friends can do, they will banish her at the very least; scarcely dare I speak of it, but even worse than banishment has heretofore befallen Romans—ay, Roman ladies too,—and these as high in birth and place as Athanasia."

"My dear Sabinus," said I, "do not imagine that now for the first time all these things are suggested to me. Imagine rather, how, unable for a moment to expel them from my mind, I have spent these miserable hours. Her friends, too, what must not be their alarm!"

"The thing was so done," quoth the Centurion, "that I think it is impossible it should have made much noise as yet. If there was in the family no suspicion that the lady had any connection with these people, they must be in perfect perplexity. I lay my life they take it for granted she has had some private intrigue, and has gone off with her lover."

"Alas!" said I, "when they hear the truth, it will be still worse than this in their eyes. Yet it appears fit that no time should be lost in making them acquainted with the real state of the case. O Sabinus, I foresee that in all these things I shall have need of your counsel and your help."

"You shall have them both, my dear boy," said he,—"you shall have them both to the uttermost. But there is no question at all about the propriety of telling the relations all you know. Licinius is probably well acquainted with them. I am almost sorry for having prevented your immediate return to the city; and yet one night will soon be over."

"But Athanasia herself——"

"Ah! that indeed is a point of some difficulty. It was merely from having remembered who the men were that rode off with you, that I was enabled to learn so soon whither you yourself had been conveyed. But the party consisted of a few men out of almost every one of our cohorts,—those, in short, that were on duty, scattered up and down in different parts of the city; and I may not find it very easy to discover who had the care of any other individual."

"But Athanasia——"

"True," said he, "I had not thought of it. There was but one female besides herself. That will furnish a clue. You may rely on it, I shall easily find out the place to which they have taken her; but then where, and at what distance that may be, Heaven only knows; for it seemed as if every prisoner were to be carried to a separate place of confinement. At all events, even if we knew where she is, we could do nothing at present. Come, cheer up, now you have unburdened yourself of all this load. I shall be ready to start as early as ever you please in the morning."

By this time the moon was in full splendour, and nothing could be more beautiful than the scenery of the native place of Sabinus, as we drew near to its precincts. A little gentle stream, which kissed our path, did not desert us as we entered the village, but murmured all through its humble street. Street, indeed, I should not say; for there were dwelling-houses on the one side only, the other being occupied with gardens, in the midst of which I saw the Doric portico of a small temple. In front of this a bridge crossed the stream, and there we were met by a troop of maidens, who seemed to be moving toward the sacred place with some purpose of devotion, for they were singing in alternate measures, and in their hands they carried garlands. Some recognized Sabinus, and, without interrupting their chant, saluted him with their laughing eyes. We halted our horses, and saw them proceed all together into the hallowed enclosure, which they did, not by means of the bridge, although they were close by it, but by wading hand in hand through the stream below; whose pebbles, as it appeared from the evenness of their motion, dared not to offer any violence to the delicate feet that trod upon them. "Happy creatures," said I to the Centurion; "of a surety they think these moonbeams shine on nothing but glad faces like their own. Alas! with what heart does poor Athanasia at this moment contemplate this lovely heaven!"—"Nay, Valerius," quoth he, "if people were not to be contented with their own share of sorrow, would the world, think ye, be worth living in? I hope Athanasia herself will ere long sing again by the moonlight.—But stop, here is my own old haunt, the abode of our village barber, and now I think of it, perhaps it might be as well that you and Dromo should remain here for a moment, till

I ride on to the house, and let them know you are coming, for the sudden sight of strange faces might alarm the old folks at this hour."

He had scarcely said so, when the tonsor himself, hearing, I suppose, the sound of our horses' feet, ran out with his razor and basin in his hand, to see what might be the matter. "Ah, good Virro," quoth the Centurion, "with joy do I once more behold your face. Well, the girls still sing, and Virro still shaves; so every thing, without question, goes well."—"The Centurion himself!" replies the barber; "so Venus smile upon me, it is Kæso Sabinus, who I began to think would never come back again.—Here, boy, bring out a cup of the best. Alight, I pray you—well, at least, you shall kiss the rim of the goblet."—"I will," said he, "I promise you, my good friend, and that in a minute or two; but I must first salute my father; and, in the meantime, I leave with you in pledge, good Virro, my excellent friend here, and the most knowing Cretan that ever landed at Brundusium.—Dismount, Valerius, I shall be with you again ere Virro can half smoothen the chin of Dromo, which even this morning shewed no small need of trimming."—"Well, well," said the tonsor, "eagles will have their own way. Be speedy."

The Centurion had set the spur to his charger; and we, in obedience to his command, submitted ourselves to the guidance of the oily-faced little barber. A stripling was already holding two horses at the door, but another came out and took care of our animals, and we entered, exchanging courteous salutations, the tonsorial penetralia.

They were occupied by as various and talkative a company, as the imagination of Lucilius ever assembled in such a place. In the middle of the room, which was spacious, though low-roofed, hung a huge shield of brass, with a dozen mouths of flame blazing around the edge of its circumference, close beside which sat a man with a napkin tucked about his neck, the one side of whose visage, still besmeared with a thick coat of lather, testified that the curiosity of Virro had induced him to abandon a yet uncompleted job. The half-trimmed physiognomy, however, displayed no sign of impatience, and the barber himself seemed not to think any apology necessary, for he resumed his operations with an air of great cheerfulness, saying, "Neighbours all, here is Kæso Sabinus, that is now the Centurion, come once more to gladden the old village with his merry face, and that, I promise you, is prettily tanned since we knew him first."

This piece of news appeared not a little to interest several of those who were sitting under the tonsor's roof. "Ha!" said one, "the noble Centurion! Well, has he brought home a wife with him at last? for the talk was, that he had been seen at the Amphitheatre, paying great court to one of the richest ladies in Rome."

"A wife?" says Virro, "no, no, centurions and barbers can do without wives. But if he is to have one, I shall be happy to hear she is rich; for centurions, after all, sometimes carry most of their silver upon their helmets, as we do most of our brass on our basins."—"Indeed," said I, "I never heard of it before."

"If it please you, friend," said another of them, "is this the same Sabinus that has lately been in Britain?"—"Britain," quoth an ancient dame; "I never heard that name before—Britain! I know it not—I know not where he hath been, but they told me it was over the sea, perhaps in Palestine."—"Tut, dame," interrupted the barber, (who was now busy on Dromo,) "you think every one goes to Palestine, because your own boy carried a spear with Titus; but you know they ruined the city, and killed all the Jews and Christians, and there is no occasion for sending Centurions thither now."—"Killed all the Jews and Christians, said you?" quoth another. "I think the old dame has the better of you as to that point at least, Virro. Not Trajan himself will ever be able to kill them all; the superstition spreads like a pestilence. It was but last night that a hundred of them were taken together in one place, eating human flesh."—"Human flesh!" quoth the barber. "Oh, ye gods, why do ye endure such barbarians!"

"Human flesh!" echoed Dromo, springing from his seat, and I looked at him, and saw that the barber in his horror had made in truth a deep incision upon the cheek of the poor man. The blood, oozing from the cut, had already traced a river of crimson upon the snowy surface of his well-soaped chin. It was this that had deranged the philosophic composure and customary phlegm of my Cretan; and no wonder; but the enthusiastic tonsor took no notice of what had occurred.—"Great Jove," he proceeded, and he pointed to the roof with his razor as he spake—"Great Jove! I adjure thee! are all thy lightnings spent; is there never a thunderbolt remaining?"

"In the meantime," quoth one of the bystanders, "they are in the hand not of Jove, but of Trajan, and he, I think, cannot now be accused of treating these wretches with too much lenity. You have all heard of that Tisias?"— "We have," cried another; "but what was a single individual to this great assembly? what a sight will it be the day they are all executed!"

"I think," said the same person who had inquired whether our Centurion were the Sabinus that had been in Britain,—"I think you are overrating the numbers of that assembly. I heard of no more than a dozen."

This stranger (for such he seemed) had probably taken that day a considerable journey, for his tunic and boots were covered with dust. He was attired in the plainest manner, but notwithstanding, there was something about him which gave one the idea of rank superior to the company in which he was seated; and his complexion was so dark that I could not help thinking to myself,—I am not the only provincial in the room; here is certainly some well-born African or Asiatic.

"You have not told me, however," said he, after a pause, "whether or not this be the Sabinus that was lately in Britain."—"Sir," said I, "it is the same; I myself came in the same ship with him, but a few days ago. He is a Centurion in the Prætorian Bands."—"Yes," replied the stranger, "I guessed in truth, it must be the same; for I remember no other of that rank bearing the same name."—"If you are acquainted with him," said I, "you may have an opportunity of seeing him immediately, for I expect him here every moment to conduct me to his father's villa, which is hard by."

"Well," quoth the barber, who by this time had ended, without fresh misadventure, the trimming of the Cretan—"well, I hope he will stay for a moment when he does come, and then we shall be sure to hear the truth as to this story about the Christian assembly. They may talk as they please, but may Jove devote me, if I had Cæsar's ring upon my finger for one night, this should be the last of them."—"And how, friend," said the stranger, "by what means, if I may ask you, should you propose so speedily to do away with this fast-spreading abomination?"—"Look ye, sirs," quoth he, "I would place myself thus in my tribunal"—(he took his seat at a little table, beside a goblet of wine, as he spake,) "I would seat myself thus in the midst of a field, as Cato and the great Censors of old used to do. I would cause Rome to be emptied—man, woman, and child should pass before me; and every one that did not acknowledge the gods as he passed, by all the gods! he should sprawl upon a tree in presence of all the people. What avails watching, prying, spying, and surprising? I should make shorter work of it, I trow."

"You may say what you will," said one who had not before spoken, "I cannot bring myself to believe every thing I hear concerning their superstition."—"Ay, goldsmith," quoth the barber, "you were always fond of having an opinion of your own; and, pray, what is it that you have had occasion to know about the Christians, more than the rest of us who hear you? If you mean that you have seen some of them die bravely in the Amphitheatre, why, that we have all heard of at least, and I think nobody disputes it."—"No, master barber," replied he, "that is not what I was thinking of. I have seen your common thief-knave, when he knew he could do no better, brace you his nerves for the extremity, and die like a Hercules. I would rather judge of a man by his living than his dying."—"True," rejoins Virro; "and pray, what have you got to tell us about the life, then, of the Christians?"—"Not much," said he, "you shall hear. My old mother (peace to her manes) was passing the Salarian one day last year, and there came by a hot-headed spark, driving four abreast in a chariot as fiercely as Nero in the Circus. He called out, that I believe, but the dame was deaf, and whether he tried to pull up, I know not, but the horses trod upon her as she fell. Another of the same sort came close behind, and I have been told they were running a race; but however that might be, on they both passed like a whirlwind, and my poor mother was left by herself among the flying dust. But the gods had mercy on her; they sent a kind heart to her aid. She was carried into one of the stateliest villas on that side of Tiber, and tended for six weeks by a noble lady, as if she had been not my mother, but her own; and this lady, friends—by Jove I suspected it not for long after—this lady was a Christian; but I shall not say how I found it out, nor would I mention the thing at all but among honest men. But where were these you spoke of taken?—I should like to know who they were."

"They were taken," said the stranger, "not far from the Appian Way, within one of the old monuments there,—a monument, it is said, of the Sempronii."—"Of the Sempronii?" cried the goldsmith, "Phœbus Apollo shield us!" and from that moment he became as silent as hitherto he had been communicative.

The swarthy stranger, the silence yet continuing, arose from his seat, laid a piece of money upon the table, and moved towards the door. The barber also rose up, but he said to him, "Sit still, I pray you, my friend;" at the same time beckoning with his finger to the goldsmith, who, with a very dejected countenance, followed him into the street. What passed between them there, we perceived not; but the artificer re-entered not the chamber till some moments after we had heard the departing tread of the stranger's horses. When he did come in again, he had the appearance of being in great confusion.

CHAPTER IX.

Shortly after Sabinus reappeared, and bidding adieu to our tonsor, we walked with him towards the paternal mansion,—and we soon reached it; for, as I have already said, it was but a little way out from the village.

The dwelling was modest enough, having no external ornament but a single portico, with a few statues ranged between its pillars. We entered by this portico, and found the feeble old man sitting by himself in an apartment immediately adjacent, wherein the beams of the moon, having partial access, were mingled with the subdued light of a painted lamp suspended from the ceiling. The father of my friend had all the appearance of sinking apace; yet he received me with an air, not of cheerfulness, but of kindness. The breeze found admission through the open pillars, and his countenance exhibited in its wan and faint lines the pleasure with which the coolness affected him. Beside him were placed baskets of roses, gathered from the abundance of his gardens. The young Vernæ, who from time to time brought in these flowers, came into the chamber with a decent appearance of sobriety and concern; but they were never long gone before we could hear them laughing again at their play.—"Poor children," quoth the old man; "why should they trouble themselves with thinking of the not remote victim of Orcus?"—To which the Centurion replied, somewhat softening that loud and cheerful tone with which he was accustomed to address all persons—"Courage, my dear father, you must not speak so. Cerberus, I perceive, has only been making an ineffectual snap at you, and you will be growing younger after all this."

At which the old man shook his head, without any external sign of emotion, and replied, in a low monotonous voice,—"Younger in the wrong way, my boy; for I become every day smaller in body, and feebler, and less able to do any thing to help myself. Nor am I unconscious that I have seen my due proportion of time. And yet, oh! fast sliding gentle brook, which I see between these paternal trees—I am still loath to exchange thee for Styx, and to lose the cheerful and sacred light of the sun and moon. I wish only I were once more able to repair with thy stream to the banks of father Tiber, that I might salute the good Emperor, who has been so kind to my son, and who would treat even an old broken-down, and long-retired soldier, like myself, with more favour than is to be expected from Rhadamanthus. As clouds let down their drops, so the many-peopled earth lets fall dismissed ghosts upon the Stygian shore."

While he was saying things in the same strain, an ancient Egyptian, who seemed to have the chief management of every thing, came into the chamber, and after desiring some of the boys to bring forth refreshments, took his place on a low stool by the foot of his master's couch. "Come, Tarna," said the Centurion, "what has become of all your philosophy? Why do you not inspire our friend with less of gloominess? Why is it that you do not bring out for his use some of those old stories, with which, when I was young, you were more willing to treat my ears than they were to attend?"

"Nay," said the invalid, before the Egyptian could make any answer,—"I liked well to listen to his Epicurean theories when I was able to walk about the fields; but now I would rather have him be silent. Do not trouble me any more, good Tarna, with any of your speeches. Allow me to believe as all my fathers did, and to contemplate not only the sepulchre in which their urns are placed, but the same dim regions in which many dear shades expect the greeting of a descendant."

"To me," said the slave modestly, "it still seems, that by the rushing shower of atoms which moves every where through space, the mind is soothed, as by the sound of a great river carrying continually the watery offspring of the mountains into the bosom of ocean. The mind, sirs, appears to me to be calmed by the contemplation of infinity, even as the ear of an Egyptian sleeper is calmed by the eternal music of rolling Nilus. It mingles itself with that which it contemplates; it perceives—it feels itself to be a liquid part of that vast endless stream of universal being: a part which has been casually arrested and detained, but which will soon mingle again and be scattered away in a thousand fragments, to wander, no one knows whither, through the great all-receiving void—not to lose existence, for in that my dear master entirely misunderstands me—but to cease from feeling as a Sabinus, or a Tarna."

The old man kept regarding his Egyptian with a placid smile; but I could not help interposing: "What is this you have said? Do you assert that I can cease to be Valerius, to feel as Valerius, and yet not lose my existence? Can I *be*, and yet not be *myself*?"

"Most easily," replied he; "the divided fragments may move about for a thousand years, before it befall any of them to be stopped in some future combination of atoms. These, it is manifest, only tremble and suffer when they form part of a soul, but are immediately released from all pain or mischance, when this confinement and cohesion are at an end, and they, being dispersed, regain liberty and wander about singly, as of yore; for, as our great dispeller of delusion says—When death is, we are not. If, therefore, Sabinus shrinks from the fear of death, it is an idle fear. Does he not perceive that when death arrives, Sabinus is no longer to be found. Whatever its effects may be, they must affect not him, but an army of innumerable disjointed essences, in no one of which could he by any means be able to recognize himself."

"To make a short story out of a very long one," interrupted the Centurion; "life, you think, is not worthy of the name of existence—that being so, it is no wonder you should think lightly of death."

"Mistake me not," quoth the sage; "no—life *is* existence; I not only admit that, but I assert that it is the business of every man, and the sole true object of wisdom, to render life, while it endures, pleasant. Earthly pleasure consists in a bland juxta-position of atoms necessarily, though not permanently, connected; the removal of pain implies that quiescence which pervades the nobleness of the unenclosed ALL. To exist in this shape, we are compelled; it is our business to render our existence as near an approach to felicity as we may."

"Fill your cup, Tarna," quoth the Centurion; "I am no great philosopher, yet methinks I can see the drift of this part of your story. Fill up your goblet, most venerable Epicurean, and see (if it be not below your dignity,) whether the atoms, which, by a fortuitous and temporary juxta-position have formed your throat, will not feel their corners very philosophically softened by the rushing of a little rivulet of good Falernian—one cup of which, saving your presence, I hold to be more worthy of wetting my guttural atoms, than all the water that ever sported its music between Memphis and Alexandria."

While the slave and the Centurion were thus discoursing, the old man appeared to taste, as it were, the pleasure of a renovated existence, in contemplating the brown health and strong muscular fabric of the inheritor of his name. The hearty masculine laugh with which my friend usually concluded his observations, was, I take leave to think, richer music to his ears than ever Egyptian heard in the dark rollings of the Nile, or Epicurean dreamt of in the airy dance of atoms. I suspect he was more reconciled to the inevitable stroke of fate, by considering that he was to leave such a representative behind him, than by any argument which his own superstition, or the philosophy of his attendant, could suggest. In return for this obvious admiration, the Centurion, without question, manifested every symptom of genuine affection. Yet, I think, the instinctive consciousness of his own strength made the piety of the robust son assume an air more approaching to that of patronage, than might have been altogether becoming. If such a fault there were, however, it escaped the notice of the invalid, who continued, till Tarna insisted upon his retiring, to gaze upon my friend, and listen to his remarks, with looks of exultation.

The Centurion withdrew with his father, so that I was left alone with Tarna for some time; and it was then that, in my juvenile simplicity, I could not help expressing my surprise at finding in servile condition a man possessed of such acquirements as his, and addicted to such pursuits.

"It would argue little," he replied, "in favour of such pursuits, if they tended only to make me repine at the place which has been allotted me—no matter whether by the decree of fate, or the caprice of fortune. And after all, I am not of opinion that any such external circumstances can much affect the real happiness of any one. Give to him that has been born a slave, what men are pleased to call his freedom; in a few weeks he will become so much accustomed to the boon, that he will cease to think of it. Heap wealth upon him; to wealth also he will gradually become habituated. Rank—power—with all it is the same. It is in the mind only that the seat of happiness is placed; and there it never can be, unless in companionship with thoughts that look down upon, and despise being affected by trifling things."

"And are such," said I, "the views of all those who follow your sect?"

"I wish it were so," he replied; "but ere you remain long in the city, you will meet with not a few, philosophers only in the name, who, having small means of subsistence, but being desirous of leading a luxurious and agreeable life, become teachers of such doctrines as may accord best with the vicious inclinations of those who are most likely to entertain them. These persons assume too often the name of Epicureans. They are seen every where at feasts crowned with myrtle, and fawning upon gouty senators; and whenever a boar's-head appears, they are sure to call it worthy of Meleager. Their conversation is made up of stale jests about Charon and his boat, and the taking of Auguries; and, when finally inebriated, they roll upon the ground like those animals, to whom, in consequence of the proceedings of such hypocritical pretenders, the ignorant have dared too often to liken the wisest of mankind. Such things I disdain—I am satisfied to remain, as I was born, in the rank of Æsop, Epictetus, Terence."

By this time the Centurion had returned. He had a lamp in his hand; and he interrupted our conversation. "Come, we start betimes, Caius; and you too, my sweet cock of Cyrene, I think you had better fold your wings, and compose yourself upon your roost."

Oh, enviable temperament! said I to myself—you liken the slave to a bird. Methinks yourself are more deserving of the simile. The light and the air of heaven are sufficient to make you happy—your wings are ever strong—their flight ever easy—and the rain of affliction glides off them as fast as it falls. Sleep softly, kind heart. It is only the troubles of a friend that can ever disturb your serenity.

CHAPTER X.

I was in bed before Dromo interrupted my reflections by saying, in a low tone of considerable confidence, "And now, Master Valerius, do you still continue, as much as two days ago, to disbelieve in philtres and despise enchantresses? You see what, with all my precaution, has come of this connection between Rubellia and the Neapolitan."

"In truth, Dromo," I replied, "it is visible that Pona had some share in leading the soldiers to the Sempronian Sepulchre; but I am doubtful if that had any thing to do with the private affairs of the lady Rubellia. As to that matter, I confess myself entirely in the dark."—"Dark indeed," quoth he, "must your observation have been, if you have yet to learn that, but for that accursed witch, nothing of all this had befallen; but if there be an edict against the Christians, there are twenty laws against sorcery; and that both Pona and she that consulted her shall know well ere long, if they do not as yet know it; or may Cretan change places with Bœotian!"—"Say on, good Dromo," I replied, "I am all ears; and as you appear to have been all eyes, I shall probably soon be more enlightened."

"Well," quoth he, "I am glad to find that you are in a mood to listen to me decently. You remember where I took my station when you mounted those unfortunate steps upon the tower. I had not stood there many minutes before I heard somebody approaching; and having no doubt it was Rubellia, I was preparing myself for giving her such a salutation as I thought would put a speedy end to her wandering for that night. On came the steps, but no Rubellia. No; it was Xerophrastes himself; and although he had laid aside the Greek mantle, and donned a boatman's black cloak for the nonce, I promise you I knew his stately gait well enough beneath all these new trappings. It was no part of my job, however, to attempt frightening the stoic."—"And so you let him pass without doing any thing?"—"I did; I confess I gave one or two groans after he had gone on a few paces, but I did not observe him much quicken his walk, and I believe, to do the man justice, he set it all down to the wind rustling among the trees. But I thought not much of him at all, to speak the truth; for, said I to myself, Well, if it be as I have suspected for these two blessed days, and this master long-beard is really in league with the widow, the chances are, she herself is not far behind him. I lay by, therefore, and expected in silence till I should hear another tread; and in the meantime I spoke to you once or twice across the path, but you made me no answer, for which you know your own reasons."—"The reason," said I, "was a very simple one, I assure you. I had fallen asleep, and no wonder, for you know how long I had been a watcher."—"Well," said he, "I guessed as much, and it was nothing but the born tenderness of my disposition, which made me cease from offering you any disturbance. I thought I should surely be enough single-handed for the widow; and besides, in case of need, I knew your waking would always be in my power."

"Admirably reasoned, Dromo," said I; "and so it seems no need came, for you certainly never awakened me; for which I may thank the bonds from which the Centurion's kindness has just set me free. But you have atoned abundantly—I pray you, get on with your tale."

"Presently," he resumed, "I heard footsteps, indeed, my good master, and not footsteps alone, but voices; and I moved from the place as hastily as I could, till I came to a tree, the branches of which, springing low on the trunk, offered an opportunity for mounting, which I should have been a Bœotian indeed had I neglected. I mounted, and hiding myself as well as I could among the boughs, awaited the arrival of the party, which consisted—ay, stare if you will—of Xerophrastes and the widow, walking in front, in earnest talk by themselves,—and the Neapolitan in the rear. They halted, and though they spoke low, I could hear them distinctly."—"And what, in the name of Heaven, said they?"

" 'Are you sure,' said the widow, 'that this is indeed the girl whom Sextus went to see at the Villa? Can there be no mistake?'—'Mistake, lady, there is none,' replied the Stoic. 'Pona was at the villa with her basket, and she saw them all walking together in the garden.'—'And this little Christian,' said the lady as if to herself, 'it is she that has cost me all this trouble! It is for this Athanasia that I have been insulted as never woman was by man, and they are both here in the tower!'—'They are, lady,' quoth the witch; 'they are both in the tower, for I saw her go in by her self first, and then in went some dozen of those muffled blasphemers, and, last of all, went in he himself. I saw him not enter indeed, but I swear to you, that I saw him here not twenty paces from hence, and he had with him that cunning slave of his, (meaning myself, sir,) whose ugly face, (the foul woman added,) I would know although it were disguised beneath all the washes that were ever mixed in the seething-pots of Calabria.'—'But what,' interrupted our long-beard, 'what will Licinius say? At least, my lady and my friend Pona will take good care that no suspicion rests upon me. Sextus is a silly boy, without taste, judgment, or discretion; but Licinius is acute and powerful.'—'Fear not,' said Rubellia; 'fear not, dear Xerophrastes. Nobody shall appear in the matter except Pona, and she tells you she has already given warning at the Capene Gate. There are always a hundred men stationed on the Cœlian. Nothing can save them!'

"These words were scarcely out of her mouth, ere the soldiers were heard approaching. Xerophrastes ascended with great agility a tree just over against mine; Rubellia retreated among the pines; and Pona alone awaited the guard. I would have periled a limb to have been able to give you the alarm; but little did I suspect, that had I sought you where I left you, I should have sought in vain.—How, I pray you, did you contrive to get into the accursed tower?"

I told him I should give him the story another time at full length, and mentioned briefly what had occurred. And then the Cretan proceeded with his narrative.

"I leave you to guess, Valerius, how my heart beat when I saw the witch lead the soldiers straight to the place where I supposed you were still sitting—with what anxiety I saw the tower surrounded—its tenants brought out,—with what astonishment I saw you led out, the last of their number.—I had neither time to think by what means all this had happened, nor the least power to interfere. I saw you all mounted—guarded—borne away. Whither they carried you, I was unable to make the smallest conjecture. I saw Sabinus speak to you, and then I had hope,—but that too failed. In brief, I did not venture from my tree till the whole assembly, not forgetting Xerophrastes, had departed; and you may judge what a story I had to tell Sextus when I reached home.

"Instead of waiting to ponder and hesitate, as he used to do when his own matters perplexed him, he went from me straight to his father. But before they had done with their conversation, Sabinus himself arrived, and he was immediately taken into the same chamber where they were. Licinius and he went out together soon afterwards, and I think they walked towards the Palatine; but whithersoever they went, they had a good deal of work before them, for the day had advanced considerably before they returned. The Centurion's horses were brought to the door shortly after; my master desired me to accompany him; and gave me letters for you, which I had almost forgotten to deliver."

Such was the story of the faithful Cretan. The letter of Licinius I have still preserved:—

"Since our Sabinus desires that I should write to you, although his own kindness renders it unnecessary that I should do so, I cannot refuse. I understand little, my Valerius, of what has brought you into this condition, from which, not without difficulty overcome, you are, notwithstanding, speedily to be delivered. I guess, that hastiness of various sorts, not, however, entirely without excuse in a person of your age, has been the means of implicating you in the affairs of a sect, equally unworthy of your communication, whether you consider the country in which their superstition originated, or the barbarities with which it is stained. But even for beauty, my young friend, it becomes not a Roman, least of all a Valerius, to forget what is due to the laws of Rome, and the will of the Prince. Consider with yourself how nearly you have escaped serious evil. Return to us, and forget what has passed, except for the lesson it must teach you. Of Rubellia and Xerophrastes I am unwilling to believe, without farther examination, what has been told me by my slave Dromo. We shall speak of that and other matters, when (which I hope will be early to-morrow) you once more give me the pleasure of seeing you. I have then much to say. Farewell."

BOOK III.

CHAPTER I.

Day was far advanced before the Centurion and myself once more drew near to the city. When we reached the first declivity beyond the Anio, the sun was about to sink behind the Janicular. The innumerable sounds of the capital, blended together into one mighty whisper, seemed only to form part of the natural music of the air, and might almost have been confounded with the universal hum of insects. We rode slowly down the hill, the base of which is ever darkened by the solemn groves of the Appian.

We advanced in silence through that region of melancholy magnificence. I scarcely knew whether I should be able of myself to recognize, among so many similar edifices, the mausoleum of the Sempronii, and some feeling rendered me unwilling to put any questions concerning it to Sabinus.

But while we were moving leisurely, we heard of a sudden a clang of cymbals among the trees, a little to the right hand, and the Centurion, saying, "What company can this be?" led the way down a narrow path branching from the main road. This path was winding and dusky, being edged on either side with pines and cypresses, so that for some space we saw nothing; and the cymbals having ceased again, the Centurion said, "I suppose it is some funeral; they have probably completed every thing, and have seen out the last gleam among the embers. Let us get on, for perhaps we may be kept back by their procession, if they are already returning." We quickened our pace accordingly, till a sharp turning of the road discovered to us a great number of persons who were standing silent, as if in contemplation of some ceremony. Several persons on horseback seemed, like ourselves, to have had their progress interrupted; but they were sitting quietly, and making no complaint. The silence of the whole assembly was indeed such, that Sabinus motioned to me to ask no questions, adding, in a whisper, "Take off your cap; it is some religious rite—every body is uncovered."

The Centurion, however, was not a person to be stopped thus, without wishing to understand farther the cause of the interruption. The one side of the road was guarded by a high wall, to the top of which a number of juvenile spectators had climbed;—the other by a ditch of great breadth, and full of water, beyond which was a grove of trees; and I saw him eyeing the ditch, as if considering whether, by passing it, it might not be possible, without disturbing the crowd, to get nearer the object of their attention, or at least to make progress in our journey. At last he beckoned to me to follow him, and the bold equestrian at one leap passed easily. I imitated the example, and so did the Prætorian soldier, his attendant, who had now come up to us; but as for Dromo, he was obliged to remain behind.

Ere we reached the bottom of the declivity, I perceived that we had come close to the Sempronian monument, and that the ceremony, whatever it might be, was taking place in front of the tower. We gave our horses to the soldier, and contrived to gain the bank over against it—the same place, in fact, where the Cretan slave had taken his station among the pine-trees, on the night when all those things occurred of which I have spoken to you. Like him, we placed ourselves as quietly as we could behind the trees, and, indeed, for our purpose, there could have been no better situation. We were contented, however, to occupy it as much as possible without attracting observation; for it was evident, in spite of the curiosity that detained so great a multitude near at hand, there must be something mysterious or ominous of nature in that which was taking place, since not one of the crowd had dared to come forward, so as to be within hearing of the officiators.

And these, indeed, were a melancholy group. For men, and women, and children of every age, to the number it may be of an hundred, appeared all standing together in garments of black; while, in the midst of them, and immediately by the base of the tower, two or three veiled priests, with their necessary assistants, seemed to be preparing for sacrifice a black bull, whose hoofs spurned the dust as they held him, and his gilded horns glittered in the light of the declining sun. Sabinus no sooner discovered the arrangement of the solemn company, than he whispered to me, "Be sure, these are all the kindred of the Sempronii. Without question they have come to purify the mausoleum, and to avert the vengeance of the violated Manes. Behold," said he, "that stately figure, close to the head of the animal on the right hand; that, I know, is Marcia Sempronia, Priestess of Apollo. Without doubt, these by her are her brothers."

"Some of her near relations they must be," I made answer; "for observe you that girl whose face is wrapped in her mourning veil, and whose sobs are audible through all its folds? I had one glimpse of her countenance, and I am sure it is young Sempronia, the cousin and companion of Athanasia,—the daughter of Lucius the senator."

"Poor girl," replied Sabinus, "from my heart I pity her. They are all joining hands, that the nearest of the kindred touching the priest, his deed may appear manifestly to be the deed of all."

At this moment, one of the officiators sounded a few mournful notes upon a trumpet. The priest who held the axe, clave at one blow the front of the bull. The blood streamed, and wine streamed with it abundantly upon the base of the mausoleum; and then, while we were yet gazing on the convulsions of the animal, the trumpet sounded a second time, and the whole company sung together, the priest leading them.

The shadows of the tower and of the pine trees lay strongly upon them, and I thought there was something of a very strange contrast between the company and their chant, on the one hand, and the beautiful sculptures, full of all the emblems of life and happiness, on the other, with which, according to the gay dreams of Grecian fancy, the walls of the funereal edifice itself had here and there been garnished. Fauns, and torch-bearing nymphs, and children crowned with garlands, and wreathed groups and fantastic dances, seemed to enliven almost to mockery the monumental marbles; but one felt the real gloominess both of death and of superstition, in the attitudes and accents of the worshippers. It was thus they sung:—

Ye Gods infernal! hear us from the gloom

Of venerable depths remote, unseen;

Hear us, ye guardians of the stained tomb,

Majestic Pluto—and thou, Stygian Queen,

On the dark bosom leaning of great Dis—

Thou reconciled Star of the Abyss.

Blood, not for you, unholy hands have poured,

Ye heard the shriek of your insulted shrine;

Barbarian blasphemies, and rites abhorred,

Pollute the place that hath been long divine;

Borne from its wounded breast an atheist cry

Hath pierced the upper and the nether sky.

With blood of righteous sacrifice again

The monumental stone your suppliants lave.

Behold the dark-brow'd bull—Behold him slain!

Accept, ye powers of the relenting grave,

The sable current of that vital stream;

And let the father's hope upon the children gleam.

And ye, that in the ever dusky glades

Of Hades, wandering by Cocytus' shore,

Ancestral spirits—melancholy shades—

With us the tresspass of the tomb deplore;

Oh! intercede—that terror and disgrace

May not possess (as now) your resting-place.

What though the liquid serpent of the deep

Between lie coil'd in many a glittering ring:

Not unobserved of your pale eyes we weep,

Nor to deaf ears this doleful chant we sing;

Strong is the voice of blood through night to go,

Through night and hell, and all the realms below.

Then hear us, kindred spirits—stately Sire

And pensive Mother! wheresoe'er ye glide;

If ever solemn pile and soaring fire

In freedom sped you to the Stygian tide,—

Have pity on your children: let the breath

Of living sorrow melt the frozen ear of death.

For Her that, sprung like us from your high line,

Hath mingled in the sacrifice of guilt,

Ye know that angry star, her natal sign,

To expiate whose curse this blood is spilt;

If not suffices this atoning blood,

Oh, steep the thought of her in Lethe's flood.

Beneath that current lazy and serene,

In whose unfathomable waters lie

The slumbering forms of horrors that have been

In Hades, and in Ocean, Earth, and Sky—

With long forgotten curse and murder old,

Steep that lost daughter's errors manifold.

Once more for you an hallowed flame there burns.

Once more for you an hallowed stream there flows;

Despise not our lustrations of your urns,

Nor let unhoused Manes be our foes!

Above the children of your lineage born,

Hover not, awful ghosts, in anger and in scorn.

These words were sung, as I have said, by the whole of this kindred there
assembled together; the first part of them distinctly, though not loudly; but

the last verses in a note so low, that no one, unless quite near, (like ourselves,) could have comprehended their meaning. But as for the young Sempronia, when they came to that part of the chant in which reference was so particularly made to Athanasia, not only did her lips refuse to join in the words, but her agitation was such that I thought the poor maiden would have screamed outright, had she not been controlled by the eye, and the hand also, of her aunt the Priestess. Sobs, however, and low hysterical groans, could not be stifled; and at last so great was her agony, that even the haughty Priestess was compelled to give way to it.

"Bring water," said she; "dash ye water upon the foolish thing: methinks it seems almost as if she had partaken in the frenzy of her unhappy———"

And before she could finish the sentence, one or two of the females that were present did take hold of Sempronia, and began, seeing there was no water nearer at hand, to bear her slender form towards the small stream of which I have already spoken, and which flowed immediately behind the clump of pine trees, amongst which the Centurion and I were standing.

She was quite passive in their hands; and they dragged her without resistance or difficulty to the place where we were standing; but they could not pass without seeing us: and no sooner did the eyes of Sempronia fall upon me, than she burst by one unexpected effort from the arms of those that were sustaining her, and ere I or any one could suspect what she was to do, there lay she at my feet, clinging with her arms around my knees. "Oh, Valerius," said she—"Oh, dear Valerius, they curse Athanasia! Where is my Athanasia? whither have they taken her? Oh, tell me, that I may go to her—that I may go to comfort Athanasia!"

"Peace!" said, before I could answer, the Priestess of Apollo—"Peace, mad, wretched thing,—has infatuation blasted the whole of our line?" And she seized Sempronia by the arm, and compelled her to spring from her knees. But the maiden still clung by her hands to me, and continued, with looks and words of misery, to demand from me that knowledge which, alas! I would myself have given so much to possess. Sabinus, however, smote me on the shoulder, as if to make me recollect myself; and I had resolution enough not to betray the feelings with which I listened to Sempronia's frantic supplication.

"What is this, sir?" then said the Priestess—"What is it that you know of Athanasia? and why is it that you have presumed to witness the secret sacrifice of a noble race?—Speak—or is there no meaning in this poor girl's frenzy? And yet, methinks I have seen you before, and that, too, in the presence of———"

"It was," said I, hastily—"it was indeed in the presence of Athanasia; but that circumstance, if you please to remember, was altogether accidental. I was with the lady Rubellia when you found her in the Temple of Apollo——"

"Yes," said she, "it was that same day when she refused to name the name of Phœbus in his own precincts! Ha! little did I imagine what thoughts were in her breast—else might we at least have been spared this open degradation. And yet you, methinks, saluted Athanasia.—What is your name, sir?—Know you, in truth, whither the lady Athanasia has been conveyed?"

"He was with her!—he was with her!" exclaimed Sempronia,—"he was with her in the tower when the soldiers came.—O Valerius! tell me where she is now,—into what dungeon have they cast my friend—my sister——"

"Ha!" quoth the Priestess, "he was with her in the tower!—Romans—kinsmen—Lucius—Marcus—hear ye this? I charge ye, seize upon this treacherous blasphemer!—It is he that has deceived Athanasia; and now must he come here to taint the smoke of our sacrifice, and pollute our prayers with his presence.—Seize him!"—And she herself grasped my cloak as she spake—"Seize, I charge ye, this accursed Christian!"

But Sabinus, when he saw the Priestess thus furious, stept forward, and said to her kinsmen, who were standing in perplexity behind her, "Sirs, I beseech you, be not you also carried away with this madness.—My friend here knows nothing of the lady Athanasia, except that she was borne away by soldiers from the very place where we are standing. I myself witnessed it also, being here with the Prætorians. Valerius is no more a Christian than she who accuses him."

"I know not, sirs, how we are to understand all this," said one of the Sempronii, in a calm voice. "Is this young man the same Valerius who is living in the house of Licinius?—Yet it must be he. I have been with Licinius this very day; and if this be he, whatever he may have known before, I am sure he knows nothing of where Athanasia is now,—and, sister, I am well assured he is no Christian."

"It is the same, sir," said Sabinus. "He is the same Caius Valerius of whom you spake, and I am Sabinus, a Centurion of the Prætorians."

"We have all heard of your name," said Sempronius, respectfully; "I perceive there is some mistake in all this matter. If it please you, let us walk aside, and understand each other."

So saying, he withdrew Sabinus to a little distance, and beckoned to me to accompany him. "Valerius," said the old man, when he perceived that we were out of hearing, "I crave you, in the first place, to forget all this trouble which has been occasioned to you by the violence of my daughter, on the one hand, and of my sister on the other. They are women; and, for different reasons, the violence of both is excusable. I have been for a considerable part of this day with Licinius, and have heard from him enough to satisfy me how guiltlessly you yourself have been involved in this affair; and your speedy liberation from confinement is more than enough to confirm my belief of all that he said. Yet there is much which I do not understand. I pray you speak openly, and fear nothing—you have, indeed, nothing to fear. Was it in consequence of any private meeting with my niece—nay, I mean not to suspect you of any thing amiss—in one word, how was it that you happened to be taken into custody with that unhappy girl?"

"Sir," I replied, "you are a noble Roman, and the near kinsman of Athanasia. You have a right to put these questions, and whatever reluctance I may have to overcome, I feel that I have no right to refuse an answer." And so I told Sempronius, plainly and distinctly, the story both of my unwilling entrance into the mausoleum, and of my forcible abduction from it. In short, I saw no reason to conceal any thing from the person who was most likely to be able to serve Athanasia, if any thing to serve her were possible.

"It is well," he said; "you speak as becomes a man of the Valerian blood. But as for poor Athanasia, I swear to you I cannot yet bring myself to believe that she hath in reality been privy to such things as have been discovered concerning these Christians."—"Discovered!" said I. "I pray you, what has been discovered concerning them? If you allude to any of the wild stories that are circulated about their religion, you may depend upon it, it is all mere madness to believe a word of it. I have read in their sacred books myself, and I swear to you, that, so far as I have seen, nothing can be more simple, benign, humane, than the morality inculcated by their leader."

"Young man," he answered, "I was not thinking of their creed, which, for aught I know or care, may be sublime enough; for there was always a mysterious sort of philosophy current among those old Asiatic nations. But I speak of the designs of these men; in one word, I speak of their conspiracy."—"Conspiracy!—What? How? Against whom? I will pledge my life, no conspiracy was sheltered beneath yon tower that night. I swear to you, they are simple people, and were thinking of nothing but their worship."—"Worship!" quoth he; "I promise you it will not be so easy to persuade me that Cotilius has suddenly become a man of so much piety, either to our gods, or to the deities (if they have any) of the Christians.— What, Cotilius? By Jove, Rome does not hold at this moment a more bold, daring, godless rascal. You may as soon try to make me believe that Capaneus came to Thebes with a hymn in his mouth. No, no—the sworn friend of Domitian will not easily gain credit for his new-sprung sanctity."—"Cotilius? That was the very name of the man that seized me, as I have told you."—"I should have guessed as much," said he;—"Yes, I promise you, how little soever Athanasia might have known, secrets they had; and Cotilius was well aware at what peril they should be revealed."

"The late example," said I, "must indeed have alarmed him."—"What," said he, "do you speak of that fanatic Syrian? You know little of Cotilius. No, no—had the worst of his fears been the necessity to worship all the deities between Euphrates and Rhine, he would have slept soundly."—"But surely," said I, "you do not believe that Athanasia had any knowledge of the man's secret designs, if he had any. He may have used Christianity, or desired to use it, as a weapon against the State; but be certain, neither she nor any of those really attached to their religion, had any notion of his purpose."

"It may be so, indeed," he answered;—"Heaven grant it may. As for Cotilius, I will speak to you more at length of him anon. I will bid adieu to my sister, and take order about my daughter; and then, if it so please you, we shall walk together to the city."

To this I agreed, but Sabinus rode on to the camp of the Prætorians. He whispered to me, however, that unless he were most necessarily detained, he should be, ere long, at the house of Licinius.

"To you," said the Senator, as we went on, "who have so lately come from your island, the whole of this expiatory spectacle is probably quite new; but I am sure Sabinus could not have been aware what was its purpose, otherwise he would not have been guilty of so grievously offending the feelings of my sister, and some of the rest of my kindred, by remaining a witness of these most private rites. The Priestess is indeed inconsolable, and her grief has set half her other passions in motion likewise. Athanasia was as dear to her as if she had been her daughter; so, in truth, she was to us all, ever since her parents died. But Cotilius, this knave Cotilius, has, I fear, blasted her hopes and ours."—"It occurs to me," said I, "and I should have mentioned it to you before, that there seemed to be no great understanding between this Cotilius and Athanasia. She was evidently displeased with many things he both said and did; and he, on his part, did not appear to relish her interference."—"True," he continued, "you have already hinted as much; and I assure you, these are some of the circumstances in the whole case that tend most to excite my hopes. Great Heavens! what would Caius have said had he dreamt that his orphan was to be suspected of having sympathy with any of the dark designs of that shame to Roman knighthood! But you, of course, are a stranger to this man's history."—"With its end, at least," I replied, "it is like we may all be soon enough acquainted."

"Yes," said he, "Heaven grant we have not cause too deeply to remember it! but I have known him from the beginning. I told you already that he was in great favour with Domitian."—"And the reverse, of course," said I, "both with Nerva and Trajan."

"Even so," he continued, "and with reason; for in all the disturbances which occurred on the accession of the last sovereign, and, in particular, in those foul intrigues among the Prætorians, which at one time brought Nerva's own life into immediate danger and compelled him to bare his neck to the soldiery at his gate, this Cotilius was more than suspected to have had a deep concern. When Petronius and Parthenius² were hacked in pieces, it needed no great witchcraft to detect some of the moving spirits that produced their catastrophe; but proof there was none at the time; and even had there been proof enough, the good old man would have been too timid to act upon it. These things, however, could not be forgotten either by Nerva or his successor. Hitherto, the strong hand has repressed every rebellious motion; but be sure that no man ever lived more an object of suspicion, than this man has done ever since Nerva adopted Trajan."

"And you think," said I, "that, among other intrigues, it had occurred to this man to make his own use of the Christians; despised and persecuted though they be, there can, indeed, be no doubt that their numbers are considerable, and that their faith is a strong bond of cohesion."

"It is even so," said the Senator. "But as yet the treason even of Cotilius rests on suspicion only, and report; and, after all, even if he were proved guilty of having nourished such schemes, the account you give of what you saw and heard at their assembly, inspires me with considerable doubts whether he can be supposed to have ever as yet ventured to invite their participation;— unless, indeed, they practised deception while you were with them. The moment I heard of what had happened, I went to the Palatine, in hopes of attaining either assistance from Urbicus, or mercy, if that were all we could look for, from Trajan. But Urbicus could give me no satisfaction, except that my niece was in a solitary and safe place. The charges, he said, against one of the leaders (he meant Cotilius) were heavy; and until these were sifted, it was impossible that access could be afforded to any one who had been thrown into confinement. The Emperor had shewn unusual symptoms of anxiety, and had even, so he hinted, been in person investigating the matter at a distance from the city, during great part of the preceding night and day. To tell you the truth, Valerius, till this thing fell out, I was wont to consider the new violence about the Christians as somewhat unworthy of the enlarged intellect of Trajan: it had not occurred to me, how easily the resources of such a superstition might be enlisted in the cause of discontent."

"Of course," said I, "nothing will be done in regard to Athanasia until all circumstances have been examined."

"Done!" said he; "has not enough been done already to justify almost in a man more than you have seen among our women? Has not a whole family been disgraced? Has not the mausoleum of their fathers been prostituted for the unholy purposes of this barbarian sect? If the Senate should be summoned, with what countenance should I shew myself among my friends?—Unhappy girl! How little did she know in what trouble she was to involve those that love her the best."

By this time we had come within sight of the house of Licinius, and the Senator took leave, with a promise that I should see him on the morrow.

I found Sextus alone in his chamber, where he embraced me with all the ardour of juvenile affection. "Alas!" said he, "my dear Caius, at any other time I might have found fault with you for taking so great a part in my griefs, and yet keeping so many of your own to yourself. But if it be indeed as Sempronia has said, I should be a strange friend to choose this hour for complaining of such trifles as regard only myself."

"Sextus," I replied, "it was only because of the greatness of your own distresses that I concealed from your kindness any of mine."

"My Valerius," he answered, "we shall talk at length to-morrow; at present, I have only time to say, that the misfortune of Athanasia was communicated to Sempronia almost immediately, by an old freedwoman, who had been in the habit of attending her when she went from home in secret, and who, going to the mausoleum to accompany her on her return, arrived there just in time to see what befel her. She saw you also, (how she knew who you were, I know not,) and when she had told her story to Sempronia, the poor girl, before speaking even with her father, sent for me to come to her in the gardens. I did so; all that passed I need not repeat; but I hope my advice was the right one. At all events, I acted for the best, and my father, who is now aware of every thing, seemed to approve of what I had done. O Valerius! were Athanasia free, and you happy, many things have occurred to make me much more at ease than when you left us. My father is evidently shocked with what Dromo told about Rubellia; and as for Xerophrastes, he had not once spoken to him either yesterday or to-day. Indeed, neither of them have been much here. My father is continually exerting himself concerning Athanasia; and Xerophrastes, I suppose, is afraid of a discovery. As for me, I am sorry I must leave you, for I promised to meet Sempronia; and although I have nothing to tell her, I cannot fail in my appointment. She must have returned before this time from the mausoleum, where an expiatory sacrifice was to be made at sunset."

Sabinus by this time had hastened to me once more, according to his kind promise. I told him that my kinsman was not at home, and that I proposed, in the meantime, accompanying his son a part of the way towards the Suburban of Capito. The Centurion insisted on going with us, saying, that he could not think of returning to the camp without having spoken with Licinius.

CHAPTER II.

The Centurion, in virtue of his office, had free access to the gardens of Trajan; so he led us by both a more delightful and a nearer path towards the Salarean Gate. Young Sextus then quitted us; and we returned slowly through the beautiful groves of the Imperial Villa, in hopes of finding my kinsman by the time we should reach his mansion. But as we were walking very quietly along one of the broad green terraces, we heard voices in an adjoining alley, separated from us by luxuriant thickets of myrtle, and Sabinus, whispering to me, "Hush, let us see what we have got here," insinuated himself with great dexterity among the verdant shrubs. I followed him with as little noise as was possible, and having found a convenient peeping place, we soon perceived two figures at some little distance from us in the moonlight.—"Come, Sabinus," I whispered, "they are lovers perhaps—I don't see what right we have to overhear."—"Peace," quoth he, "if you stir, they will detect us, and it is nothing unless it be known."

With some reluctance I remained where I was; but my scruples were at an end the moment I perceived who they were.

"Most noble, most illustrious lady," said Xerophrastes, "this matter has indeed been conducted unfortunately, yet no reason see I why you should give way to so many groundless apprehensions. The only thing, after all, that you have lost, if indeed you have lost it, is the good opinion of Licinius; for, as to that foolish boy——"—"Name him not," replied Rubellia, "name not the stripling. Surely madness alone can account for my behaviour."— "Madness!" quoth the Stoic; "yes, truly, and who, at certain moments, is free from such madness? As Euripides has expressed it, Venus, if she come in wisdom, is the wisest; if otherwise, the most frenzied of influences. The greatest have not been exempt from such visitations. Banish it from your heart, noble lady, or replace it by something more worthy of your discernment. There is, I think, but one pair of eyes in Rome that could have been blind to such perfections."—"O Xerophrastes!" said she, "speak not to me of perfections. Alas! I was born under a deceitful star—a star of apparent splendour and real misery."—"Noble lady," he replied, "I swear to you that what tincture of philosophy I have imbibed, is unable to sustain my serenity when I hear such words from your lips. You are surrounded by all that externals can minister. It is your part to compose your mind, and then how should it be possible for you to taste of unhappiness? Think no more of that boy."

The philosopher took her hand with an air of the deepest sympathy, and at the same time drew the end of his mantle over his face, as if to conceal the extent of his participation in her distresses.—"Alas! lady, this is, after all, a miserable world. There is no rest but in the affections, and behold how they are harassed on every hand by the invidious accidents of life. Philosophy proclaims her antidote, but the poison is every where; and it is all one course of being wounded to be cured, and being cured only to be more easily wounded again."

Our friend continued in an attitude of pensive contemplation. The moonbeams fell full on his high brow and the large massy features of his countenance, and on the robust limbs which emerged from below the stately folds of his mantle; and I could not help thinking that there was something almost heroic, which I had never before remarked, in the whole of his appearance. Rubellia kept her eyes fixed steadfastly upon him.

"I should have known nothing of it," he resumed, "had I never deserted my paternal valley for the vain pleasures of Athens, and the magnificence of Rome."—"You repent," said she, "that you ever visited Italy? I pray you deal with me openly. If it be your wish to leave Rome, speak, and I shall put it in your power to retire to Greece as handsomely as you could ever have hoped to do from the family of Licinius. Of wealth, as you well know, I have enough both for myself and for my faithful friends, among whom, be sure, I place you in the first rank. Control your feelings, I pray you once more—and speak freely."

Hastily and fervently he pressed his lip upon the beautiful hand of Rubellia, and whispered something into her ear. She started, and I think blushed in the moonlight; but neither seemed offended very deeply with what he had said, nor with the gesture he had used.—"Softly, softly," whispered the Centurion, "be not ashamed, fair lady, of the love of thy servant."

But (whether the echo of his Horatian parody had reached her ear or not, I cannot tell,) scarcely had these words been uttered, ere Rubellia started from her seat, and began to move pretty quickly down the shaded alley, as if towards the entrance of the gardens. Xerophrastes sate still for a moment, even after the lady had arisen, covering his eyes, and part of his broad forehead with his hands, as if buried in his own thoughts too deeply to be with ease affected with a sense of things passing around him. Then, at last, he arose, and uttering an exclamation of surprise, walked after the noble dame, taking heed, however, (it did not escape our observation,) to arrange, as he rapidly followed her, the massive folds of his mantle into a graceful drapery.

Sabinus restrained himself till they were beyond the reach of his voice; but he then made himself ample amends. "Ha!" said he, "is this to be the end? Most pensive ghost of Leberinus, is this to be thy successor?"—"Good heavens!" said I, "Sabinus, do you think it possible she should make the pedagogue her husband—she that was but yesterday so desperately enamoured of the beautiful young Sextus?"—"My dear islander," quoth the Centurion, "do you remember the story of a certain beautiful boy, called Adonis?"—"To be sure," said I, "who is ignorant of the story of Adonis, or of the beautiful verses of Bion—

"I weep for fair Adonis—for Adonis is no more,

Dead is the fair Adonis—his beauty I deplore;

His white thigh with a tusk of white the greenwood monster tore,

And now I weep Adonis—for Adonis is no more.' "

"Well spouted," quoth the soldier; "and with an excellent gravity: But think you Venus never altered the burden of her ditty? Have you never heard of Mars the blood-stained, the destroyer of men, the leveller of city walls—nor of Anchises, the Dardan shepherd, wiser in his generation than one who inherited both his station and his opportunity; no, nor even of Vulcan, the cunning Artificer, the Lord of the One-eyed Hammerers, the Lemnian, the Chain-maker, the Detector, the awkward Cup-bearer, whose ministration, as honest Homer confesses, fills Olympus with inextinguishable laughter. Have you heard of all these, and I take it of a few more besides; and yet do you talk as if Venus, after the white boar's tusk had pierced the white thigh of her Adonis, had made no use of her beautiful girdle, but to wipe the tears from her pretty eyes withal?—her girdle, of which, heaven pity your memory, I know not how many blessed ages after Adonis had fallen, the same faithful bard said,

'In it is stored whate'er can love inspire:

In it is tender passion, warm desire,

Fond lovers' soft and amorous intercourse;

The endearing looks and accents that can fire

The soul with passionate love's resistless force,

'Gainst which the wisest find in wisdom no resource.'

I was there the night she espoused Leberinus, and I pitied her very sincerely, when I saw the pretty creature lifted over the old man's threshold in her yellow veil, which I could not help thinking concealed more sighs, if not more blushes, than are usual on such occasions. But I promise you the glare of her new torches shall affect me with different emotions."

Such talk passed as we were leaving the gardens of Trajan. But as we advanced into the more peopled region, we found the streets full of clamour, insomuch that quiet discourse could no longer be carried on. The evening was one of the most lovely I had ever seen, and the moon was shedding a soft and yellow light upon the lofty towers and trees, and upon all that long perspective of pillars and porticos. Yet groups of citizens were seen running to and fro with torches in their hands; while many more were stationary in impenetrable crowds, which had the air, as it seemed to us, of being detained in the expectation of some spectacle. Accordingly we had not jostled on much farther, ere there arose behind us a peal of what seemed to me martial music; but my companion, as soon as the sounds reached him, warned me that a procession of the priests of Cybele must be at hand.

At last they came quite close to us, and passed on dancing around the image of the Goddess, and singing the chaunt of Atys. A path being opened for them by the crowd all along, they made no halt in their progress, but went on at the same pace, some of them leaping high from the ground as they dashed their cymbals, and others dancing lowly while they blew the long Phrygian trumpets and crooked horns of brass. The image itself was seated in a brazen chariot, to which brazen lions also were fastened, the whole being borne on the shoulders of some of the assistants. Behind it came others, beating great hollow drums; and then again more, leaping, and dancing, and singing, like those who preceded it. They were all clad in long Asiatic vests, with lofty tiaras; and their countenances, as well as their voices, intimated sufficiently that they were ministers of the same order to which the hapless Atys had belonged. Yet nothing but enthusiasm and triumph could be discovered in their manner of singing that terrible hymn.

They had not advanced much beyond the spot where we were standing, ere they stopped of a sudden, and, placing the chariot and image of Cybele between the pillars of one of the porticos that run out into the street, began a more solemn species of saltation. When they had finished this dance also, and the more stately and measured song of supplication with which it was accompanied, the priests then turned to the multitude, and called upon all those who reverenced the Didymæan mysteries, to approach and offer their gifts. Immediately the multitude that were beyond formed themselves into a close phalanx, quite across the street, and torches being conveyed into the hands of such as stood in the foremost rank, there was left in front of the image an open space, brightly illuminated, for the convenience, as it seemed, of those who might come forward to carry their offerings to the foot of the statue. And, indeed, it appeared as if these were not likely to be few in number; for the way being quite blocked up by those torch-bearers, no one could hope to pass on easily without giving something, or to pass at all without being observed. Not a few chariots, therefore, and litters also, having been detained, the persons seated in these vehicles seemed to be anxious, as soon as possible, to present their offerings, that the path onward might be cleared to them by command of the priests. It was necessary, however, as it turned out, that each person in advancing to the chariot of Cybele, should imitate the motions practised by the Galli themselves; and this circumstance, as may be imagined, was far from being the most acceptable part of the ceremony to some of those who had thus been arrested. A few of the common sort, both men and women, stepped boldly into the open ring, and with great appearance of joy went through the needful gesticulations. But, at first, none of the more lordly tenants of the chariots and litters seemed to be able to prevail on themselves to follow the example. At length, however, the impatience even of these dignified persons began to overcome their reluctance; one and another red-edged gown was seen to float in lofty undulations across the torch-lighted stage, and when a handful of coin was heard to ring upon the basin of the Goddess, doubt not the priests half-cracked their cheeks in blowing horn and trumpet, and clattered upon their great tambarines as violently as if they had made prize of another Atys. But how did the Centurion chuckle when he observed that one of the next chariots was no other than that of Rubellia herself, and perceived that she and the Stoic were now about to pass onwards like the rest, at the expense of exhibiting their agility before the multitude.

"Jove in heaven!" cried he, "I thought the garden scene was all in all; but this is supreme! Behold how the sturdy Thracian tucks up his garment, and how, nodding to the blows of the tambarine, he already meditates within himself the appropriate convolutions. And the pretty widow! by the girdle of Venus, she also is pointing her trim toe, and, look ye! better and better, do you not see that she has given her veil to the Stoic, that so she may perform the more expeditely?"

At this moment, some one from behind laid hold of my arm, and whispered my name. I looked round, and perceived an old man, wrapped in a very large and deep mantle, the folds of which, however, were so arranged that I could see very little of his features. Stepping a pace or two backwards, he beckoned to me with his hand. I hesitated; but his gesture being repeated, I also entered within the shade of the pillars, and then he, dropping his mantle on his shoulders, said, "Valerius, do you not remember me? We met last at the tomb of the Sempronii."—"At the tomb of the Sempronii!" said I; and recognized, indeed, the features of the Christian priest, who had treated me on that eventful evening with so much courtesy; but my wonder was great to find him in such a situation; for I had seen him conveyed away between armed guards, and I could not imagine by what means he, of all others, should have so soon regained his freedom. He observed my astonishment, and said, in a low voice, "My friend, perhaps I might have as much reason to be surprised with seeing you here, as you have in seeing me. But follow me into this house, where we may communicate what has occurred."

The hope of perhaps hearing something concerning Athanasia determined me. I cast a look towards Sabinus, and saw him attentively engaged in witnessing the performance; and hoping that he might continue to amuse himself so for a few minutes longer, I permitted the old man to lead me into the vestibule. The slaves, who were waiting there, seemed to receive him with much respect. He passed them, saying, "Do not trouble yourselves—I shall rejoin your master;" and shortly ushered me into a chamber situated over the hall of entrance, where a grave personage was reclining by the open window. He perceived not our approach till we had come close up to his couch, for he was occupied with what was going on without. When the old man accosted him, and said, "Pontius, I have been successful. Here is my friend, Caius Valerius," the stranger rose up, and saluted me with kindness. "Caius Valerius," said he, "will pardon me for being desirous of seeing him here, when he learns that I was one of his father's oldest friends, and served with him many campaigns both in Germany and Britain. I should have been ill pleased had I heard that you had been in Rome, and departed without my having an opportunity of retracing, as I now do, the image of my comrade."

I had to answer not a few questions concerning the situation of my mother and myself, before I could lead the conversation into the channel I desired; and at length, indeed, it was not so much any thing I said, as the readiness of the priest himself, which gave to it that direction; for the first pause that occurred in the discourse between Pontius and myself, he filled up, by saying, "And now, will Valerius pardon me for asking, if he has ever looked again into the narrative of Luke, or whether his curiosity, in regard to these matters, has been entirely satisfied by the adventures of one unfortunate night?"

The manner in which Pontius regarded me when the priest said this, left me no doubt that he was at least favourably inclined to the opinions of the Christians; so I answered without hesitation, "My curiosity, instead of being satisfied by what I saw that evening, received new strength; but you may easily believe that the troubles in which I was involved, and still more the troubles with which I know others yet to be surrounded, have hitherto taken away from me both the means and the power of gratifying my curiosity as I would wish.—But tell me, I pray you, by what means is your imprisonment at an end?"—"My friend," replied the priest, "you speak naturally but rashly. I believe you yourself are the only one of those surprised in the tower, whose imprisonment has as yet terminated. Yet hope, good hope is not absent,— above all, I trust there is no reason to despair concerning that dear child who interfered in your behalf, when a bold, and, I fear me, a false man, had drawn his weapon to your peril. As for me, I have but gained the liberty of an hour or two, and long ere dawn I shall be restored again to my fetters."—"Your fetters!" said I, "am I to understand, that, by the connivance of a Roman jailor, you are this night at liberty to perambulate the streets of Rome?"— "Young man," answered the priest, "he is a Christian."—"Even for his sake," said I, "the name is honourable."

"Valerius," said he, "I pray you speak not things which may hereafter give pain to your memory. Already you have read something of the life of ONE, for whose sake our name is indeed honourable—of Him I trust you shall ere long both read and think more; but how shall I bless God, that threw my lot, since captivity it was to be, into a place where such authority was to have the superintendence of me? Yet more, how shall I be sufficiently grateful, that She, in all things so delicate, although in nothing fearful, has shared the same blessing?"

"Heavens," said I, "what do I hear!—Is Athanasia indeed lodged in the same prison with yourself, and may she also go abroad thus freely?"

"Think not," he replied, "that I embrace such freedom for any purposes of mine own. What I do for the service to which I am bound, think not that Athanasia will ever desire to do for herself. She abides her time patiently where the lot hath been cast for her; in due season, if such be the will of the Lord, she shall regain that in truth, of which this is but the shadow."

"God grant our prayer," said Pontius, "and not ours only, but the prayer of all that know her, and have heard of this calamity!—Whatever the exertions of her family and their friends can accomplish, most surely shall not be awanting. Would that those who are linked to her by ties yet more sacred had the power, as they have the will, to serve her! Yet Hope must never be rejected. The investigations of this very night may produce the true accomplices of Cotilius; and then Trajan will be satisfied that the Christians stand guiltless of that treason."

"Alas!" said I, "if this faith be a crime, how can any one hope to follow it without being continually liable to accidents as unfortunate? In Rome, at all events, what madness is it thus to tempt the fate which impends over the discovery of that which it must be so difficult, so impossible to conceal?"

The aged Priest laid his finger on his lips, and pointed to the window. I listened, and heard distinctly the shrill voices of the mutilated dancers, as they brake forth above the choral murmurs of the drums and cymbals, and I perceived that the bloody legend of Atys was once more the subject of their song.

The ancient waited till the voices were drowned again in the clamour of the instruments, and then said to me, "Young man, do you know to what horrid story these words of theirs refer? Do you know what sounds all these are designed to imitate? Do you know what terror—what flight—what blood— what madness are here set forth in honour of a cruel demon—or rather, I should say, for the gain of these miserable and maimed hirelings? Do you know all these things, and yet give counsel of flight and of cowardice to me, upon whose head the hand of Christ's holy apostle hath been laid? Read, dear Valerius, read and ponder well.—My prayers, and the prayers of one that is far purer than me—they are ever with you. But now since I have introduced you to Pontius, why should I delay here any longer? He, both for your father's sake and for your own, and for that of the faith, (of which you have had some glimpses) will abundantly aid you in all things. Deal not coldly nor distantly with him. I commit you into his hands, as a brand to be snatched from the burning."

Pontius reached forth his hand and grasped mine in token of acquiescence in all the old man expressed. He, by and by, looking into the street, said, "These jugglers have now departed to their dens, and the gaping multitudes have dispersed. But I still see one person walking up and down, as if expecting somebody; and it seems to me that it is the same, Valerius, who was in your company." I perceived that it was indeed Sabinus, whistling to himself on the bright side of the pavement. I therefore bade them adieu, saying, "Dear father, when shall I see you again, and when shall I hear farther of Athanasia?"—The old man pausing for a moment, said, "To-morrow at noontide be in the Forum, over against the statue of Numa. You will there find tidings."

The Centurion plainly intimated that he took it for granted I had been engaged in something which I wished to keep from his knowledge; but such affairs made no great impression on him; and after laughing out his laugh, he bade me farewell by the portico of Licinius.

CHAPTER III.

In the morning I found my kinsman and his son extremely uneasy, in consequence of the absence of Xerophrastes, who had not returned during the night; but Sabinus came in while they were talking to me, and narrated, without hesitation, all he had seen and heard both in the garden of Trajan, and at the procession of the Galli. Young Sextus could scarcely be restrained by respect for his father, from expressing, rather too openly, his satisfaction in the course which the affairs of the disappointed lady appeared to be taking; while the orator muttered words which I thought boded not much of good to the ambitious pedagogue. The Centurion alone regarded all these things as matters of mere amusement, or so at least he seemed to regard them; for, as I have already hinted, I was not without my suspicion, that he was at bottom by no means well pleased with the contemplation of the future splendour of the Stoic.

However, after many jests had been exchanged between Sextus and the Centurion concerning this incongruous amour, Licinius said, he was in so far much relieved by what he had heard, as it satisfied him that both the widow and Xerophrastes were now otherwise occupied, than in prosecuting their designs against the niece of his friend Capito.

"I myself," he continued, "was all yesterday, as well as the day before, exerting every means in my power for her extrication from this unfortunate confinement. Cotilius, without question, has indeed been a traitor; but I believe the Prince himself is, by this time, well inclined to absolve, not only the young lady, but by far the greater part of those who were taken with her, from any participation in his traitorous designs. The charge, however, of which it rests with them alone to exculpate themselves, is one of a nature so serious, that it is impossible to contemplate without much anxiety the pain to which so many families—above all, the noble and excellent Sempronii— may still be exposed. But this day Cotilius will, in all likelihood, pay the last penalty of *his* crimes—and then we shall see what intercession may avail. Would to heaven there were any one who could obtain access to the deluded lady, and prevail with her to do that which would be more effectual than I can hope any intercession to prove. This infatuation—this dream—this madness—is, indeed, a just source of fear; and yet, why should we suppose it to be already so deeply confirmed in a breast young, ingenuous, so full, according to report, of every thing modest and submissive? Surely this affectionate girl cannot be insensible to the affliction of those who love her.—But you still shake your head, Valerius; well, it is in our hands to do what we can; as for the issue, who can hope to divert Trajan from doing that which he believes to be just? Our best hope is in his justice——"

"And in his clemency," interrupted the Centurion; "you will scarcely persuade me that Cæsar can meditate any thing serious concerning a young beauty, who has been guilty of nothing but a little superstition and enthusiasm. Nobody will confound her case with that of any obstinate old fanatic. In the meantime, what avails it to distress ourselves more than is necessary? Licinius is able to do something; and as for Valerius, the best thing he can do is to get on horseback, and go with Sextus and myself to inspect the cohorts that have arrived from Calabria."

Young Sextus, on all occasions fond of military spectacles, embraced this proposal; and fain would they both have prevailed on me to accede to it likewise. I knew, however, that it would be impossible, if I accompanied them, to keep my appointment with the old Christian; and that I was resolved on no account to forego. I therefore retired to my chamber, there to await the approach of the hour; and spent the time till it drew near, in perusing once more the volume which had been restored to me by Athanasia. This volume, and the letter which I have before mentioned, I placed together in my bosom, before I went forth into the city.

I entered the Forum, and found it, as formerly thronged with multitudes of busy litigants and idle spectators. A greater concourse, indeed, than was usual, crowded not it only, but the avenues to it, and the neighbouring streets, by reason of a solemn embassy from the Parthian, which was to have audience that day in the Senate. But I, for my part, having discovered the statue of Numa Pompilius, resolved to abide by it, lest, being mingled in the tumult of the expecting multitudes, I should, by any mischance, escape the notice of the old man, who, I doubted not, meant to seek me there in person. The time, however, went on—senator after senator entered the temple—and, at last, the shouts of the people announced that Trajan had arrived. And immediately after he had gone in, the pomp of the embassy appeared, and every eye was fixed upon the long line of slaves, laden with cloth of gold and rich merchandise, and upon the beautiful troop of snow-white horses, which pawed the ground, in magnificent caparisons, before the gate of the Senate-house. But while all were intent upon the spectacle, I observed a little fair-haired girl standing over against me, who, after looking at me for some moments, said with great modesty, "Sir, if you be Caius Valerius, I pray you, follow me."

I followed her in silence up the hanging stairs, and, in a word, had soon reached the level of the Capitol, from whence, looking back, I could perceive the whole array of the forensic multitudes far below me. The child paused for a moment at the summit, and then, still saying nothing, conducted me across two magnificent squares, and round about the Temple of Jupiter, until, at length, she stopped at one of the side doors of an edifice, which, from the manner in which it was guarded, I already suspected to be the Mammertine.

The girl knocked, and he who kept the gate, saluting her cheerfully, allowed us to pass without question into the interior of the prison. My companion tripped before me along many passages, till we reached at length a chamber which was arranged in such a manner that I could with difficulty believe it to belong to a place of punishment.

Here I was soon joined by the old priest, (whose name, if I have not before mentioned it, was Aurelius Felix,) together with a mild-looking man of middle age, whom he desired me to salute as the keeper of the prison, saying, "Here, Valerius, is that Silo, of whom yesterday evening you spake with so great admiration. But I hope the benevolence of a Christian will ere long cease to be an object of so much wonder in your eyes."

"My father," said the jailer, "methinks you yourself say too much about such little things. But, in the meantime, let us ask Valerius if he has heard any thing of what has been determined by Cæsar."

I answered by telling what I had just heard from Licinius; upon which the countenance of the old man was not a little lightened; but Silo fixed his eyes upon the ground, and seemed to regard the matter very seriously. He said, however, after a pause, "So far, at least, it is well. Let us hope that the calumnies which have been detected, may turn more and more of discredit upon those that have gone abroad concerning that which is dearer to you, my father, and to all your true companions, than any thing of what men call their own. But, alas! these, after all, are but poor tidings for our dear young lady."

"Fear not," answered Aurelius: "have I not told you already oftentimes, that strength of heart goes not with bone and sinew, and that my gentle child is prepared for all things? She also well knows that the servant is not greater than the master."

The old man motioned to us to remain where we were, and withdrew. I sate for some minutes by the side of Silo, who was, indeed, manifestly much troubled, until at length the same modest little damsel opened the door, and addressing the jailer as her father, asked leave to conduct me to Aurelius.

The child led me, therefore, into the adjoining chamber, and tapped gently at a door on the other side of it. The voice of the old priest bade us come in, and Athanasia arose with him to receive me. She was dressed in a white tunic, her hair braided in dark folds upon her forehead; her countenance was calm, and, but for the paleness of her lips, I should have said that her gravity scarcely partook of sadness. When, however, we had exchanged our salutations, it was evident that some effort had been necessary for this appearance of serenity; for when she spoke to me her voice trembled in every tone, and, as she stooped to caress my young guide, who had sate down by her feet, I saw the tear that had been gathering drop heavily, and lose itself among the bright clusters of the little damsel's hair. I took her unresisting hand, and imitated as best I could the language of consolation. But it seemed as if my poor whispers only served to increase the misery. She covered her face with her hands, and sobs and tears were mingled together, and the blood glowed red in her neck, in the agony of her lamentation.

The old priest was moved at first scarcely less than myself by this sorrowful sight. Yet the calmness of age deserted him not long, and after a moment there remained nothing on his countenance but the gravity and tenderness of compassion. He arose from his seat, and walked quietly towards the end of the apartment, from which when he returned, after a brief space, there was an ancient volume open in his hand. And standing near us, he began to read aloud, in the Greek tongue, words which were then new, and which have ever since been in a peculiar manner dear to me.

God is our refuge and strength; a very present help in trouble. Therefore will not we fear though the earth be removed; though the mountains be carried into the midst of the sea; though the waters thereof roar and be troubled; though the mountains shake with the swelling thereof.

Athanasia took her hands from her face, and gradually composing herself, looked through her tears upon the old man as he proceeded.

There is a river, the streams whereof shall make glad the city of God; the holy place of the tabernacles of the Most High.

God is in the midst of her; she shall not be moved; God shall help her, and that right early.

The heathen raged; the kingdoms were moved. He uttered his voice; the earth melted.

The Lord of Hosts is with us. The God of Jacob is our refuge.

The blood had mounted in the countenance of Aurelius, ere he reached these last words. The tears also had been dried up on the pale cheek of Athanasia; and although her voice was not heard, I saw that her lips moved fervently along with those of the priest. Even in me, ignorant of their source, the words of the royal prophet produced I know not what of buoyance and emotion, and perhaps my lips, too, had involuntarily essayed to follow them; for when he paused from his reading, the old man turned to me with a face full of benignity, and said, "Yes, Valerius, it is even so; Homer, Pindar, Æschylus— these, indeed, can stir the blood; but it is such poetry as this that alone can sooth in sorrow, and strengthen in the hour of tribulation. Your vain-glorious

Greeks called all men barbarians but themselves; and yet these words, and thousands not less precious than these, consoled the afflictions, and ennobled the triumphs of the chosen race of Israel long, long years, ere ever the boasted melody of Ionian or Doric verse had been heard of. From this alone, young man, you may judge what measure of candour inhabits along with the disdain of our proud enemies:—how fairly, without question, or opportunity of defence, the charge of barbarity is heaped upon what they are pleased to call our *superstition*;—how wisely the learned and the powerful of the earth have combined in this league against the truth which they know not,—of which they fear or despise the knowledge. Surely the truth is mighty, and the gates of hell shall not prevail against her."

"But, alas! my dear father," said Athanasia, "I fear me this is not the place, nor the situation, in which Valerius might be most likely to listen to your words. It may be that his own narrow escape, to say nothing of our present danger, has rendered him even more cautious than he was before."

"And who, my dear child," he replied hastily,—"and who is he that shall dare to blame caution, or to preach, above all in such things as these, the rashness that is of folly? Valerius will not believe that we, like the miserable creatures whose impious songs he heard last night, are studious only of working upon the fears of the ignorant, and harassing, with dark and lying dreams, the imaginations of the simple. *Here* are no wild stories of blood-thirsty deities, and self-sacrificing maniacs. *Here* is that which Socrates vainly sought by all the ingenuity of reason. *Here* is that of which some faint and mysterious anticipations would appear to have been shadowed forth in the visions of Plato. *Here* is that which, as that Mighty Martyr who died in this very city hath said, innumerable prophets and kings of the old time desired to see, and yet saw not. Do nothing rashly, young man; but it is possible, as you yourself well know, that this may be the last opportunity I shall ever have of speaking with you; and therefore, before we part, I must needs charge you solemnly, that henceforth, if your knowledge increase not, the sin shall be upon your head. I charge you, Valerius, that when you return to your island, you blot not from your memory the things that you have seen and heard in this great city of light and of darkness. Examine—judge—ask aid, and aid shall not be refused you. I take Athanasia to witness, that I have given you the warning that is needful."

"Oh, sir!" said Athanasia, "I am sure it shall not be in vain that you have done so. I am sure Valerius will never forget this hour——"

She gazed in my face, and a tear was again visible, yet on all her countenance there was no other semblance of passion. The venerable Aurelius clasping his thin hands together, whispered,—"Would to God that I were here alone! Shall the axe be laid to the root of the fair young tree that hath but begun to blossom, when so many old trunks stand around withered with the lightnings, and sore broken by the winds?—The will of the Lord be done!"

"Amen!" said Athanasia, taking the old man by the hand, and smiling, I think, more cheerfully than I had yet seen her—"My dear father, I fear you yourself, after all, are teaching Valerius to take but a sad farewell of us."

"Alas! my child," he replied, "he must have a hard heart that could look unmoved on that sweet face in this hour of sadness. But we are in the hands of a greater than Trajan. If so it please Him, all may yet go well with us even here upon the earth. You may live to see many happy years among your kindred—and I, (the old man smiled most serenely,) and for me, my gray hairs may be laid in bloodless dust. Whatever awaits us, blessed be the name of the Lord!"

So saying, the old man retired from the chamber, and once more I was left alone in the presence of Athanasia. I took from my bosom the book and the letter which I had placed there, and laid them upon her knee. She broke the seal, and read hastily what Tisias had written, and then concealed the scroll within her tunic, saying, "Alas! Valerius, little did the brave old soldier suspect how soon his peril was to be mine—Will you permit me like him to make you my messenger?—will you seek out my cousin, my sister, and tell Sempronia in what condition you have found me?—no, not in what you found—but in what you now see me. Will you go, Valerius, and speak comfort to my poor friend? Her pity, at least, I am sure is mingled with no angry thoughts; and yet she only has reason to complain, for her secret thoughts were not hid from me, and, alas! I concealed mine from her."

"I have already seen her," said I, "and you do her no more than justice. But, indeed, Sempronius himself thinks of you even as gently as his daughter."

"I doubt it not, Valerius; but, alas! there are many others besides these; and I know not what relic of weakness it is, but methinks I could have borne the worst more easily, had it not been for what I picture to myself of their resentment. Alas! I am cut off for ever from the memory of my kindred." She threw open the lattice, as if that she might inhale the free air, and her eyes wandered to and fro over all the magnificent prospect that lay stretched out below us,—the temples and high porticos of the Forum—the gleaming battlements and long arcades of the Palatine—the baths, and theatres, and circuses between and the river—Tiber winding away among fields and groves—and the sky of Italy extending over all things its arch of splendour. When the trumpets were blown by the gate of the Senate-house, the sound floated upwards to us as gently as if it had been borne over the waters. The shouts of the multitude were faintly re-echoed from the towers and the rocks. The princely pageant shewed like a pomp of pigmies; spear, and helmet, and eagle glittered together, almost like dews upon the distant herbage. Athanasia rested her eye once more upon the wide range of the champaign, where fields and forests were spread out in interminable succession—away towards the northern region and the visible mountains. She raised her hand, and said, "Valerius, your home lies far away yonder. I must give you something which you shall promise me to carry with you, and preserve in memory—of Rome."

Before I had time to make any answer, she had taken out of a casket that stood beside us, a scroll of parchment, bound with a silk ribbon, which she immediately put into my hands, and—"To-morrow," said she, "Valerius, our fate, they tell us, must at length be determined;—if we share the fate of Tisias, the last gift of Tisias shall be yours. If, however, any mercy be extended to us, I cannot part with that memorial of a dying martyr. I must keep to myself the old man's favourite volume, for it was for me he had designed it. But I have made a copy of the same book for yourself. I have written it since I came hither, Valerius, and you must not despise it because the Mammertine has not furnished the finest of materials. Take this, Valerius, and take with it my thanks—my prayers. I know you will not forget my message to my dear sister.—Sextus and she—may many happy days be theirs—and yours."

I kissed the sad gift, and placed it in my bosom.

"Valerius," she said, "dry up your tears. You weep for me because I am a Christian; forget not that the Roman blood flows in my veins, and think not that its current is chilled, because I have forsworn the worship of idol and demon, and am in peril for the service of The Living God."

"Athanasia!" said I,—"I weep for you, but not for you alone. I ask nothing— I hope nothing—but I could not bear to part with you thus, and not to tell you that when I part from you, I bid farewell to all things. Pardon me—once more pardon me."

A single flush of crimson passed over her face, and I saw her lips move, but the syllables died ere they were uttered. She continued for a moment gazing on me, pale, and trembling; and then at last she fell upon my neck and wept— not audibly—but I felt her tears.

Athanasia was still folded to my bosom in that strange agony of sorrow and of confidence, when Silo, the jailer, entered the apartment, abrupt and breathless.

"Oh, sir!" said he, "your sufferings are mine—but it is necessary that you should leave us, and on the instant, for the Prefect is already at the gate, and unquestionably he will examine every part of the prison; and should you be recognized as the person who was taken in the Mausoleum, you see plainly to what suspicions it might give rise. Come then, sir, and let me secure your escape—we shall take care to warn you of whatever occurs, and we shall send for you, if there be opportunity."

Athanasia recovered herself almost instantly, when she heard what Silo said.

"We shall meet again," said I.

"Once more," she replied—"at least once more, Valerius."

And I tore myself away from her; and the jailer having once again committed me to the guidance of his child, I was in a few moments conducted to the same postern by which I had been introduced. In a word, I found myself in the court of the Capitol, at the instant when the Prefect, with all his attendants, was entering by the main gate of the Mammertine.

CHAPTER IV.

On reaching home, I was told that Licinius was still absent; and found at the same time a billet upon the table, which informed me that Sabinus had carried Sextus with him to his quarters, and that both expected I would join them there immediately upon my return. I knew not how to refuse compliance, and yet I could not bear the thought of being so far from the Capitol, in case of any message being sent to me from the prison. Since I could do no better, however, I charged Boto to remain in my apartment till sunset, and bring me, without delay, any letter or messenger that might arrive in my absence. Should none such appear within that space, I gave him a note, which I desired him to deliver into the hands of Silo; and having, as I thought, furnished him with sufficient directions how to discharge this commission, I myself took the path to the Prætorian Camp, where I thought it very probable that I might gather some new intelligence as to Cotilius.

The Prætorian who had accompanied Sabinus at my release from the rustic tower, recognized me at the gate, and conducted me immediately to the Centurion, who, to my surprise and displeasure, had directed that I should be ushered without delay to, not his own apartment, but the general table. Here I was received most courteously, however, and hoping the feast was nearly over, took my place near my friend.

Several of those high-fed warriors who had more than once disposed of the empire, were reclining upon rich couches around the board; and their effeminate exterior would, perhaps, have made them less formidable in my eyes, had I not remembered the youth of the great Cæsar, the Parthian retreat of Antony, and the recent death of Otho.[2] There were present, besides, a few casual visiters like ourselves; among others, a sleek Flamen, who reclined on the right hand of the presiding Tribune, and a little bald Greek, who seemed to think it incumbent upon himself to fill up every pause in the conversation, by malicious anecdotes or sarcasms, of which last it was easy to see that the Flamen opposite was a favourite subject. Neither wit nor impiety, however, could make speedy impression upon the smooth-faced Flamen, who seemed to think, if one might judge from his behaviour, that the most acceptable service he could render to the deities, was to do full and devout justice to the gifts of their benevolence.

A very animated discussion concerning the review of the newly-arrived cohorts, (which, I have told you, had taken place that morning by the river side,) relieved for some time the patient Flamen from the attacks of this irreverent person, and engaged the zealous participation of those who had hitherto been the most silent of the company. Sabinus, among the rest, was ready with a world of remarks upon the equipments, the manœuvres, the merits, and the demerits of the troops in question; but something he said was quite at variance with the sentiments of one of his brother Centurions, who disputed with him rather warmly than successfully for a few moments, and at last ended with saying,—"But why should I take so much trouble to discuss the point with you, who, we all know, were thinking of other matters, and saw not much more of the review than if you had been a hundred miles off from it?"

The Centurion coloured a little, and laughed, as it seemed to me, with rather less heartiness than usual; but the disputant pursuing his advantage, said, "Yes, you may laugh if you will; but do you think we are all blind, or do you suppose we are not acquainted with certain particulars? Well, some people dislike the Suburra, but for my part I agree with Sabinus; I think it is one of the genteelest places in Rome, and that there are some of the snuggest houses in it too—and if old men will die, for me, I protest, I don't see why young men should not succeed them." The Centurion laughed again, and natural ruddiness of complexion was, I thought, scarcely quite sufficient to account for the flush on his countenance, as he listened to these innuendos. But the master of the feast cut the matter short, by saying that he had a health to propose, and that he expected all present should receive it with honour.— "Here," said he, "is to the fair lady Rubellia, who is never absent when the Prætorians turn out, and may all things fair and fortunate attend her now and hereafter." I whispered to Sabinus,—"My friend, I think you have really some reason for blushing. If you had no pity on Xerophrastes, you might at least have had some for the pretty widow."

He made no answer to this, and looked, if possible, more confused than ever; but, just at that moment, a soldier came in, and delivered a billet to the presiding Tribune, who handed it to Sabinus immediately after he had read it, and said, loud enough to be heard by all those who sate near him, "I wish the Prince would give some of this work to these new comers. But, indeed, I wonder what Lictors are good for now-a-days; but every thing that these Christians are any way concerned in seems to be a matter of importance."

Sabinus, having read the billet, handed it back again to the Tribune, and said aloud, "*Exit* Cotilius!—Who would not be of the chorus at the falling of that curtain?"

The Tribune shrugged his shoulders, whispered something into the ear of the messenger, and then, dashing more wine into his cup, said, "Rome will never be a quiet place, nor the Prætorian helmet a comfortable head-piece, till these barbarians be extirpated."

The Flamen tossed off a full goblet, and, smiting with his hand upon the table, said, "There spake a true Roman, and a worshipper of the Gods. I rejoice to find that there is still some religion in the world; for, what with skulking Jews on the one hand, and bold blasphemous Cyrenæans on the other, so help me Jupiter, the general prospect is dark enough!"

"In my opinion," quoth the bald Greek, putting on an air of some gravity, "the Jews will have the better of the Cyrenæans. Indeed, I should not be much surprised to see this Christian superstition supplant every other." The Flamen half started from his couch. "You observe, gentlemen," proceeded the Greek,—"what great advantage any new superstition has over any thing of the same sort that is old. We all know, for example, that Isis and Cybele have for many years past left comparatively few worshippers to Mars, Apollo,—even to Jupiter. It is lamentable; but it is true. I have heard that unless on some very great day, a gift is now quite a rarity upon the altar of any of the true ancient deities of Rome. Egypt and Mount Ida have done this; and why should not Palestine succeed as well as either? In the meantime, the enlightened contemplate every different manifestation of the superstitious principle with equal indifference; and, I confess to you, I have been a little surprised to perceive how far Trajan is from imitating their example. But that Chæronæan master of his, that Plutarch, was always an old woman; and I fear the Prince has not been able to shake off the impression of his ridiculous stories."

"Hush!" quoth the master of the day, "if it please you, nothing can be said here against either Trajan or his friends; and, as for Plutarch, he was one of the pleasantest fellows that I ever met with."

Sabinus, desirous of restoring the harmony of the assembly, called forthwith on a musical senior, to join him in a song. The gentleman required solicitation, but at last announced his consent to attempt the female part in the duet of Horace and Lydia. Sabinus, always ready, began to roar out the tender words of regret and expostulation which the most elegant of poets has ascribed to himself; and the delicate squeaking response of our wrinkled Lydia formed an agreeable contrast.

All, in short, were once more in perfect good humour, when another soldier appeared behind the couch of the president, and handed to him what seemed to be another billet of the same complexion. He tossed the paper as before to my friend, who looked very serious as he read it.—"Caius," he whispered, "an additional guard is ordered to the Palatine—and the reason is said to be that the rest of the Christian prisoners are to be examined, within an hour, by the Emperor himself."

I had scarcely had a moment to compose myself, when one of the slaves in attendance signified that a person wished to speak with me in the antichamber. It was Dromo.—"Sir," said he, "I have no time for explanation. Silo wishes to see you—I left Boto with him at the Mammertine."

As we walked from the camp, Sabinus, with his guard, passed without noticing me; and I received some explanations which I must give to you very briefly. Boto, mistrusting his recollection of my instructions, had requested Dromo to assist him in finding his way to the Mammertine; and the Cretan had come to be witness of a scene, which, in spite of his sarcastic disposition, he could not narrate without tokens of sympathy. I mentioned to you that my faithful slave, in coming with me to Rome, had indulged the hope of meeting once more with a brother, who many years before had been carried off from Britain. I smiled when the poor man expressed confidence that he should find out this ere he had been many days in the metropolis of the world. But now, in truth, a fortunate accident had recompensed much ill-regulated search. He had found his brother, and he had found him in the Mammertine. That very brother was Silo, to whose kindness I, and one dearer than myself, had been so deeply indebted. The Cretan, himself a slave and an exile, had partaken in the feelings of the long-lost brothers, and hastened to bring me from the camp, that Boto might be spared the pain of immediately parting from Silo.

CHAPTER V.

I had hurried along the darkening streets, and up the ascent of the Capitoline, scarce listening to the story of the Cretan. On reaching the summit, we found the courts about the Temple of Jupiter already occupied by detachments of foot. I hastened to the Mammertine—and before the postern opened to admit us, the Prætorian squadron had drawn up at the great gate. Sabinus beckoned me to him. "Caius," said he, stooping on his horse, "would to heaven I had been spared this duty! Cotilius comes forth this moment, and then we go back to the Palatine; and I fear—I fear we are to guard thither your Athanasia. If you wish to enter the prison, quicken your steps."

We had scarcely entered the inner-court, ere Sabinus also, and about a score of his Prætorians, rode into it. Silo and Boto were standing together; and both had already hastened towards me; but the jailer, seeing the Centurion, was constrained to part from me with one hurried word:—"Pity me, for I also am most wretched. But you know the way—here, take this key—hasten to my dear lady, and tell her what commands have come."

Alas! I said I to myself, of what tidings am I doomed ever to be the messenger!—but she was alone; and how could I shrink from any pain that might perhaps alleviate hers? I took the key, glided along the corridors, and stood once more at the door of the chamber in which I had parted from Athanasia. No voice answered to my knock; I repeated it three times, and then, agitated with indistinct apprehension, hesitated no longer to open it. No lamp was burning within the chamber, but from without there entered a wavering glare of deep saffron-coloured light, which shewed me Athanasia extended on her couch. Its ominous and troubled hue had no power to mar the image of her sleeping tranquillity. I hung over her for a moment, and was about to disturb that slumber—perhaps the last slumber of peace and innocence— when the chamber-walls were visited with a yet deeper glare. "Caius," she whispered, as I stepped from beside the couch; "why do you leave me? stay, Valerius." I looked back, but her eye-lids were still closed; the same calm smile was upon her dreaming lips. The light streamed redder and more red. All in an instant became as quiet without as within. I approached the window, and saw Cotilius standing in the midst of the court; Sabinus and Silo near him; the horsemen drawn up on either side, and a soldier close behind resting upon an unsheathed sword. I saw the keen blue eye as fierce as ever. I saw that the blood was still fervid in his cheeks: for the complexion of this man was of the same bold and florid brightness so uncommon in Italy, which you have seen represented in the pictures of Sylla, and even the blaze of the torches seemed to strive in vain to heighten its natural scarlet. The soldier had lifted his sword, and my eye was fixed, as by fascination, when suddenly a deep voice was heard amidst the deadly silence—"Cotilius!—look up, Cotilius!"

Aurelius, the Christian priest, standing at an open window, not far distant from that at which I was placed, stretched forth his fettered hand as he spake:—"Cotilius! I charge thee, look upon the hand from which the blessed water of baptism was cast upon thy head. I charge thee, look upon me, and say, ere yet the blow be given, upon what hope thy thoughts are fixed?—Is this sword bared against the rebel of Cæsar, or a martyr of Jesus?—I charge thee, speak; and for thy soul's sake speak truly."

A bitter motion of derision passed over his lips, and he nodded, as if impatiently, to the Prætorian. Instinctively I turned me from the spectacle, and my eye rested again upon the couch of Athanasia—but not upon the vision of her tranquillity. The clap with which the corpse fell upon the stones had, perhaps, reached the sleeping ear, and we know with what swiftness thoughts chase thoughts in the wilderness of dreams. So it was that she started at the very moment when the blow was given; and she whispered—for it was still but a deep whisper—"Spare me, Trajan, Cæsar, Prince—have pity on my youth—strengthen, strengthen me good Lord!—Fie! fie! we must not lie to save life. Felix—Valerius—come close to me, Caius—Fie! let us remember we are Romans—'Tis the trumpet——"

The Prætorian trumpet sounded the march in the court below, and Athanasia, starting from her sleep, gazed wildly around the reddened chamber. The blast of the trumpet was indeed in her ear—and Valerius hung over her—but after a moment the cloud of the broken dream passed away, and the maiden smiled as she extended her hand to me from the couch, and began to gather up the ringlets that floated all down upon her shoulder. She blushed and smiled mournfully, and asked me hastily whence I came, and for what purpose I had come; but before I could answer, the glare that was yet in the chamber seemed anew to be perplexing her: and she gazed from me to the red walls, and from them to me again: and then once more the trumpet was blown, and Athanasia sprung from her couch. I know not in what terms I was essaying to tell her what was the truth, but I know that ere I had said many words, she discovered my meaning. For a moment she looked deadly pale, in spite of all the glare of the torch-beams; but she recovered herself, and said in a voice that sounded almost as if it came from a light heart,—"But Caius, I must not go to Cæsar, without having at least a garland on my head. Stay here, Valerius, and I shall be ready anon—quite ready."

It seemed to me as if she were less hasty than she had promised, yet many minutes elapsed not ere she returned. She plucked a blossom from her hair as she drew near to me, and said, "Take it: you must not refuse one token more; this also is a sacred gift. Caius, you must learn never to look upon it without kissing these red streaks—these blessed streaks of the Christian flower."

I took the flower from her hand, and pressed it to my lips; and I remembered that the very first day I saw Athanasia, she had plucked such an one, when apart from all the rest, in the gardens of Capito. I told her what I remembered; and it seemed as if the little circumstance had called up all the image of peaceful days; for once more sorrowfulness gathered upon her countenance. If the tear was ready, however, it was not permitted to drop; and Athanasia returned again to her flower.

"Do you think there are any of them in Britain?" said she; "or do you think that they would grow there? You must go to my dear uncle, and he will not deny you, when you tell him that it is for my sake he is to give you some of his. They call it the Passion-flower—'tis an emblem of an awful thing. Caius, these purple streaks are like trickling drops; and here, look ye, they are all round the flower. Is it not very like a bloody crown upon a pale brow? I will take one of them in my hand, too, Caius; and methinks I shall not disgrace myself when I look upon it, even though Trajan should be frowning upon me."

I had not the heart to interrupt her; but heard silently all she said, and I thought she said the words quickly and eagerly, as if she feared to be interrupted.

The old priest came into the chamber while she was yet speaking so, and said very composedly, "Come, my dear child, our friend has sent again for us, and the soldiers have been waiting already some space, who are to convey us to the Palatine. Come, children, we must part for a moment—perhaps it may be but for a moment—and Valerius may remain here till we return to him. Here, at least, dear Caius, you shall have the earliest tidings, and the surest."

The good man took Athanasia by the hand, and she, smiling now at length more serenely than ever, said only, "Farewell, then, Caius, for a little moment!" And so, drawing her veil over her face, she passed away from before me, giving, I think, more support to the ancient Aurelius than, in her turn, she received from him. I began to follow them, but the priest waved his hand as if to forbid me:—the door closed after them, and I was alone.

CHAPTER VI.

I know not, my friends, how to proceed with the narrative of what followed. Thoughts, passions, fears, hopes, succeeding so rapidly, give to that strange night, when I look back upon it through the vista of years, the likeness of some incoherent, agonizing dream. Much, without doubt, of what passed within my own mind I have forgotten; but it seems to me as if what I saw or heard were still present in the distinctness of reality. That chamber in the Mammertine! Its walls are before me blazing with the reflection of torch-light, and then again, all dim and shadowy—the stars shining feebly upon them from the twilight sky—every thing around lonely and silent, except the voice of Silo's little maiden,—bewailing no doubt in her privacy the departure of Athanasia.

Her father after a little time rejoined me. "Sir," said he, "all is now quiet here; will you walk with me towards the Palatine, that we may at least be near to know what is reported of their proceedings? My brother will stay here till we return."

We soon had descended from the Capitoline, passed through the silent Forum, and gained the brow of the opposite eminence, where, as shortly before at the Mammertine, all was light and tumult. Every court was guarded with soldiery, and groups of busy men were passing continually about the imperial gates and porticos. Silo led me round and round the buildings, till we reached what seemed an abandoned wing. "Sir," said he, "you do not know more familiarly the house in which you were born and reared, than I do every corner within these wide walls. But I have not crossed the threshold since the day Cæsar died.—I was the slave of Domitian, and he gave me my freedom.—He was kind to his household."

We entered beneath a small portico—and Silo drew a key from his bosom. The lock, after two or three trials, yielded to its pressure. A large empty hall received us, the circumference of which was scarcely visible by the light of the newly-risen moon, streaming down from a cupola.

Another and another sombre chamber we in like manner traversed, till at length Silo opened one so comparatively light, that I started back, apprehending we had intruded farther than he intended. A second glance, however, seemed to indicate that we were still in the region of desolation, for a statue lay in the midst of the floor, one of its limbs snapped over, as if it had fallen and been permitted to remain.

"Where are we, Silo?" I whispered, "what means this unnatural light among so many symptoms of confusion?"

"Sir," said the freedman, "this is the place in which alone Domitian used to eat and sleep, and walk about for the last months of his life, when he was jealous of all men; and he contrived these walls, covered all over with the shining Ethiopian stone, that no one might be able to approach him without being discovered. Even when a slave entered, he would start as if every side of the chamber had been invaded by some host of men; fifty different reflections of one trembling eunuch. It was, they say, behind this shattered piece of marble that he ran when he had felt the first treacherous blow. Yonder in the corner is the couch he slept upon, and he had always a dagger under his head, and he called to the little page that was waiting upon him to fetch it from the place; but the scabbard only remained; and then in came Parthenius and Claudianus, and the gladiator, and the rest, who soon finished what the cunning Stephanus had begun. Let us go on;—we have not yet reached the place to which I wished to bring you—but it is not far off now."

With this Silo walked to the end of the melancholy chamber, and pressing upon a secret spring, where no door was apparent, opened the way into a room, darker and smaller than any of those through which we had come. He then said to me, "Now, sir, you must not venture upon one whisper more— you touch on the very heart of Domitian's privacy. It is possible that the place I have been leading you to may have been shut up—it may exist no longer; but the state in which all things are found here makes me think it more likely that Trajan has never been master of its secret. And in that case, we shall be able both to see and to hear, without being either seen or heard, exactly as Domitian used to do, when there was any council held either in the Mars or the Apollo."

I started at the boldness of the project which now, for the first time, I understood; but Silo laid his finger on his lip again,—cautiously lifted up a piece of the dark-red cloth with which this chamber was hung,—and essayed another spring in the pannelling beneath. Total darkness appeared to be beyond; but the jailer motioning to me to remain for a moment where I was, and to keep up the hanging, glided boldly into the recess. I wondered how he should tread so lightly, that I could not perceive the least echo; but this no longer surprised me, when I had the sign to follow. The floor felt beneath my foot as if it were stuffed like a pillow; and, after I had dropped the hanging, every thing was totally dark, as it had at first appeared to me, except only at certain points, separate and aloft, which let in gleams of light, manifestly artificial. Silo, taking hold of me by the hand, conducted me up some steps towards the nearest of these tiny apertures; and, as I approached it, I heard distinctly the voices of persons talking together in the room beyond. I did not draw my breath, you may well believe, with much boldness; but my eye was soon fixed at one of the crevices, and, after the first dazzle was over, I saw clearly. Silo took his station by my side, gazing through another of these loop-holes, which, that you may understand every thing, were evidently quite concealed among the rich carved-work of an ivory cornice.

The chamber was lighted by three tall candelabra of silver, close beside one of which was placed a long table covered with an infinity of scrolls and tablets. One person, who had his back turned towards us, was writing, and two others, in one of whom I instantly recognized the Emperor, were walking up and down on the other side.

"No, Palma," said Trajan, for it was that old favourite whom he addressed—"I have made up my mind as to this matter. I shall never permit any curious inquisition as to private opinion. Every man has a right, without question, to think—to believe—exactly what pleases him; and I shall concede as much in favour of every woman, Palma, if you will have it so. But it is totally a different affair, when the fact, no matter how, is forced upon my knowledge, that a subject, no matter who or what he be—a subject of the Roman empire, refuses to comply with the first, the elemental, and the most essential of the laws. The man—aye or the woman—that confesses in my presence contempt for the deities whom the commonwealth acknowledges in every step of its procedure—that person is a criminal; and I cannot dismiss him unpunished, without injuring the commonwealth by the display of weakness in its chief. As for these poor fanatics themselves, it is the penalty of my station that I must control my feelings."

"But you are satisfied, my lord," said Palma, "that these people are quite innocent as to Cotilius's designs; and as it was upon that suspicion they were apprehended, perhaps it may be possible——"

"Yes, Palma," interrupted the Prince; "quite possible and quite easy, provided they will condescend to save themselves by the most trivial acknowledgment of the sort which, I repeat to you, I do and must consider as absolutely necessary. And women too—and girls forsooth—I suppose you would have me wait till the very urchins on the street were gathering into knots to discuss the nature of the Gods.—Do you remember what Plato says?"—

"No, my lord, I do not know to what you refer."

"Why, Plato says that nobody can ever understand any thing accurately about the Deity, and that, if he could, he would have no right to communicate his discoveries to others; the passage is in the Timæus, and Tully has translated it besides. And is it to be endured that these modest fanatics are to do every hour what the Platos and the Ciceros spoke of in such terms as these? I think you carry your tolerance a little farther than might have been expected from a disciple of the Academy."

"I despise them, my lord, as much as yourself; but, to tell you the truth, it is this young lady that moves me to speak thus—and I crave your pardon, if I have spoken with too much freedom.—Her father was one of the best soldiers Titus had."

"The more is the pity, Palma. Have you ever seen the girl yourself? Did you give orders that she should be brought hither? I have not the least objection that you should have half an hour, or an hour if you will, to talk with her quietly; perhaps your eloquence may have the effect we desire."

"I doubt it, my lord, I greatly doubt it," he replied; "but, indeed, I know not whether she be yet here—Did you not send to the Mammertine?"

The man writing at the table, to whom this interrogation was addressed, said, "I believe, sir, both this lady and the old man that was in the same prison are now in attendance." And upon this Trajan and Palma retired together towards the farther end of the apartment, where they conversed for some minutes in a tone so low, that I could not understand any thing of what was said. Trajan at length turned from his favourite with an air, as I thought, of some little displeasure, and said aloud, coming back into the middle of the room,—"I know it is so; but what is that to the affair in hand? I am very sorry for the Sempronii, but I doubt if even they would be so unreasonable as you are."

"Will you not see the poor girl yourself, Cæsar?"

"You do not need to be told, that my seeing her would only make it more difficult for me to do that, which, seeing or not seeing her, I know to be my duty. Do you accept of my proposal? Are you willing to try the effect of your own persuasion? I promise you, if you succeed, I shall rejoice not less heartily than yourself; but it is rather too much to imagine that I am personally to interfere about such an affair as this—an affair which, the more I think of it, seems to me to be the more perfectly contemptible. Nay, do not suppose it is this poor girl I am talking of—I mean the whole of this Jewish, this Christian affair, which does indeed appear to me to be the most bare-faced absurdity, that ever was permitted to disturb the tranquillity of the empire. A mean and savage nation have but just suffered the penalty of obstinacy and treachery alike unequalled, and from them—from the scattered embers of this extinguished fire, we are to allow a new flame to be kindled—ay, and that in the very centre of Rome. I tell you, that if my own hand were to be scorched in the cause, I would disperse this combustion to the winds of heaven; I tell you, that I stand here Cæsar, and that I would rather be chained to the oar, than suffer, while the power to prevent it is mine, the tiniest speck to be thrown upon the Roman majesty. By all the Gods, Palma, it is enough to make a man sick to think of the madness that is in this world, and of the iron arguments by which we are compelled to keep those from harming us, that at first sight of them excite no feeling but our pity. But I am weary of these very names of Palestine—Jew—Christian. Go to this foolish girl, and try what you can make of her; I give you fair warning—no breeders of young Christians here."

CHAPTER VII.

Cornelius Palma, after the Prince retired, was apparently for some space busied with his reflections. He then talked in a whispering manner with the secretary, and moved towards an extremity of the chamber. But the moment Silo perceived this, he plucked my sleeve, and drew me to the other end of our closet, where, as I have told you, the light had admittance in a similar manner. Here another of the imperial apartments was visible in equal distinctness; and in it appeared Athanasia and her friend, as waiting now at length in entire composure the moment when they should be summoned.

Palma entering, both rose, and he, returning their salutation, remained before them for a moment in silence, his eyes fixed on Athanasia. It was to Aurelius, nevertheless, that his first words were addressed:—"From what has been reported of your behaviour at the execution of Cotilius, I fear there is nothing to be gained by speaking to *you*, concerning the only means by which your own safety can yet be secured. You are obstinate, old man, in your superstition?"—"Noble Palma," said the priest, "contempt is the only thing I fear from men. But I thank my God, that it is the only thing I have it in my power to avoid."—"I will not argue with you," answered Palma, pointing to a door near him:—"It was not with any purpose of bending you, that I undertook this painful office. I desire to speak in freedom with one whose case is, I trust, less hopeless."

The old man, pointing to his fetters, said meekly, "Let them guard me whither it pleases you."

"Sir," said Athanasia, "I pray you let Aurelius remain; imagine not that I shall either hear or answer less freely because of my friend's presence."

"He will, at least, retire to the other end of the chamber," said Palma—"and interfere no farther."

The priest drew back;—Athanasia, on her part, seeing that Palma hesitated, and seemed at a loss how to begin, said to him in a tone of modest composure:—"Noble sir, if your purpose be indeed as kind as I think it is, I pray you spare me at least the pain that is needless, and spare yourself what I am sure is painful to you. You see my youth and my sex, and it is not unnatural for you to think as you do; but know that my faith is fixed, and that I hope I shall not be deserted, when I strive even at the last moment to do it no dishonour."

"This gray beard," said Palma, "has made you, then, thoroughly a Christian?"

"I would it were so," she answered—"I would to God it were so!"

"Lady," resumed Palma, "we have knowledge both of your father's high character, and of your own amiable dispositions. If you persist in this manner, you will give grief to Cæsar; and as for your family, have you yet seriously considered into what misery they must be plunged?"

"Sir," she replied, "this is cruel kindness. I have considered all things."

"Young maiden," continued Palma, "the touch of the physician's knife is painful, yet his hand must not falter. But I have sent for those, who, I hope, may speak more effectually."

The Senator turned from the pedestal on which he had been leaning, and walked to the door over against where Aurelius was sitting: and after a moment had elapsed, there entered, even as I had anticipated, both her uncles, Lucius and Velius. Behind them came, wrapped in her consecrated veil, the Priestess of Apollo; and last of all, gazing wildly around, her apparel disordered, the friend of her youth, the sister of her bosom,—she to whom in all things, save one, Athanasia's heart had ever been laid open. The two Patricians advanced, deeply dejected, towards the place where Athanasia stood waiting their approach. The stately Priestess, walking yet more slowly, lifted the veil from her face, which was pale and calm as marble. But when the youthful companion at last rested her eye upon her friend, and the fettered hands clasped together on that bosom, she rushed past them all, and was folded in a cold embrace; for though Athanasia pressed Sempronia to her bosom, I saw also that she trembled from head to foot, and that her eyes were riveted on those who approached with seriousness more terrible than the passion of young sympathy.

"Athanasia," said Lucius, taking her by the hand, "look not upon us thus; we come as to a daughter."

"Dearest," said old Velius, "listen to thy true friends. Do you put more faith in the words of strangers than in the blood of kindred—the affection of your father's brothers—the guardians of his dear orphan?"

"Wo is me!" said Athanasia—"O God, strengthen me! Why, oh, why am I forced to wound these kind hearts! Have pity upon me, have pity upon me— you know not what you speak of, else you would all be silent."

"Weep," said the Priestess; "weep, and weep largely. There is yet time to repent. Abjure this madness; let the last of your tears be shed upon the altars of your paternal Gods, and they also will be merciful. Nay, tremble not when you hear my voice, Athanasia. I love you as tenderly as the rest, and if you have deceived me also, I have long since pardoned."

The Priestess kissed her forehead; and she bowed her head, weeping at length audibly. But Athanasia speedily recovered herself, and gently removing the hands of Sempronia, stood erect again in the midst.

"Dear friends," said she, "the moments you have to be with me are numbered; what avails it that they should be spent in words that can have no effect? I have been baptized in the name of the one true God—I have partaken of the symbols of the Christian mystery—and I have no more power to bring myself out of this peril, than he that stands in the front rank—without sword or buckler—deprived of all things but his honour."

"Athanasia!" said Velius, "alas! my dear girl, what madness is this? Do you hold yourself wiser than all the wise men, and all the good, and all the great men that have ever lived in Rome? Do you deem yourself able to penetrate mysteries from which all the sages of the earth have retreated with humility? Consider with yourself—remember the modesty that might be becoming in your tender years—and, I must speak the truth, your ignorance."

"Oh, sir!" she answered, "believe not that I have been brought into this place, because of my being puffed up with emptiness of conceit. I know well that I am a poor, young, unlearned creature; but God gives not according to our deserts; and because I am poor and ignorant, must I therefore reject the promise of his riches, and the great light that has been manifested to me,—which, would to God it had also been to you, despite the perils which a dark world has thrown around it."

"O Athanasia!" said young Sempronia, "I know the secrets of your heart, although you have kept from me some of them. Think, dear sister, of all the love that we bear to you—and, oh! think of Valerius."

"The more, then, is the sacrifice!" said Athanasia. "Caius Valerius also is a Christian—at least I hope in God he will soon be sealed into our brotherhood."

"Amen! amen!" said Aurelius.

The Priestess turned round when he uttered this, and observing that he also was fettered, "Blasphemer!" cried she, "behold the end of your frenzy. Your eyes are dim, your clay is already yearning, it may be, to be sprinkled into ashes; but behold your victim. Ye Gods that see all things, have mercy upon the errors of deceived, ensnared, murdered youth! Hoary Apostate! feeble though you be, may strength be given to you in anger, that you may taste the full struggle and the true agony. May you be strong to wrestle, that you may fall slowly, and feel your fall! Would to the Gods, just and merciful, that you might struggle and fall alone!"

"Rash woman," said the manacled Saint, "most surely your last wish is mine. But why is it that you have come hither with cruel words, to imbitter equally the last moments of a life that is dear to you, and a life that you despise? You speak of ignorance and of deceit. Little know ye who are the deceived. We are the servants of the living God, whose light will soon shine abroad among the nations, and quench glimmering tapers, fashioned with the hands of men, with which, hitherto, ye have sat contented amidst darkness. Cæsar may bind and slay—but think ye that the spirit is his to do with it what he will? Think ye that chains and dungeons, and the sword of man can alter the course of things that are to be, or shake from its purpose the will of Him, in whom, blind and ignorant, ye refuse to behold the image of the Maker of all—shutting eyes, and ears, and your proud hearts; and blaspheming against the God of heaven, whose glory ye ascribe to stocks and stones, and to the ghosts of wicked and bloody tyrants, long since mouldered into dust,—and to the sun, and the moon, and the stars of the sky, which God set there to rule the day and the night, even as he lets loose his winds to scatter the leaves of the forest, and to lift up the waves of the great deep?—Leave us, I beseech you.—The young and the old are alike steadfast, for God is our strength, and he bestows it on them that ask for it in the name of the Redeemer."

"Peace, thou accursed!" said the Priestess; "I serve the altar, and came not hither to hear the Gods of heaven and earth insulted by the lips of hardened impiety.—Athanasia! will you go with us, or will you stay here, and partake the fate of this madman?"

"O God!" cried the maiden; "how shall I speak that they may at length hear me!—Friends—dear friends—if you have any love, any compassion, I pray you kiss me once, and bid me farewell kindly, and lay my ashes in the sepulchre of my fathers—beside the urn of my mother. Fear not that I will disturb the repose of the place—I shall die in anger against no one, and I shall have rest at length when I am relieved from this struggle. Pardon, if in any thing besides I ever gave you pain—remember none of my offences but this—think of me kindly. And go now, dear friends; kiss my lips in love, and leave me to bear that which must be borne, since there is no escape but in lying, and in baseness, and in utter perdition here and hereafter. May the Lord strengthen his day soon, and may ye all bless the full light, although now ye are startled by the redness of the dawn! Farewell—kiss me, Velius—kiss me, Lucius—my aunt also will kiss me."

They did kiss her, and tears were mingled with their embraces; and they said no more, but parted from her where she was. Palma himself lifted the desolate Sempronia from the ground, and he and her father carried her away senseless, her tresses sweeping the pavement as they moved.

The prisoners were alone. "The moment is come," said Silo; "now, sir, prepare yourself to risk every thing where every thing may be gained."

He did not whisper this, but spake the words boldly; and ere I could either answer any thing, or form any guess as to his meaning, he had leaped down from my side, and thrown open another secret spring. Silo rushed in, and I followed him. It was all done so rapidly, that I scarce remember how. I cannot, indeed, forget the wild and vacant stare of Athanasia, the cry which escaped from her lips, nor the fervour with which she sunk into my embrace. But all the rest is a dream. The door closed swiftly behind us;—swiftly I ran, bearing the maiden in my arms through all the long course of those deserted chambers. Door after door flew open before us. All alike, breathless and speechless, we ran on. We reached the last of the chambers, the wide and echoing saloon, ere my heart had recovered from the first palpitation of surprise; and a moment after we breathed once more the free air of heaven.

"Stop not," said I, "for the sake of God. Hasten, Silo, it is you that must guide us."—"Ha!" said he, "already have they perceived it? Great God! after all, is it in vain?" We heard shout echoing shout, and the clapping of doors. "Treachery, treachery! Escape, escape!"—and trumpet and horn mingled in the clamour of surprise, wrath, terror. "Ride, ride," screamed a voice high over all the tumult—"ride this instant—guard every avenue—search every corner—the wing of Domitian!"

"We are lost," said Silo;—"we can never reach the gate."

"To the Temple of Apollo!" said I; "the Priestess will shelter Athanasia."

"Thank God," whispered Silo, "there is one chance more."—And so we began again to run swiftly, keeping close beneath the shaded wall of the edifice, and then threading many narrow passages of the hanging gardens of Adonis, we reached indeed the adjoining court of the Palatine, and found ourselves, where all was as yet silent and undisturbed, under the sacred portico. The great gate was barred. Athanasia herself pointed out a postern, and we stood within the temple.

It was filled as before, (for here the alternations of day and night made no difference,) with the soft and beautiful radiance proceeding from the tree of lamps. But the fire on the altar burned high and clear, as if recently trimmed, and behind its blaze stood one of the ministering damsels. Her hand held the chain of the censer, and she was swinging it slowly, while the clouds of fragrant smoke rolled high up above the flames;—and the near light, and the intervening smoke, and the occupation with which she was busied, prevented her from at first perceiving what intrusion had been made on the solitude of the place. Athanasia ran on, and clasping the knees of the astonished girl with her fettered hands, began to implore her by the memory of old affection and companionship, and for the sake of all that was dear to her, to give escape, if escape were possible—at least to give concealment. The girl had dropped the censer from her hand, and seemed utterly confused, and unable to guess the meaning of what she saw and heard. "Lady!" cried Silo, falling by the side of Athanasia—"Oh, lady! stand not here considering, for this is the very moment of utmost peril. Behold these fetters—they tell you from what her flight hath been."

The girl grasped the hands of Athanasia, and gazed upon the manacles, and still seemed quite amazed and stupified; and while Silo was renewing his entreaties, we heard suddenly some one trying to open the postern which the freedman had fastened behind us. Once and again a violent hand essayed to undo the bolt, and then all was quiet again. And in a moment after, the great gate was itself thrown open, and the Priestess entered, followed by her two brothers, who supported between them the yet faint and weeping young Sempronia.

In a moment Athanasia had rushed across the temple, and knelt down with her forehead to the ground, close by where the feet of her haughty kinswoman were planted.

"Unhappy!" said she; "by what magic do I behold you here? How have you escaped? and why—oh! why fled hither? Think ye, that here, in the Temple of Apollo, the priestess of an insulted God can give shelter to blasphemy flying from the arms of justice? Ha! and he, too, is here!—Outcast! how durst thou? Speak, unhappy Athanasia—every thing is dark, and I see only that you have brought hither———"—"Friends, friends—oh! blame them not," interrupted the maiden—"Oh! blame them not for venturing all to save me. Oh! help us, and help speedily—for they search every where, and they may speedily be here."

"Here?" cried the priestess—"who, I pray you? Ha! run, fly, bolt the door. If Cæsar speaks, I answer."

The ring of arms, and voices of angry men, were heard distinctly approaching. In a moment more we could hear them talking together beneath the very portico, and trying, in their turn, to thrust open the massive valves of the temple. "Who calls there?" cried the Priestess—"Who calls and knocks? If a suppliant approaches, let him come as a suppliant."—"Castor! We are no suppliants," answered a rough voice:—"Dead or alive, you must give up our pretty Christians. Come, come, my sly masters; yield, yield, there is no flying from Cæsar."

"Peace, insolent!" quoth the Priestess—"peace, and begone! This is the Temple of Apollo, and ye shall find no Christians here. Turn, rude man, and dread the arm that guarded Delphos!" And saying so, she at length lifted up Athanasia, and moved towards the other extremity of the fane, where, as I had occasion once to tell you before, the private chamber of the Priestess was situated on the right hand beyond the statue of Apollo. In passing the image she halted an instant, laid her hand on her eyes, and kissed its feet, with a murmur of supplication; but that was her only utterance: and the rest gave none.

She thus led us across the chamber in which, on a former day, I had heard Athanasia sing; and in like manner, having taken a lamp in her hand, on through the long passages which conduct towards the receptacle wherein the Sybilline prophecies are said to be preserved. She opened the door which she had, on that earlier day, told me led into the repository of those mysterious scrolls. Two inner doors appeared before us; that to the left she opened likewise, and we perceived, descending from its threshold, a dark flight of steps, as if down into the centre of the rock.

"Here," said she, as she paused, and held the lamp over the gloomy perspective—"here, at last, I leave you, having already done too much, whether I think of the God I serve, or of Trajan, or of myself. But for the blood of kindred not little may be dared. Go with her, since you have come with her. More I cannot do. Here—take this lamp; the door at the bottom is fastened only from within; let it fall behind you, and make what speed you may."

"One thing," said Silo, "had better be done ere you depart;" and so, very adroitly, he, by means of his jailer's key, relieved both of them from their fetters. He then whispered, "Go no farther, Valerius; you may rest assured that no one suspects us." I saw that he designed to return into the courts of the Palatine, and so proceed homewards, as if ignorant of every thing that had occurred. The good freedman had no other course to pursue, either in duty to himself or to his family. But for me, all my cares were here. I squeezed by the hand both Lucius and Velius, and both warmly returned my pressure. The Priestess gave the lamp into my hand, and the door was shut upon us; and we began, with hearts full of thankfulness, but not yet composed enough to taste of lightness—with thankfulness uppermost in our confused thoughts, and with no steady footsteps, to descend into the unknown abyss.

CHAPTER VIII.

The steps were abrupt and narrow; but in a few minutes our feet became accustomed to them, and we descended rapidly. After we had done so for some time, we found ourselves in a low chamber of oblong form, in the midst of which an iron stake was fixed into the floor, having chains of ponderous workmanship attached to its centre, and over against it, a narrow chair of the same metal, it also immoveable. I asked Athanasia to repose herself here for a moment; for it was evident that the tumultuous evening had much worn out her strength. But she said, shuddering, "No, not here, Valerius; I never saw this place before, but the aspect of it recals to me fearful stories. Here, wo is me, many a poor wretch has expiated offences against the dignity of the shrine, and the servants of its Demon. My father knows, I doubt not, some humble Christian roof, beneath which we may be safe until the first search be over. Let us breathe at least the open air, and He who has hitherto helped will not desert us."

"No, my children," said Aurelius; "let us not linger here. Christian roofs, indeed, are known to me, both humble and lofty; but how to know how far suspicion may already have extended?—or why should we run any needless risk of bringing others into peril, having by God's grace escaped ourselves, when all hope as to this life had been utterly taken away? Let us quit these foul precincts—let us quit them speedily—but let us not rashly be seen in the busy city. There is a place known to me, (and Athanasia also has visited it heretofore,) where safety, I think, may be expected, and where, if danger do come, it shall find no unnecessary victim. Let us hasten to the Esquiline."

"Thanks, father!" said Athanasia; "there no one will seek us: there best shall our thanksgivings and our prayers be offered. We will rest by the sepulchre of our friend, and Valerius will go into the city, and procure what things are needful."

We began the descent of another flight of steps, beyond the dark chamber. This terminated at length in a door, the bolts of which being withdrawn, we found ourselves beneath the sky of night, at the extremity of one of the wooded walks that skirt the southern base of the Palatine—the remains of the Assyrian magnificence which had once connected the Golden House of Nero with the more modest structures of his predecessors. I wrapped Athanasia in my cloak, and walked beside her in my tunic; and Aurelius conducted us by many windings, avoiding as far as was possible the glare of the Suburra, all round about the edge of the city, to the gardens which hang over the wall by the great Esquiline Gate.

"Is it here," said I, when he paused—"is it in the midst of this splendour that you hope to find a safe obscurity?"

"Have patience," replied the old man; "you are a stranger:—and yet you speak what I should have heard without surprise from many that have spent all their days in Rome. Few, indeed, ever think of entering a region which is almost as extensive as the city itself, and none, I think, are acquainted with all its labyrinths."

So saying, the priest led the way into one of the groves. Its trees formed a dense canopy overhead; nor could we pass without difficulty among the close-creeping undergrowth. At length we reached the centre of the wide thicket, and found a small space of soil comparatively bare. The light of moon and star plunged down there among the surrounding blackness of boughs, as into some deep well, and shewed the entrance of a natural grotto, which had, indeed, all the appearance of oblivion and utter desertedness. "Confess," said he, "that I did not deceive you. But there is no hurry now; let me taste once more the water of this forgotten spring."

I had not observed a small fountain hard by the mouth of the grotto, which, in former days, had evidently been much cared for, although now almost all its surface was covered with leaves. The marble margin shewed dim with moss; nor had a statue just within the entrance of the grot escaped this desolation. Damp herbage obscured its recumbent limbs, and the Parian stone had lost its brightness. "You can scarcely see where the inscription was," said Aurelius, "for the letters are filled up or effaced; but I remember when many admired it, and I can still repeat the lines—

'Nymph of the grot, these sacred springs I keep,
And to the murmur of these waters sleep;
Ah! spare my slumbers, gently tread the cave,
And drink in silence, or in silence lave.'[4]

Little did they, who graved this command, conjecture how well it was to be obeyed. But there should be another inscription.—Ay, here it is," said he, stepping on a long flat piece of marble among the weeds. I was advancing to examine the stone, but the old man stopped me:—"What avails it to spell out the record? Do you remember the story of Asinius? It was within this very cavern that the man was butchered;[5] and now you see both he and his monument are alike sinking into forgetfulness. I believe, however, the monument itself must bear the blame in part; for I have heard my father say that he had been told this was a favourite fountain until that slaughter."

Athanasia meantime had sat down by the grotto, and was laving her forehead with the water of the solitary fountain. Aurelius, too, dipped his hands in the well, and tasted of the water, and then turning to me, he said, with a grave smile, "Valerius, methinks you are religious in your regard for the slumbers of the nymph." He whispered something into the ear of Athanasia, and received an answer from her in the same tone, ere he proceeded:—"Draw near—fear not that I shall do any thing rashly—we owe all things to your love—we know we do; but speak plainly.—Do you indeed desire to be admitted into the fellowship of the true Faith? Let not the symbol of regeneration be applied hastily. Without doubt, great were my joy might my hands be honoured to shed the blessed water of baptism upon the brow of dear Valerius."

"Caius," said Athanasia, "I know God has touched your heart; why should this be delayed any longer? You have shared the perils of the faithful. Partake with them in good as in evil. Hesitate no longer; God will perfect what hath been so begun."

"Dearest friends!" said I, "if I hesitate, it is only because I doubt if I am yet worthy. Surely I believe that this is the right faith, and that there is no God but He whom you worship."

"Acceptable is humility in the sight of Heaven," said the priest; and he rose up from the place where he had been sitting, and began, standing by the margin of the well, to pour out words of thanksgiving and supplication, such as I have never heard equalled by any lips but his. The deep calm voice of the holy man sounded both sweet and awful in the breathless air of midnight. The tall black trees stood all around, like a wall, cutting us off from the world, and from the thoughts of the world; and the moon, steady in the serene sky, seemed to shower down light and beauty upon nothing in all the wide earth, but that little guarded space of our seclusion. I stepped into the cool water of the fountain. The old man stooped over me, and sprinkled the drops upon my forehead, and the appointed words were repeated. Aurelius kissed my brow, as I came forth from the water, and Athanasia also drew slowly near, and then hastily she pressed my forehead with trembling lips.

We sate down together by the lonely well; and we sate in silence, for I could not be without many thoughts partaken by none but myself, at the moment when I had thus, in the face of God and man, abjured the faith of all my fathers, and passed into the communion of the despised and persecuted Few; nor did either the priest or Athanasia essay to disturb my meditations.

There were moments (for I must not conceal from you my weakness) in which I could scarcely help suspecting that I had done something that was wrong. I thought of my far distant mother; and I could not reflect without pain upon the feelings with which I had every reason to suppose that she, kind as she was, and merciful in all things, would have contemplated the scene which had passed. I thought of my dead parent too; and that was yet more serious and awful. The conviction of my own mind, in obedience to which I had acted, relieved me, however, from any feelings of self-reproach.—My father is dead, said I to myself—He died in ignorance, and he has not been judged according to the light, which never shone upon him. But now—Oh, yes! it must be so—the darkness has passed from before his eyes; and, if the spirits of the departed ever visit, in the dim hours of silence, those who were dear to them upon this earth, surely his venerable shade stood by smiling while the forehead of his son was laved with these blessed waters.

Meantime, minutes—hours, perhaps, glided away, while troubled, and solemn, and tender thoughts thus occupied by turns my bosom. The old priest sate by me, his arms folded on his breast, gazing upwards upon the spangled glories of the firmament. Athanasia was on the other side, close by the statue of the Sleeping Naiad. From time to time, she too would fix her eyes for a moment upon the untroubled beauty of the moon; and then, stooping over the brink of the fountain, once and again I saw its calm dark waters rippled beneath her by the dropping of a tear.

"My children," said, at length, Aurelius, "methinks more sadness is amongst us than might suit the remembrance of what Providence has done for us, since the sun that went down upon fear and sorrow is about to rise upon many fair hopes. I am old; the world lies behind me, save a remnant I know not how brief. It lies all before you, and you have a light whereby to look upon it, which my early day wanted. I trust that soon, very soon, ye shall both be far from this city—I say both, for I know well, go where ye may, ye will go together. As for me, my lot is cast here, and here I will remain. Caius, you must leave us betimes—you must return into the city, and consult with your friends and hers, how best Athanasia may be conveyed safely beyond the bounds of Italy. Cæsar, indeed, rules every where; but at a distance from Rome suspicion is, at least, less watchful; and there is no precept given by which ye are bound to seek unnecessary perils."

"Aurelius," said I—"dear father, think not but that I have already been considering all these things anxiously. As soon as I have seen you safely placed within the retreat of which you have spoken, I shall hasten to Licinius, my kinsman, who already, indeed, must be feeling no small anxiety from my absence. I shall speak with him, and with both the Sempronii. My own errand to the capital I value as nothing, and I shall be ready on the instant, if Athanasia herself will consent to partake my voyage."

"Yes, Caius," said the father—"this child of God will be your wife, and ye will both serve the Lord many days, amidst the quiet valleys of your far off island.—Nay, daughter, do not weep, for these are not common days, and you must follow without fear the path which God's providence points out.

Before ye go, my children, I myself shall join your hands in the name of our God."

Athanasia heard his words, and saw me gaze upon his face, but she made no reply, except by the tears which Aurelius rebuked, and a timid, yet grave and serious pressure, with which she, when he had made an end of speaking, returned the fervid pressure of my hand upon hers.

"Children," said the old man, "there is no need of words when hearts are open—the tears that ye have shed together are the best earnest of the vows that ye shall ere long, I trust, pronounce. Yet, let no rashness attend your steps. The dawn must now be near, and Athanasia and I had better retire into our protecting covert. Valerius will leave us, and return at eventide. Till then, fasting and praying, we shall give thanks for our deliverance, and ask the aid that alone is precious for the time that yet remains."

I had, fortunately, brought all the way with me the lamp which lighted our steps down the mysterious staircase, from the shrine of Apollo. Some little oil still remained within it, and Aurelius soon struck a light, and, taking it in his hand, began to enter before us the dark cavern, by the mouth of which we had all this while been sitting. You, perhaps, have never heard of those strange excavations, the whole extent of which has probably never been known to any one person, but which appear, indeed, as the priest had said, to be almost co-extensive with the great city beneath which they are placed. For what purpose they were at first dug, is a subject which has long exercised the conjectures of those fond of penetrating into the origin of things, and the customs of antiquity. By some it is supposed, that in such caverns, winding far away into unseen recesses, the first rude inhabitants of Italy, like the Troglodytes of Upper Egypt and Ethiopia, had fixed their miserable abodes. Others assert, that they owe their origin merely to the elder builders of the visible Rome, who, to avoid marring the surface of the earth, were contented to bring their materials of sand, clay, and stone, from these subterraneous labyrinths, which so grew with the progress of diligence, and with the extension of the city itself. Perhaps both conjectures may have some foundation in truth; but be that as it may, there is no question, that, in succeeding times, these catacombs had been widened and extended, to serve as places of burial for the mortal remains of the poor citizens. And now is it to be wondered at, that here, in regions so obscure and dismal, the persecuted adherents of the Faith should have frequently sought not only resting-places for the bodies of their dead, but even shelter for themselves, amidst the terror of those relentless days? Hither, more than once, the aged priest said, he had fled to escape the pursuit of his enemies—here once more he hoped the shield of safety would lie over his peril—here, at last, by whatever death he should die, his brethren had promised to lay his bones in the earth, beside Tisias of Antioch, and many more that, in the bloody times of Nero and

Domitian, had already, in the sight of all that heartless city, merited the crown, and the spotless robe, and the palm-branch of martyrdom, by patient endurance of the last insolence of man.

Our father, therefore, held the lamp before us, and we entered those gloomy regions, wherein alone the servants of the Son of God could at that troubled era esteem themselves in safety from the hot pursuit of contemptuous power. We passed along beneath the arches of the rock-hewn roof, and between the endless winding walls, on either side of which appeared many humble inscriptions, recording the virtues of the departed and the regrets of the surviving poor. Of these last, however, as it appeared, all must long since have been gathered to the ashes of those they lamented, for there was no semblance of any new monument among all that we observed, and most of them, to judge from the shape of the letters upon them, must have been set up at least as long ago as the period of Asinius. After traversing many of these subterraneous galleries, we came, at last, to one more low-roofed than the rest, into which Aurelius struck aside, saying, "Here Tisias lies, but no inscription marks the place where a martyr finds repose. Here is the spot; with my own hands I lent feeble help in digging the grave. Athanasia, too, knows it well, for she also did not fear to assist in rendering the last honours to that soldier of Christ."

A flat thin stone, without mark or epitaph, indicated the spot.

"Father," said Athanasia, "let me rest here. I am weary and worn—but here I shall fear no evil. Conduct Caius back to the grotto; it is time he should go."

Thus leaving her by the funeral-stone, Aurelius and I retraced our steps to the mouth of the catacomb.

"Already," said he, "the sky is red eastward—walk cautiously through the gardens, and regain with all speed the house of your kinsman. Go, my son; may all blessings attend your steps. Come back at the rising of the moon, and cast a stone into the fountain, and I shall be within hearing. Go, and fear not."

CHAPTER IX.

I passed without disturbance through the gardens of the Esquiline, and the streets of the city, in which no one was as yet moving, except a few rustics driving asses laden with herbs to the market-place. When I reached the house of my kinsman, however, it was evident that sleep did not prevail within its gates; lights were visible in the vestibule, and there I found several of the slaves sitting in conversation. My own could not conceal the extravagance of his satisfaction on seeing me enter among them in safety; so that I had no doubt his brother had informed him, in so far at least, of what had passed after our leaving him in the Mammertine. Dromo received me also with warm demonstrations of joy, and conducted me to the chamber of Licinius, in which, with the orator himself, were Sextus, pale with watching, Sabinus, still habited in military attire, with a goblet of wine before him on the table, and Lucius Sempronius, who was reclining at some little distance from the rest. It was he that eagerly began to question me; and I perceived from the style in which he spoke, that all present had already been made aware of the manner in which Athanasia had been withdrawn from the council-chamber. A few words informed them of what had followed after we quitted the Temple of Apollo.

"I thank the gods," said Sempronius,—"so far at least it goes well—but if this strictness, of which the Centurion speaks, shall be adhered to, there still must be no small difficulty about conveying her beyond the city."

"In truth," quoth Sabinus, after a little pause, "I am afraid this is scarcely a matter in regard to which I should be consulted. I know not but already I have done several things that could not be quite reconciled with my duty. I shall, in all probability, be set on the watch myself, and if so—much as I must regret the necessity—it certainly will be most necessary for me to discharge what is committed to my trust. Is there no possibility, think you, of inventing some impenetrable disguise? Depend on it, it is quite impossible the young lady should remain any where in Rome, without being ere long discovered. The first thing is to have her safe beyond the city-walls."

"I myself," said I, "shall embark instantly for Britain. Sempronius, Athanasia must go with me—Surely it may be possible to have her carried unobserved to the shore."

"You!" said Licinius—"you embark instantly for Britain?—You know not what you speak; your law-suit has been determined this very afternoon. Every thing that Cneius left is your own."

"O Jove!" cried Sabinus, "did ever mortal receive such news with such a face! But come, here is health to the heir of the Valerii, and may this Massic choke me, if I love him not the better for his gravity."

"Would to heaven!" said Sempronius, "our young friend had loved under other auspices! No, Valerius must stay and take possession, destined, as I hope he is, to equal, under the favour of the gods, the noblest name in his lineage. My dear niece—let us trust she may be concealed somewhere in safety from the pursuit. Separated from this fanatic crew, she will, ere long, without question, abandon the dreams they have filled her mind withal; and on some happier day, our friend may perhaps have no reason either to fear or to blush, for lifting her over the threshold of the Valerii."

I drew near to the old man, and, receiving his embrace, whispered into his ear, "Sempronius, you speak generously; but know that this very evening I also have become a Christian."

"Heavens!" cried he, "what limits shall be affixed to this contagion! Rash boy! have you not seen already to what consequences this must lead?"

"What?" says Licinius—"what new calamity is this? Have my ears deceived me? Speak, dear Caius—for the sake of all the blood in your veins—you have not embraced this frenzy?"

"My friends," said I, "why should I speak to one, when all of you are, I well know, alike interested? In all things else I bow to age and understanding so much above my own; but here I have thought for myself, and my faith is fixed."

Licinius heard me with a countenance of painful and anxious emotion. In the eye of young Sextus I saw a tear ready to start, and his whole aspect was that of one sad and bewildered. Sempronius leaned his brow upon his hand, and turned himself away from me. But as for the Centurion, he preserved his usual air; and after a moment, all the rest continuing silent, said, "Valerius, I have been in love ere now, and perhaps am not out of the scrape at present; but you have thrown a new light upon the matter. What do you fancy to be the great merits of the present age, that it should be treated with more favour than all that have gone before it? And, if you come to speak of the Jews, every body knows they are a most pitiful, mean, knavish set of creatures. They were always by the ears among themselves; but I think it is rather too much that they should have the credit of bringing their betters (by which I mean all the world besides) into confusion. You are but green yet; all this will blow over anon, and you will laugh more heartily than any one else when you think of your weakness. But look up, good friend, I don't think you are listening to me."

"My dear Sabinus," said I, "I do listen, but I think it is rather to the gay Prætorian, than to the patient friend I had expected to find in you."

"Come!" said he again, "you take every thing so seriously. If you are resolved to be a Christian, I am very sorry for it; but even that shall not stand between me and a true friend. I hope you will soon see the thing as I do—I know you will; but, in the meantime, Valerius, you may count upon me."—And the kind man squeezed my hand with his customary fervour.

He then turned round to the rest of our friends, and began to propose for their consideration a dozen different schemes of escape, that had already suggested themselves to his imagination.

Licinius took advantage of the first pause, to suggest that the Centurion seemed in a hurry to get rid of me. He then passed into an account of the speech he had delivered on the preceding afternoon before the Court of the Centumvirs, and of the unhesitating manner, so gratifying to his feelings, in which its judgment had been pronounced. For some moments, in his detail of these proceedings, he seemed almost to have lost sight of the present situation and views of the person most interested in their termination. But when, in the progress of his story, he came to enlarge upon the magnificence of my new possessions—the domains in Africa—the rich farms in Sicily— the numerous slaves engaged in their cultivation—the Spanish silver mine— and, last of all, the splendours of the great villa upon the banks of the Tiber— it was not difficult to perceive that he could scarcely restrain his indignation at the purpose I had been expressing. "And such," said he, "are the realities which our young friend quits for the reasons he has mentioned! Well, every man must judge for himself. If it must be so, let it be so."

I heard him patiently to the end, and then said, "You have well summed up the whole matter, my dear Licinius. It must indeed be so. I go immediately to Britain, and I trust she—for whom I would leave all these things, were they greater than they are—shall, by the aid of your kindness, go with me in safety. There is one request only which I have, in addition to all this, to lay before you; and that you may hear it the more patiently, it does not concern myself.

"In a word, then," I continued, "should happier days arrive, I hope once more to be among you here in Rome. The wealth which, thanks to your zeal, Licinius, is this day mine, can be of little use to me in the British valley, to which, for the present, I retire. Above all, this beautiful villa of which you speak,—why, because for a time I am unable to occupy it, should the mansion of my fathers stand empty, when there are others among their descendants, who lie not under the same necessity of exile? Till I am enabled to breathe in freedom the air of Italy, I trust Licinius will consent to let Sextus represent me in my villa. There, too, I hope Sempronius will permit his daughter to be. It will give pleasure to Athanasia, to think that those halls contain the dearest of our friends. When we come back, if ever we do so, they will not grudge to make room for us beneath the same roof with themselves. Licinius—Sempronius—what say you?"

They were both silent for a moment; but Sabinus was at hand to answer for them:—"By all Olympus! I shall knock down any man henceforth, that in my presence abuses Christianity as a destruction of men's hearts. Let it be, good friends, as our Caius says. I know, Sextus, I have at least your voice upon my side. Let it be so; and, for heaven's sake, let it be immediately. A wedding is the very thing to divert attention from these troubles in both kindreds."

Our conversation was interrupted by Dromo, who told me that Silo the jailer had come to see me, and was below in the hall. There I found the humane man, with his little daughter in his hand, and walked aside with him into the inner portico of the house. I told him how the escape, for which his zeal alone was to be thanked, had been terminated—and to what resolution I had now come;—and then inquired whether no suspicion had been attached to himself, in consequence of his absence from the Capitoline. Having assured me that he had no reason to think so,—"The oath which I had taken to Trajan," said he, "prevented me from adopting the simpler course of setting open for our dear friends the gates of the Mammertine; and I trust that I did not offend against that oath by acting as I did, after they had been taken away for the time from my keeping. But both they and you must be aware of the pain which I suffered during their confinement, and of the dangers which I have encountered by their escape. I am resolved no more to be subject to such struggles. I cannot preserve my faith as a Christian, and my honour as a servant of Trajan. This very day I resign my charge in the Mammertine; this very night, if it so please you, I am ready to accompany you and my dear young lady, in your flight to Britain."

I need not say with what gladness I heard this proposal. Returning to my friends, I informed them of what I had just heard, and perceiving now at last that there was no chance of diverting me from my project, they entered, like true friends, into serious consultation respecting the best method of carrying my project into execution. The aid of Silo, who had already given such proofs both of presence of mind, and of prudence, and courage, was regarded by them as of the highest importance. He was shortly summoned to take part in our deliberation, and it was resolved, that after resigning in a formal manner the office he held, and transferring his property for the present into the custody of Licinius, he should forthwith repair to Ostium, and there hire and put in readiness, for immediate use, a small vessel, the lightest he could find, in which the fugitive party might transport themselves at least as far as Corsica. To this the zealous Silo without hesitation assented. It was agreed that he should have the mariners on their benches by the coming on of night, and that he himself should be waiting for us by a certain ruined tower, which stands conspicuously by the river side, about a mile and a half above Ostium. We left it to Silo himself, to stock the bark with any merchandise which he might deem best adapted to deceive the superintendents of the haven.

Partly from the necessity of making provision of various kinds for this voyage, but still more in consequence of the law-suit, with the termination of which you have just been made acquainted, I had no leisure that day, from which to work out unnecessary pain either for myself or for others. I had to assist Licinius in looking over an infinity of deeds, and to superintend the drawing out of others. In the next place, I had to go to the Forum for the purpose of manumitting some slaves, (such a largess being naturally expected); and while I was occupied with this, need I tell you, that my own poor Briton was not forgotten? Licinius having, at the joint request of Sextus and myself, accorded that morning to the Cretan also the well-merited gift of his liberty, Boto and Dromo were seen strutting about the Forum together for some moments, each arrayed in that worshipful cap which had formed the most prominent object in their day-dreams of felicity. I shall not trouble you with needless particulars. Let it suffice, that the greater part of the day was thus spent in unavoidable business.

Towards evening, I stole privately from my kinsman's house, being willing to avoid a formal farewell, and repaired to Sabinus, who received me with very lively emotion. What he dwelt upon most fervently, however, was the probability—the certainty he seemed to esteem it—that a persecution of this nature could not be long persisted in by such a prince as Trajan; and the pleasure with which, that being all at an end, he should see me come back to Rome, and take due possession of the inheritance of my fathers. After expatiating most fluently for some minutes on the expected delights of that day, he paused suddenly, and then added, in a tone of some little hesitation, "And as for me, I wonder in what state you shall find me. Rich or poor—married or single—Centurion or Tribune—one thing is certain, that I shall, in all circumstances, be not a little rejoiced to see you."

"You had better marry, my good captain," said I.

"Marry! me to marry? I have not the least thought of such a thing. You did not put any faith, did you, in the raillery of those waggish fellows of yesterday?"

"A little—a very little, Sabinus."

"Poh! poh! now you are jesting."

"And much, very much, Sabinus, in the conscious looks of a certain blushing Centurion, yesterday."

"Come," quoth he, "there is more cunning in these British eyes than I ever should have dreamt of. Fill your cup to the brim, boy, and since you are to leave us so speedily, I shall have no secrets for you. I have seen service;— true, but what of that? I have kept a light heart in all my campaigns. But my day, it must be confessed, begins to wear a little, a very little, towards the evening; and, Castor! if you allow supper-time to slip over, I don't know but you must go to bed with a light stomach. Now or never was the word, my boy; and the widow is mine own."

"And Xerophrastes?" said I.

"And as for the most sagacious and venerable Xerophrastes, why, to tell you the truth, I see nothing for him but that he should allow his beard to curl as it pleases, drop his long cloak over his ambitious pair of shanks, forswear moonlight, purchase for himself a dark lantern instead, and see whether he can't find, within the four walls of Rome, an honest Greek, and a constant widow, to make one blessed wedding withal. That is my advice to the Stoic— Stoic no longer—but, if there be hoops upon a tub, the most cynical of all Cynics."

When it was at last necessary that I should move—"Dear Caius," said the Centurion, "you know the Prefect has set a price on their heads, and I promise you it is such a temptation as no virtue, that keeps watch beneath any common prætorian breast-plate, could well be trusted to wrestle with. But hope, and dare. And here, take once more this helmet, and cloak, and sword, and with them share the password of the night."

Sabinus then gave private orders to one of his troop, and walked with me towards the Esquiline.—But why should I linger over what little remains of this story? Why pain you with the parting which I witnessed between my Athanasia and the holy Aurelius, afterwards numbered among the martyrs of Christ?—Behold us at last issued from the Catacombs, and mounted on the trusty horses which our friend had caused to be waiting at no great distance from the thicket that clothed their entrance. Behold us arrived without interruption at the Ostian Gate of Rome.

The soldiers on guard challenged us cheerily as we came up to them.

"The word, comrades?"

"*Titus!*" quoth the Centurion.

"Pass on—whom bear you with you, comrades!"

"A Christian—a Christian prisoner," said I.

"By Jove, that's worth gold to you, brother," quoth the guard.—"Open the gate there;—pass on, friends. I hope I shall have luck one day myself."

FINIS.

Footnotes

<u>1.</u>

"Concerning the nature of the Bacchic Stimulus."

<u>2.</u>

These were the principal conspirators by whom Domitian was slain. They were afterwards butchered by the Prætorians, who regretted the tyrant; and it was supposed to be chiefly in consequence of that slaughter, and its shameful consequences to himself, (for he was compelled, among other insults, to return public thanks to the butchers,) that Nerva called to his aid the personal vigour and high military genius of Trajan.

<u>3.</u>

————Catonem
Novisti moriens vincere, mollis Otho.

<u>4.</u>

So Pope has rendered the beautiful lines:
Hujus Nympha Loci, sacri custodia fontis,
Dormio, dum blandæ sentio murmur aquæ;
Parce meum, quisquis tangis cava marmora, somnum
Rumpere; sive bibas, sive lavere, tace.

<u>5.</u>

Asinius autem brevi illo tempore quasi in hortulos in *arenarias* quasdam juxta portam Exquiliniam perductus, occiditur.—Cic. *Pro Cluent.*

Milton Keynes UK
Ingram Content Group UK Ltd.
UKHW030740071024
449371UK00006B/703

9 789362 099549